The Reagan-Gorbachev
Arms Control Breakthrough

MEMOIRS AND OCCASIONAL PAPERS
Association for Diplomatic Studies and Training

In 2003, the Association for Diplomatic Studies and Training (ADST) created the Memoirs and Occasional Papers Series to preserve firsthand accounts and other informed observations on foreign affairs for scholars, journalists, and the general public. Sponsoring publication of book series is one of the ways in which ADST, a nonprofit organization founded in 1986, seeks to promote understanding of American diplomacy and those who conduct it. Together with the Foreign Affairs Oral History program and ADST's support for the training at the State Department's Foreign Service Institute, these efforts constitute the Association's fundamental purposes. *The Reagan-Gorbachev Arms Control Breakthrough* is the twenty-first volume in the series.

The Reagan-Gorbachev Arms Control Breakthrough

The Treaty Eliminating Intermediate-Range Nuclear Force (INF) Missiles

David T. Jones, Editor

With contributions by:
Ronald Bartek
Roger Harrison
Geoffrey Levitt
Leo Reddy
John Woodworth

ASSOCIATION FOR DIPLOMATIC STUDIES AND TRAINING
MEMOIRS AND OCCASIONAL PAPERS SERIES

Washington, DC

VELLUM/New Academia Publishing 2012

The opinions and characterizations in this book are those of the author and do not necessarily represent official positions of the Government of the United States or the Association for Diplomatic Studies and Training.

Printed in the United States of America

Library of Congress Control Number: 2012948560
ISBN 978-0-9860216-3-3 hardcover (alk. paper)
ISBN 978-0-9860216-4-0 paperback (alk. paper)

 An imprint of New Academia Publishing

 New Academia Publishing
PO Box 27420, Washington, DC 20038-7420
info@newacademia.com - www.newacademia.com

Dedication

This volume of memoir and observation on the INF Treaty
is dedicated to
Ambassador Maynard "Mike" W. Glitman (1933–2010).

Mike was the principal INF Treaty negotiator, the inspiration for
and leader of the INF delegation, and the key to the INF Treaty's
successful completion and ratification by the U.S. Senate.

Isaiah Berlin is credited with dividing humanity into "foxes"
and "hedgehogs." The hedgehogs know one great truth;
the foxes pursue many. Mike was the consummate "hedgehog"
and the strengthening of the NATO Alliance in all its dimensions
his great truth.

The INF Treaty was just the most obvious element of his
professional success.

Ambassador Maynard Glitman

Contents

All of the pieces not otherwise identified are the work of David T. Jones

Preface

In recognition and commemoration of the 25th anniversary of the signing on December 8, 1987, of the Intermediate Range Nuclear Forces (INF) Treaty, the following essays and observations recount elements of the Treaty's creation. Readers should keep in mind that most of these essays are contributions by members of the INF negotiating team written at the time of and immediately after the treaty signing and recount views they held then. The first two, however, are from 2011–12, when the book was being assembled.

While most of this analysis was aimed at predicting and improving relations with the Soviet Union, there are lessons contained therein still applicable for modern arms control negotiations, not only with today's Russian Federation but with China, North Korea, and Iran. These analyses, combined with an assessment of the Senate ratification of the INF Treaty and prospective "next steps" for arms control, also provide a case study of the seminal benchmark for NATO Alliance security and arms control relations with Moscow, both during and after the Cold War.

The INF Treaty—formally, the *Treaty Between the United States of America and the Union of Soviet Socialist Republics on the Elimination of Their Intermediate-Range and Shorter-Range Missiles*—is unique. It was warmly received when signed at the December 8, 1987, Washington Summit and, following Senate ratification on May 27, 1988, moved through implementation so smoothly that its progress was all but unremarked by national or international media. Other arms control negotiations covering virtually every weapon from ballistic missiles to bread knives subsequently basked in the diplomatic sunshine whose rays first fell on the INF Treaty.

Consequently, the authors and editors of this study believe there is much to examine and learn from the INF Treaty experience. However, rather than undertake a traditional chronological account fulsomely footnoted and scholarly in approach, we have elected to examine a number of specific elements of the Treaty experience, such as the respective "endgames" in Washington and Geneva and the U.S. Senate's advice-and-consent process. Likewise, there were lessons to be learned from the INF experience. These were immediately applicable for dealing with the Soviets until 1991 (when history and politics transformed them into Russians) but remain largely effective in addressing relations with modern Moscow. Additionally, the views of less involved Asian states are reviewed—and these lessons remain topical. We have also provided individual chapters on key elements of the treaty: legal problems; the "elimination" of INF systems; and the mechanisms for monitoring treaty compliance. Finally, to demonstrate that treaties are human, not mechanical, products, we have interspersed the chapters with anecdotal vignettes drawn from the memories of the Geneva endgame.

The authors have had wide experience in government and arms control, which they brought to bear on the treaty negotiations. Subsequently, they have moved to other assignments and/or other careers. The following brief biographic notes identify their roles during the INF negotiations.

- Ambassador MAYNARD W. GLITMAN. The INF negotiator and principal administration witness during Senate ratification testimony.
- Ambassador JOHN WOODWORTH. The INF deputy negotiator and DOD representative.
- RONALD BARTEK. State Department representative on the INF Delegation and principal negotiator for the INF Treaty Elimination Protocol.
- ROGER HARRISON. Deputy Assistant Secretary of State for Politico-Military Affairs and Chairman on the INF Interagency Group.
- DAVID T. JONES. Special Assistant to Ambassador Glitman and Deputy for the State Department INF Treaty Ratification Task Force.
- GEOFFREY LEVITT. State Department lawyer addressing end game elements of the INF Treaty.
- LEO REDDY. State Department representative at the INF negotiations in Geneva.

Much of the initial drafting and editing of this manuscript was assisted financially by the Una Chapman Cox Foundation, whose generous sabbatical program for Foreign Service officers at the Department of State made this effort possible. Personally, we have been strongly supported by many friends and colleagues throughout the "interagency community" of arms control experts. Their information, comments, and insights substantially improved the quality of the work. Of special note is the assistance given by Stanley Riveles, former ACDA member of the INF Delegation (1985–86) and Inter-agency Backstopping Chair (1986–88), Robert Scott Dean, a State Department Foreign Service officer who provided the missile photos, and Lexie Miller, who converted hundreds of pages of typed manuscript into usable digital form.

Finally, on behalf of all the authors, our appreciation to friends and family for their support and encouragement is immeasurable.

Twenty-Five Years Later:
Where INF Has Gone

David T. Jones

There is a tide in the affairs of men.
Which, taken at the flood, leads on to fortune;
Omitted, all the voyage of their life
Is bound in shallows and in miseries.
On such a full sea are we now afloat,
And we must take the current when it serves,
Or lose our ventures.
— Brutus, *Julius Caesar*

It is not the purpose of the following remarks to attempt to sort out the labyrinth of international arms control over the twenty-five years since the signing of the U.S.-Soviet INF Treaty. A phalanx of researchers, spear-tipped by a generation of graduate students, are already mining the memories of individual negotiators and the diplomatic archives of nations to extract nuggets of knowledge and insight from the dross of deadly dull commentary. Nevertheless, there are some useful perspectives looking back from a future that has now arrived, but which was often not even a glimmer in December 1987. Indeed, much has changed unalterably, and much is in the process of continuing to change.

Geopolitical Constants

We say, somewhat ruefully at times, that "change is the only constant." It is also useful, however, to note what has *not* changed in the intervening quarter century since the signing of the INF Treaty.

First, the global security arrangements of fifty years ago remain structurally recognizable today. Essentially, the political-social-economic structure of the West (the NATO "sixteen" of the time) and key non-NATO allies (Japan, India) continues unaltered. There have been no political revolutions among these countries: the structures of their governments remain the same. We even have the same Queen Elizabeth II presiding over an ever-diminishing British Empire. Almost none of the countries of the NATO Alliance of 1987 (Germany being the obvious exception) have changed geographic boundaries. "Canada" is still one country, and not separated into two or more nation states; the "United States" likewise remains territorially unaltered, still an *Unum* and not a *Pluribus*. Thus the NATO Alliance, although substantially expanded numerically (and bereft of the USSR/Warsaw Pact threat) continues; continental North American defense and security, epitomized by the North American Aerospace Defense Command (NORAD), remains a concern.

Next, economies (despite the battering from the Great Recession) remain committed to free market capitalism. The lessened role and comparative strength of the United States does not eliminate the reality that the USA remains first (and still without equals).

Additionally, many of the "intractable problems" of 1987 are still such today. The Middle East looks no closer to a solution. Cyprus remains deadlocked. India and Pakistan persist at daggers drawn (now with nuclear "daggers") over Kashmir and most other elements of their bilateral relationship. Until the 2011 Arab Spring, many local actors (Mubarak, Qadaffi) and the power families in Tunisia, Syria, and Yemen had been unaltered since 1987. Even many of our enemies (or should we say competitors?) remain the same, specifically the Peoples Republic of China, Russia, North Korea, Iran, and Cuba. To be sure, the classic diplomatic axiom that that we have neither eternal friends nor eternal enemies remains pertinent, but at the twenty-five to fifty year mark, it sometimes seems like an eternity.

So What Has Changed?

It is also useful to recognize and appreciate the quotation from Shakespeare's *Julius Caesar*. There *are* times and tides in the affairs of men and the history of nations that the fortunate seize, and others regret. One cannot argue that had the United States and Soviet Union not acted adroitly to conclude an INF Treaty, something comparable would never have come to pass. But the aphorism that it takes two to make peace and only one to make war remains accurate. Without a credible interlocutor, no actor is willing to risk failure. It is even more difficult when the actors had a history of intense suspicion and mutual distrust (although happily never direct armed combat). Nevertheless, the opportunity to move productively toward agreement on intermediate range ballistic missiles was one that both Washington and Moscow elected to seize.

The first, most obvious change has been attitudinal. The "Doomsday Clock" in the *Bulletin of Atomic Scientists* (an always overrated "viewing with alarm" mechanism) has long ago backed away from its "one minute to midnight" nuclear holocaust setting. The palatable tension that gripped NATO nations for much of the Cold War, the idea that World War III was only a trivial miscalculation away from being a horrible reality, is now gone. The Soviet Union is history; its Khrushchevian era predications that the USSR would "bury" us is no longer remembered, let alone cited by the post-1989 generation.

The generation that took the baton from the hand of the World War II "greatest generation" was imbued with the almost desperate concern that the West might have to fight outnumbered and win against Soviet tank armies rushing through the Fulda Gap. The generation that executed the INF Treaty also had that constant fear in mind. It is a fear almost impossible to communicate to later generations, just as the horrors of WWI trenches are barely muddy memories today, and the survivors of Nazi holocaust still struggle against blithe "deniers." It is perhaps the modern concept of a "reset" in Russo-American relations (albeit attenuated by a revanchist Russia) that has made war in Europe today seem such an unthinkable circumstance. It permits continued operation of a NATO Alliance with the flexibility to operate "out of area" at greatly reduced strength without the concern that an instant of inattention could result in Soviets on the banks of the Rhine.

Next, it would be to ignore the proverbial elephant in the living room not to specify the obvious: the collapse of the Soviet Union. Its replacement by the Russian Federation and an assembly of spin-off states, from those as large as Ukraine to miniatures such as the Baltics (Lithuania, Estonia, and Latvia) is unquestionably the most basic and dramatic change in global foreign policy in the past twenty-five years. Just as we continue to sort out the collapse of the Austro-Hungarian Empire, virtually a century after the end of World War I, so we will continue to address the ramifications of the Soviet Union aftermath into the indefinite future. The most positive outcome thus far has been that these offspring are more or less democratic, mostly not a threat to neighbors, and without armament at a level to disconcert other European/Central Asian states. Is there a democracy in Russia's future with or without President Putin? No one can tell, but at least the chances for a Russian state not militarily aggressive appear relatively good; if the future holds a "jaw, jaw" rather than a "war, war," we can accept such an outcome.

No More Yugoslavia

If the disintegration of the Soviet Union came without bloodshed, the collapse of Yugoslavia was another story. The artificial construct that Josef Broz Tito created by grafting various Balkan elements around a Serbian nation simply could not hold. Its violent collapse may be the most regrettable development of the past 25 years; but one in which it is impossible to see how disaster could have been avoided. Despite the efforts of some of the most creative and dedicated diplomats available in the West, the shards of former-Yugoslavia have continued to fracture. The ethnic groups not "cleansed" from territory in which they are now a minority appear to have little future; there are more tragedies waiting to happen.

A Quarter Century of Arms Control

I met a traveler from an antique land
Who said: Two vast and trunkless legs of stone
Stand in the desert. Near them, on the sand,
Half sunk, a shattered visage lies, …;
And on the pedestal these words appear:
"My name is Ozymandias, king of kings:
Look on my works, ye Mighty, and despair!"

Nothing beside remains. ...
The lone and level sands stretch far away.
   — Percy Bysshe Shelley
   The Examiner, London, January 11, 1818

There was a touch of arrogance in the builders of the INF Treaty. We were venturing into the unknown: an "agreement" with a most disagreeable adversary. Moscow historically had never adhered to such an agreement; violations great and small with all range of partners were the hallmark of agreements with the Soviets. At one point, there was even the perhaps apocryphal claim that Moscow had *never* fully honored an agreement. Hence, the frequently cited Reagan sobriquet, "Trust but verify" was constantly on our minds.

Nevertheless, we hoped that the INF Treaty would be the benchmark "first" in a series of defining arms control agreements; that we would break the pattern and start a relationship between Moscow and the West that would accord with NATO's objectives since its 1949 inception: enhanced security at a lower level of armament. What we feared was that the INF Treaty would be a "one off" (a phrase not then invented) exercise; that it would at best be a stepping stone to nowhere, or at worst another failed agreement in which the Soviets were identified as having cheated on various treaty provisions, discrediting further arms control negotiation.

Instead, we have had an agreement that indeed met our hopes rather than our fears; a building block that has led to further agreement on conventional forces, strategic nuclear systems (most recently "New START"), and agreements to eliminate chemical and biological weapons. Likewise, following the collapse of the USSR, there have been agreements to secure fissile material and to assure that weapons in parts of the old Soviet Union that became separate independent states were returned to Russian control.

The process has neither been fast, inexpensive, nor comprehensive. We failed in efforts to secure Senate ratification of a Comprehensive Test Ban Treaty, and there is still no anti-satellite agreement (the PRC demonstrated ability to shoot down a satellite in 2007). We are still far from agreement on a strategic antimissile defense agreement (our deployments in Alaska remain a point of difference). Efforts to devise a theater antimissile system, protecting NATO allies against prospective attack from rogue states such as Iran, have encountered many political and technical difficulties. In this regard, the U.S. government has struggled not only with internal policy conflicts in the transition from the Bush to the Obama administrations, but also second thoughts by possible basing countries in Europe, and relentless hostility to such a system from Moscow.

New Threats

The passage of a quarter century has sparked developments that did not even qualify as the proverbial "cloud the size of a man's hand" on the politico-military horizon of 1987. In effect, technical progress has created and produced "INF" missiles in a series of countries: India; Pakistan; North Korea; and Iran. Significantly, China also retains such capabilities. Obviously, none are constrained in any way by the U.S.-Soviet INF Treaty. Nor is there any serious likelihood that these states, either individually or corporately, would accept the INF Treaty provisions. For most of them, the INF Treaty eliminating ground launched missiles between the ranges 500 and 5,000 kilometers would eliminate their entire missile force.

Although India and Pakistan are focused on each other, North Korea and prospectively Iran are potentially threats to many neighbors and even relatively distant states. Certainly, the prospect is that both North Korea and Iran will continue to develop and expand their missile forces (and concurrently nuclear weapons—despite Iranian demurs that it has no nuclear weapons program). This circumstance prompts the question whether the INF Treaty remains valid, so far as its purpose was eliminating the threat to Europe and Asian allies from INF range missiles. To be sure, the threat is no longer Soviet missiles; however, while Soviet missiles might have been regarded as an ancillary threat to Asian allies such as Japan, Taiwan, and the Republic of Korea but more of a concern to the PRC, a North Korean ballistic missile force is a direct threat to Japan and the ROK. Likewise, sanguine observers might regard an Iranian nuclear ballistic missile force as primarily designed to be a deterrent against action by nuclear armed neighbors and a surety against U.S. attack; however, more skeptical governments throughout the Middle East and Europe could see it as a direct threat for which they have no obvious deterrent. One need only attempt to factor in the Israeli nuclear program to move a simple headache to migraine status, contemplating resolving the Middle East political problems simultaneously with nuclear security issues.

Conclusion

Perhaps political analysts should simply accept the axiom that "sufficient onto the day is the evil thereof" and avoid any vast prescriptions based on half-vast conclusions. Contemporary historians, perhaps from self-indulgent hubris, repeatedly conclude that every bend in the political road is a seminal turning point in the sweep of history (see *Romance of the Three Kingdoms*, a saga of Chinese political military action 2,000 years ago, expressing a full range of human drama with its parallels into the twenty-first century). In that context, the INF Treaty remains a useful, functional agreement that has enhanced the midterm security of those negotiating and concluding it. It is not necessary to ask for more.

Vignette: Welcome to Geneva

The newcomer arrives in Geneva. A basic question is where to stay. The tradeoffs are proximity to the U.S. Mission or price. Proximity or price. The closer to the Mission, the more expensive the accommodations. After weighing the best local advice, the newcomer chooses the hotel Mon Repos.

Upon entering the hotel, the newcomer is immediately greeted and escorted, bag and baggage, via a small creaking elevator to his seventh floor room. He enters the room. The effect is palatable, like a blow. It is without question the deadest room he has ever entered. Without a single ostensible fault, the psychology of the room is remarkable: all brown motif, brown threadbare rug, brown bedspread, tan walls. Battered furniture (brown, naturally), featuring a brown lacquered armoire serving both as dresser and closet. No pictures on the walls, not even the traditional undistinguished reproductions. No TV, no postcards, envelopes, or paper, no "sundries," dull lighting, and walls thin enough to transmit the intimacies of neighboring life.

In short, there is nothing that could be stolen. There is virtually nothing that could be additionally damaged or worn by anything less than deliberate strong-armed action. But clean. Yes, clean, clean, clean as only Switzerland produces. A room whose life had been cleaned away. A bathroom that could have been a surgical operating room. A husk available to greet the next client, and the next, and the next.

"Well," he says to himself, this room is not going to give me anything when I get back at night." And, as soon he is working a minimum of thirteen hours a day, seven days a week, little is required.

Welcome to Geneva.

Why INF?

The NATO Alliance suffered through INF deployments. It triumphantly struggled to remain unified through the long years of INF negotiations. It placidly observed INF eliminations through years of observing, monitoring, and inspecting empty INF facilities, ending only in 2001. This drama, which in its conclusion played out over more than twenty years, is and will continue to be the subject of graduate students' detailed dissertations.

The following chapters of this study deal with some of the specific aspects of the INF Treaty, among them the "end game" in Geneva, the "lessons learned" from these negotiations, the U.S. Senate and INF ratification. Thus instead of an intensively detailed chronological explanation of diplomatic exchanges, the focus of the material in the manuscript is on episodes and elements of the Treaty. It attempts to show some of the problems and issues faced by the negotiators and how they were resolved. It is useful, however, to put the INF deployments and negotiations into context, at least as the authors saw them, to provide a backdrop for the subsequent material. While much of the information should be familiar to even a casual reader, as INF was the politico-military issue of the 1980s, there well may be slants and interpretations—highlighting so to speak—that reflect our idiosyncratic views. The following exposition attempts to provide an overview of the historical context of the INF negotiations, a few of the major issues involved and how they were negotiated both in Geneva and Washington, the role of the U.S. Senate in Treaty ratification, and how implementation of the INF Treaty evolved.

The Background

Intermediate-range and shorter-range (500–5,500 kilometer) nuclear missiles, let alone INF-range weapon systems, were hardly new military phenomena for military forces in Europe. As well as nuclear capable aircraft, the U.S. deployed Jupiter and Thor intermediate range ballistic missiles (IRBM) respectively in Turkey and Italy in the late 1950s. These IRBMs were withdrawn following the 1961 Cuban missile crisis, in an unannounced (and denied at the time) *quid pro quod* for Soviet missile and aircraft withdrawals from Cuba. Still earlier, the United States had deployed Regulus missiles of an ancient cruise missile variety. In contrast, the Soviets deployed considerable numbers of SS-4 and SS-5 missiles, which had sufficient range to cover a wide assortment of European targets.

Nevertheless, during the period of SS-4 and SS-5 deployments, Europeans were essentially sanguine about these Soviet missiles. Strategically they believed themselves protected by massive U.S. superiority in intercontinental range missile systems. Tactically, they determined that SS-4/SS-5 facilities were primarily "soft" bases on launch pads and not installed in hardened silos. They were also slow to prepare for launch, carried only a single warhead and were believed to be inaccurate. Consequently, there was a perception that such Soviet systems were vulnerable and could be effectively attacked by NATO aircraft should war break out.

The SS-20, however, was a new development. It was mobile; it had three, more accurate warheads; and Europeans anticipated that it would be deployed in large numbers beginning in 1977, after having been tested for several years previously. Its mobility ended the implicit NATO military rationale that the systems could be caught on the ground prior to launch.

Moreover, its improved accuracy, range, and three warheads put many more European targets at risk. Even so, if Moscow had limited itself to simply replacing the warheads carried by SS-4/5, the SS-20 might have been explained away as a "modernization" not significantly different from existing Soviet INF systems and even, due to its mobility and hence reduced vulnerability, more "stabilizing" in a potential nuclear crisis. But it was clear, virtually from the beginning, that the Soviets did not intend simply to match earlier

SS-4/5 deployments (they steadily surpassed regularly revised official estimates) but to far exceed them and to keep substantial numbers of SS-4/5 on active duty as well, despite their liabilities.

These anticipated Soviet deployments took place against the backdrop of U.S.-Soviet strategic nuclear equivalence, with the Soviets viewed as having matched previous U.S. superiority. Regardless of precise warhead numbers in the strategic balance (which still favored the United States in absolute numbers), Europeans perceived that the United States and Soviets had reached rough parity. They concluded from this new strategic equivalence that, short of a direct attack against the continental United States, Washington would be highly reluctant to use its strategic systems against the Soviet Union no matter how high the stakes, e.g., the loss of Europe, for fear of Soviet retaliation against U.S. cities. The Soviets were already viewed as having an advantage in conventional forces. Thus in European eyes, an unanswered Soviet dominance in intermediate range systems might convince Moscow that there could be a crisis and conventional battle in which the Soviets could threaten to use SS-20s against European targets without stimulating a "linkage" of U.S. strategic nuclear forces against Soviet targets.

Soviet capability vs. US and allies	Strategic	Conventional	INF
	Equivalence	Advantage	Dominance

Fig.1 *Soviet capability vs. U.S. and Allies*

This calculus would result in loss of credibility for the deterrent ability of NATO/U.S. conventional and nuclear forces and Soviet political domination of Europe.

This theory was both impressionist and unverifiable; deterrence is ultimately in the minds of the beholders. Nevertheless, the judgment reflected honest European concerns in the mid-1970s over the U.S. commitment to Europe and worries that the SS-20 could have real political and psychological effects not "today or tomorrow" but over a period of years. Thus in the spring and summer of 1976, the Europeans pressed the need to redress the "Euro-strategic balance."

The United States initially accepted neither the European concerns nor their solutions. In the U.S. views of the day, and in accord with NATO's (still existing) "flexible response" defense strategy, deterrence was a seamless web. The composite forces of NATO defenses, from the frontline rifleman to the silo-based Minuteman, were equal elements of deterrence. To attempt to draw out one element of this balance, for example, "Euro-strategic" missiles, for separate calculation, would weaken the logic of the "flexible response" doctrine.

Consequently, during the summer of 1976, the USG twice sent briefing teams led by the Department of Defense's Defense Nuclear Agency head, Donald Coter, to brief allies at NATO headquarters on U.S. nuclear forces and commitments. Coter argued persuasively that NATO did not need a specific counter for the SS-20, that any Soviet threat from the SS-20 would be deterred by U.S. strategic systems, and that U.S. conventional and nuclear forces were firmly linked to the defense of Europe. Following these briefings, U.S. authorities were convinced that NATO allies had heard, understood, and agreed, and that the "Euromissile" issue was effectively resolved.

Wrong. European concerns were not assuaged. In his famous March 1977 speech to the International Institute of Strategic Studies in London, FRG Chancellor Helmut Schmidt returned to the SS-20 threat and the theme that these systems had to be countered. It was clear that action was now being demanded at the highest political levels. Taking a deep bureaucratic breath, the equivalent of a substantive sigh, the U.S. agreed.

TNF Modernization

In the mid-1970s, simultaneous with Russian development of the SS-20, the United States was examining through internal studies the need for "theater nuclear force (TNF) modernization." At that juncture, NATO's theater nuclear forces consisted of aging U.S. and FRG Pershing IA missiles (range 740 km) and aircraft that could deliver nuclear bombs. These systems suffered from a perception that they lacked survivability and flexibility. This judgment was particularly acute for key types of aircraft, which had the dual responsibility for delivering conventional (high explosive) and nuclear weapons. As aircraft and nuclear weapons are concentrated at a relatively limited number of sites whose locations were widely regarded as known to the Soviets, these airbases were perceived as particularly inviting targets for attack. Thus, at bureaucratic working levels, the United States was considering various options for TNF modernization that would improve the flexibility and survivability of such nuclear systems and also permit the full commitment of aircraft to any conventional combat.

The systems under consideration for TNF modernization were the Pershing II ballistic missile (a modernization with extended range of the long-deployed Pershing IA) and the ground launched cruise missile (GLCM), the latest in U.S. advanced technology able to hit targets with high accuracy while flying close to the ground albeit at subsonic speeds. Each system had its advocates based on technical and/or financial considerations. The Schmidt IISS appeal, however, catapulted a relatively routine U.S. domestic military-technical discussion into a high political drama.

To address the military questions stimulated by TNF modernization, NATO created a High Level Group (HLG) with a U.S. chairman. The HLG was to recommend to NATO foreign and defense ministers a concept for theater nuclear modernization. The structure of the INF force ultimately recommended and agreed (464 GLCM and 108 PII missiles) was constructed within parameters which concluded that the Soviets would regard fewer than 200 INF warheads as insignificant. A force larger than 600 warheads would be considered an attempt to match the Soviet SS-20 force directly, rather than to add to the deterrent aspect of the entire range of NATO defense forces. The final figure of 572 warheads on the same number of missiles reflected totals from the hypothetical table of organization and equipment (TOE) structures of projected INF Pershing II and GLCM missile units, rather than any abstract calculation that 572 (instead of 571 or 573) was the perfect number to deploy. That is, NATO totaled the unit strengths for forces to be deployed rather than deciding on a specific number to be deployed and then creating units to match that figure. The proposed deployments can be found in the following table.

Basing Country	Unit Strength
FRG (West Germany)	96 GLCM and 108 PII
United Kingdom	160 GLCM
Italy	112 GLCM
Belgium	48 GLCM
Netherlands	48 GLCM

Fig.2 Basing Countries' Unit Strength

In 1979 Bonn noted an additional political requirement: one European continental state other than the FRG, i.e., not the UK, would have to commit itself to accept U.S. INF deployments to permit Bonn to accept such deployments. Otherwise, Bonn argued, the FRG would be isolated ("singularized") and in direct opposition to Moscow on the INF issue. This FRG requirement was not peripheral as while the military calculations of the HLG were well advanced, and hypothetical deployment numbers were being bandied about, clear political commitments to accept deployments had substantially lagged. Indeed, the Belgian, Dutch, and possibly other NATO member commitments were speculative rather than concrete. There was a conviction that one or another ally would "come through" to meet Bonn's demand but in early 1979, there was no pronounced eagerness among the Allies to take that first step.

Fortunately for the Alliance, however, in May 1979, the Italian government did make the commitment. INF deployments in Italy were a conscious decision by Rome to raise its status within NATO and to seek a position equal to that enjoyed by Bonn, Paris, and London. As a consequence of that early decision, Bonn's political requirement was met, and the forthcoming INF Ministerial-level deployment decision guaranteed to be a success. Indeed, it was fortunate for NATO that it had the Italian commitment in hand, as even down to the final days prior to the 12 December 1979 meeting of Foreign and Defense Ministers, there was no assured decision to accept INF deployments by any other continental ally. Subsequent Italian performance on INF deployments and consultation on negotiations was exemplary. No "basing country" worked harder to make INF a success.

The Second Track

At this point, the planning and decision making for TNF modernization was well under way; but even late into 1979, little thought
had been given to a political, arms control "track." This oversight
was understandable—without agreement on what U.S. systems
could be deployed and where, there was little utility in discussing
their control, let alone control of Soviet systems. Moreover, there
was an implicit U.S. belief that the case for INF deployments to
counter SS-20s (in response to European requests) was so compel-
lingly self evident that it did not need to be "sold" to European
publics wrapped in a parallel arms control proposal.

The Dutch thought otherwise. Arguing that modernization
was only supportable for certain elements of their population if
accompanied by an arms control offer, they urged the creation of
a "second track" to convince Allied publics that while the Soviets
were committed to threatening the Alliance, NATO was focused on
peaceful deterrence. Thus the NATO official decision to deploy U.S.
INF systems by late 1983 was accompanied by an Alliance call to
eliminate INF missiles; a promise not to deploy, if the Soviets destroyed their INF missiles.

At best, such a plea was a very faint hope. There were, however,
those who both sought to be good allies and still avoid deployments. They anticipated that ratification of SALT II would provide
impetus for negotiations on INF range system and that the four
years between the NATO official commitment and the projected
deployments would suffice sufficiently to limit or even eliminate
Soviet SS-20s and make U.S. INF deployments unnecessary. Such
a prospect, however, was regarded with utter cynicism by most,
who regarded the arms control "track" as the veil behind which
INF deployments would proceed. Then there was the series of cri-
ses immediately following the INF deployment decision (namely
the Soviet invasion of Afghanistan and the Polish suppression of
Solidarity leading to the nonratification of SALT II), which made
any agreement to avoid INF deployments even less likely. To the
Soviets, the NATO proposal undoubtedly was risible—an offer to
trade a bucket of diamonds for an empty bucket.

Failed Negotiations: 1981–83

It probably is safe to assume that the opening set of INF nego-
tiations labored under the burden of substantial cynicism. U.S.
Ambassadors Paul Nitze and Maynard (Mike) Glitman and Soviet
Ambassador Yuli Kvitsinsky led these negotiations. The internal
U.S. bureaucratic battles over negotiating positions for these negotiations are effectively developed in Strobe Talbot's *Deadly Gambits*.
In essence, to simplify enormously, an essentially "conservative"
U.S. political administration under President Reagan had replaced
a more "liberal" one under President Carter. The new U.S. admin-
istration was convinced through both historical and contemporary experience that Moscow viewed the West in general, and the
United States in particular, with a hostile ill will that would be fatal
in the absence of improved defenses and heightened vigilance. And
it set about attempting to strengthen itself and its allies and counter
Soviet moves in every possible forum.

Brezhnev's and Andropov's Soviets were not Gorbachev's
Soviets. If the Soviets were not the "Evil Empire" of rhetoric, neither
were they flexible negotiating partners interested in offering mutually advantageous compromises. Soviet SS-20 deployments had
given them a substantial political and military advantage, which
they intended to exploit. Moscow of the early 1980s had yet to come
to terms with the economic failures and foreign policy blind alleys
that, to the retrospective judgment of a decade later, appeared to be
so obvious. Moreover, the West had yet to display the unity and determination in defense and foreign policy commitments that doubtless were a conditioning factor in Soviet decision making.

Thus, in perspective, the 1981–83 negotiations appear fore-
doomed to failure. Throughout this period, the Soviets were seeking to preserve an effective INF monopoly by breaking NATO's will
to deploy a counterforce. The most persistent claim by the hysteri-
cal European left was that U.S. INF deployments would prevent
any agreement and thus, at all costs, deployments should be post-
poned if not cancelled entirely. The kindest judgment that history
can give is that such critics were misguided, and that the British
women protesters camped outside Greenham Common inveighing
against missile deployment have increased their chances of rheu-
matism in later years. In fact, the intensity of the criticism from the

European left demonstrates the political effectiveness of the SS-20, which, by its very existence, had conditioned elements of European publics to argue that NATO should not take an action that was easily justifiable as a proportionate response to a Soviet threat.

In the end, the Soviets sadly overplayed their hand. While the United States was attempting to negotiate an agreement, the Soviets continued to deploy SS-20s. Whatever the merits of the June 1982 informal "walk in the woods" proposal by Ambassadors Nitze and Kvitsinsky (which would have set equal number of INF launchers in Europe, prohibited Pershing II deployments, and frozen SS-20 deployments in Asia), Moscow also rejected it and did not follow up with anything comparably attractive. On the eve of the first U.S. deployments on 23 November 1983, the Soviets had deployed 360 SS-20s with 1,080 warheads. These deployments in the UK and FRG prompted a Soviet walkout—ultimately a gross tactical error by Moscow. NATO now had the perfect foil to domestic criticism and could easily rally popular opinion by pointing to Soviet intransigence: Moscow's refusal to negotiate because NATO sought to protect itself. Those who opposed deployments had simultaneously to justify Moscow's bullyboy negotiating tactics as well as the invasion of Afghanistan and the proxy crushing of Solidarity.

Nevertheless, the Soviets may have calculated that their walkout was a "no lose" tactic. It increased pressure on each of the basing countries by emphasizing to their publics the ostensibly unacceptable nature of the U.S. deployments. Indeed, over the period of deployments, each of the basing countries fought—and won—an election in which their opponents pledged to reject U.S. INF deployments. This was also true in the United States where the 1984 Presidential primary election saw skepticism by some Democratic candidates, e.g., Senator Cranston, over the utility of INF deployments. The Soviets could reasonably have wondered whether "President Mondale" would have been a more congenial negotiating partner.

Successful Negotiations: 1985–1987

The Soviets followed the election returns. With the reelection of President Reagan, Moscow was confronted with the ever-rising likelihood that it would ultimately face 572 deployed U.S. INF warheads and had to balance such an eventuality against negotiating an acceptable agreement. The first requirement was a structure for negotiations—something that would do the job but permit the Soviets to claim that they had not simply returned to the negotiating with tail between their legs. The decision was a relatively simple expansion of the Geneva INF arms control negotiations to include parallel but independent negotiations on strategic armaments (START) and "star wars" antimissile systems (Defense and Space [D&S]). The agreement to resume negotiations under the new rubric of the "Nuclear and Space Talks" (NST) was announced on 24 November 1984 and resumed officially on 12 March following a January Geneva meeting between Secretary of State Shultz and Soviet Foreign Minister Gromyko. During the next several years for personal or professional reasons, there were changes in the leadership of START (Senator John Tower, Ambassadors Ronald Lehman, and Read Hanmer) and D&S (Ambassadors Max Kampelman and Hank Cooper). The INF negotiations, however, were headed by Ambassador "Mike" Glitman, Nitze's deputy in the 1981–83 negotiations. Glitman provided an unparalleled depth of background and focused competence and dynamism in the Geneva negotiations that was a major determinant of their success.

Not that the negotiations were, so to speak, "condemned to success." It is a truism that in any negotiation between essentially antagonistic interests, the sides start from very different positions and move by fits and starts (if at all) to an agreement satisfying at least the minimum requirements of each. It is not for this account to describe the tit-for-tat cycle of proposal and counter proposal leading to this final agreement. These lasted two and a half years, with hundreds of official meetings, and generated thousands of official reports and documents. Human memories being what they are, there is no one alive who recalls every detail of the negotiations, and even points that were major issues for months have faded from the recollections of many. It may be useful to note, however, that the United States, representing in these negotiations NATO Alliance consensus, determined early in the process some specific requirements for an acceptable final agreement:

- *Equality.* U.S. and Soviet systems were to end at equal levels. Reductions by equal percentages or equal numbers— long time Soviet positions—were unacceptable.
- *Globality.* All INF systems worldwide had to be included. We would not, for example, let increased security for Europe disadvantage Asian friends and allies by permitting the Soviets to transfer INF systems from Europe to Asia.
- *Exclude Conventional Forces.* Systems under discussion were strictly limited to ground-based missiles. The Soviets sought various devices to include nuclear capable aircraft and aircraft carrier-based systems under an INF agreement.
- *Exclude British and French Nuclear Forces.* The Soviets sought either directly to include UK and French nuclear forces (essentially their SSBN forces) or to be compensated for them in some manner. We insisted that a bilateral agreement should not deal with third country forces.
- *Verifiability.* The United States had to be confident that it could confirm Soviet adherence to (or violation of) Treaty provisions.

The United States and the NATO Alliance take justifiable satisfaction in having achieved all of these objectives and establishing as a consequence a number of principles of considerable utility for future U.S./NATO Alliance negotiators. These include but are not limited to "asymmetrical reductions" (recognition that the side with more assets must reduce more) and intrusive verification (creation of a schema of on-site inspections to reduce the risk that Treaty violations could escape undetected). As well as being employed in START, these principles have effectively defined the parameters of the chemical weapons negotiations in the UN-sponsored Conference on Disarmament and the Conventional Armed Forces in Europe (CFE) negotiations.

It was not by chance that NATO unity endured during the negotiations. There was a basic recognition on both sides of the Atlantic that while we could have an Alliance without an INF Treaty, we could not have an INF Treaty without the Alliance. U.S. negotiators also recognized that while the systems involved were "our systems," we were operating on a European playing field and would require willing NATO agreement every step of the way. Thus the "care and feeding" of the Alliance absorbed a substantial part of U.S. diplomatic action throughout the negotiations with a steady stream of briefings, consultations, and discussions at NATO headquarters, in Washington, and in NATO capitals, on a month-to-month, ultimately year-by-year basis. To this day, there has never been a NATO effort more thoroughly and intensively discussed and agreed upon. INF set the mold for intra-Alliance consultations on arms control.

End Games

The final weeks and months of many successful negotiations bring with them their own dynamic. No matter how intensive the pace and serious the negotiators, the bulk of a negotiation has a degree of form and predictability both at the negotiating table and in the capitals of the negotiators. At the negotiating table, the sides arrange a schedule for meetings; they exchange documents explaining national positions, and discuss points of difference. In capitals, the issues are reviewed by appropriate agencies, decided as necessary by higher authorities, and "guidance" is drafted for the negotiators. The pace if hardly leisurely is at least measured and reasonably predictable. Bureaucracy is in control (there will be a plenary session on Thursday, a working group on Tuesday, etc). Under such a regime, if the negotiators are skillful and substantive differences amenable to compromise, there is steady progress toward agreement.

Almost as if predictability is unacceptably dull, however, many of our arms control negotiations have moved into highly charged "endgames" as a reaction to forcing events such as scheduled U.S.-Soviet summit meetings. This was the case for the INF negotiations. In both Geneva and Washington, work proceeded for several months leading up to the 8 December 1987 Washington summit at a pace that would make the Coyote-Roadrunner cartoons appear almost tranquil. The bureaucracy was left to harrumph a bit: "Yes, we are making progress, but it is not being done in the right way."

Parkinson's Law suggests that work expands to fill the amount of time available in which to do it. This is also true of negotiations as diplomats can always find ways to tighten, polish, and improve their product. Thus a forcing event such as a summit by foreign ministers or heads of state can be a salutary mechanism to focus minds and energies on the forthcoming "hanging," so to speak. Despite its intensity, the endgame is not normally the forum in which cosmic issues are addressed. With one exception (how to monitor production of the SS-25 first stage after it was discovered to be effectively identical to an SS-20 stage), INF endgame issues were important, but not equal to those critical problems already resolved such as global elimination of all INF missiles, inclusion and elimination of shorter range (500–1,000 kilometer) missiles, and a range of on-site inspections. In Geneva, the endgame issues were primarily the "nuts and bolts" problems of creating procedures to implement the critical decisions already taken and to fill in corollary material, such as numbers of inspectors, their rights while inspecting, the specific processes to "eliminate" a given system. As the negotiators were breaking entirely new ground in inspection, data exchange, and elimination of systems, every word set a precedent and was subject to nervous second and third thoughts.

As earlier mentioned, the very late discovery that the SS-25 first stage was "outwardly similar but not interchangeable with" the SS-20 first stage raised the potential for the Soviets cheating by claiming that secretly produced SS-20s were SS-25s. In Geneva, part of the end game was purely procedural/mechanical: assuring that the text was correct in two languages, free from typographical errors, and properly printed on the official treaty paper of each country.

In contrast, the end game in Washington required maintaining interagency consensus at a point when time was critical, but Treaty skeptics were critical also. How much inspection is enough? What elements of supporting infrastructure for INF systems should be destroyed? Are the data supplied by the Soviets on their INF systems acceptable? While the U.S. negotiators in Geneva were speaking with one voice and making unified recommendations, Washington agencies had to grapple with disagreement; and, equally distracting, they had to address the problems posed by having equally intelligent people compete to provide a solution.

The Senate and Ratification

"If the Executive proposes, then the Senate disposes." Nothing has been chancier in recent history than presenting an arms control Treaty to the United States Senate. The Senate has been the political equivalent of a black hole for many U.S.-Soviet treaties, from SALT II limits on strategic weapons to the Threshold Test Ban Treaty to restrict nuclear testing. No body is more scrupulous of its prerogatives or convinced of its ability to detect and rectify executive branch error than the Senate. Beyond the normal institutional tensions between the Executive and Legislative branches, the INF Treaty also had to counter (a) the political realities of a Democratic-controlled Senate being asked to provide its Republicans opponents with an election year bonus; (b) the institutional challenge of what information the Executive Branch is required to provide the Senate and who can subsequently interpret a Treaty's meaning; and (c) substantive issues such as conventionally armed cruise missiles and the role of future technology for INF.

Ultimately, the Senate did attack and resolve each of these challenges. The overwhelming public impression that the INF Treaty was a "good thing" had early affected the views of individual senators and the Treaty remained overwhelmingly popular throughout the Senate's review. Rarely does a document enjoy such a wide spectrum of support ranging from the Veterans of Foreign Wars to Women's Strike for Peace. Ratification thus was a downhill fight. The problem was not battling for the votes for ratification, as absent a substantive catastrophe demonstrating massive negotiating incompetence, a two-thirds majority was assured. The only question was whether external factors (renewed Soviet adventurism) or procedural creativity by the handful of outspoken Treaty critics and a few less vocal sympathizers could tie up and defer Senate action long enough to weaken support. The politics of the 1988 election year were obvious and the intricacies of the Executive-Legislative encounter over "treaty interpretation" will undoubtedly provide grist for Legal Review articles for years. However, the substantive points associated with the conventional GLCM and "futuristic" technology as applied to INF systems can benefit from some introductory discussion.

Conventional GLCM and "Futuristic" INF Technology

Essentially each of these topics addresses hypothetical U.S. ability to employ technological advances creatively to military advantage. The conventionally armed cruise missile already existed in both air and sea launched forms. Defense Department officials, most prominently Assistant Secretary Richard Perle and his successor Frank Gaffney, argued vigorously for several years that this option should be extended to ground launched cruise missiles, to permit the great accuracy possible for high tech cruise missiles to bolster NATO's conventional forces. Perle, Gaffney, and Defense Secretary Caspar Weinberger were eventually overruled (after repeated reclamas and delays) by the arguments of the rest of the government that (a) after extensive investigation the United States had concluded it was impossible to verify that a "conventional" cruise missile could not be quickly converted into a nuclear armed missile by switching the warhead, and (b) the U.S. military had no plans and no requirement for a "conventional" ground launched cruise missile. Perle and Gaffney deigned to argue the facts, but simply contended that the U.S. military was traditionally short sighted with regard to technological innovation. Carrying this argument to the Senate, they did stimulate a Senatorial resolution emphasizing that a START agreement should not ban conventionally armed cruise missiles.

The "futuristics" argument was more abstract. Essentially, it was posed as a question by then Senator Quayle as to whether future technologies such as microwaves, lasers, or Star Trek's "phasers," whose applicability as weapons is as yet no more than a gleam in the eyes of science fiction writers, could be used on INF range weapons. As drafted, the INF Treaty was not explicit on future systems, but the negotiators believed that by addressing "weapons," the Treaty covered everything in that category: past, present, and future. The negotiating record included statements by Soviet officials supporting that belief. Senator Quayle was clearly attempting to keep open the door for such weapons—at least a crack. By pressing the potential ambiguity, however, he forced other senators, particularly Senator Nunn, to nail down prohibition of "futuristic" INF range systems to an almost absurd degree through a series of repeated letters and exchanges of diplomatic notes, prior to a final reaffirmation in the Senate's instrument of ratification.

Lessons Learned

Every successfully completed negotiation spawns a horde of "lessons" that those who participated in the experience want to impress on successors. Some of these expositions are not much more than the "look how smart I was" garden variety of back patting. It is hard, however, to determine how much experience is applicable to the future and how much unique to the personalities and circumstances present at an instant of time. Lessons that appear obvious, such as a requirement that the West have real assets, negotiating "chips" or whatever one might call them, to induce serious Soviet proposes and compromises are also expensive, as they imply construction of such assets only to bargain them away. That expenditure appears wasteful to any abstract observer in times of multiple demands on scarce resources. The tendency certainly is to convince the other side to accept the "will" to build and deploy such assets for the deed.

Likewise, the lesson of determining clear objectives and sticking to them appears self evident: that is, until internal debate arises (as it always does) over whether negotiating persistence is a disguise for stubborn avoidance of creative compromise. ("I am consistent, he is stubborn, you are bull headed"). Other lessons can be learned too well. Our intensive INF consultation with NATO members was vital to preserve Alliance cohesion. Such intensive, detailed coordination is now seen as the template for constructing future negotiating positions and has subsequently become a factor distinctly restricting Alliance flexibility in responding to Moscow's initiatives. NATO seems to be caught in a cleft stick of either spending the six to twelve months necessary to coordinate fully a new Alliance initiative while suffering the consequent public impatience, or else having the United States act virtually unilaterally with "consultation" (more of a wink and a nod) and Alliance members tempted to opt out if the consequences of such a U.S. initiative look less than stellar.

Finally, some lessons can be transitory. In the INF negotiations in Geneva, the Soviets were less flexible than the U.S. team due both to technological short comings (virtually no word processors or high speed Xerox equipment) and inadequate numbers of personnel. These are not systemic weaknesses and can be quickly overcome.

There are, of course, even longer-term consequences from INF. The long standing NATO nuclear doctrine of "flexible response," which suggests that any Warsaw Pact aggression could be met with an incalculable NATO response ranging from conventional defense to strategic nuclear strikes, may need revision following the elimination of INF Treaty systems and European reluctance to modernize short range nuclear missiles. The West also had basic questions to ask itself concerning the reliability of Moscow as a negotiating partner. In this regard, the INF Treaty was a "test drive" agreement. It addressed systems that were important, even critical in European perceptions, but not on the level of strategic nuclear weapons or conventional force balances. The arms control negotiating experience since July 1987 suggested that the Soviets were willing to conclude agreements that had mutual advantage, specifically those that increased security at a lower level of armament. Soviet proposals in START, chemical weapons negotiations, and the Conventional Armed Forces in Europe (CFE) negotiations were serious in tone with a minimum of the self congratulatory bombast that used to mark Moscow's maneuvers.

In the end, the INF Treaty roundly deserves its "historic" label. The weaponry addressed was not the most powerful or the most numerous. Initially it stood as a pillar in an empty plain. It had the potential of any pillar either to be one element in a larger structure or a *de facto* tombstone for the hopes of wider accomplishment.

ZERO ZERO

The INF Treaty:
Its Origins, Content and Promise

MAYNARD W. GLITMAN

Maynard W. Glitman was the United States Negotiator for Intermediate-Range Nuclear Forces. The article was originally published in the Winter 1987–88 edition of Disarmament, *prior to Senate ratification of the treaty. It has been edited to reflect subsequent developments.*

The signing of the INF Treaty by President Reagan and General Secretary Gorbachev on 8 December 1987 marked the culmination of a negotiating process whose immediate origins dated back more than a decade. In the United States, the Senate must first give its "advise and consent" before the treaty can enter into force. This article assesses what has been accomplished in this area.

The INF Treaty comprises 125 pages of single-spaced text. The Treaty proper is accompanied by an Inspection Protocol outlining the detailed modalities of the inspection regime, an Elimination Protocol covering how each item banned by the Treaty will be eliminated, and a Memorandum of Understanding on data, declaring type, number and location of each item to be eliminated, along with photographs of the systems and diagrams of the sites to be inspected.

The Treaty is a legal document, and its detail and phrasing reflect this. In essence, it contains the basic arms-reduction goals and policy that the United States, in close consultation with its allies, has pursued since the formal INF negotiations opened in late 1981. These goals and policy were based in turn in NATO's 12 December,

1979 decision to overcome the challenge posed to the security of the alliance by the Soviet intermediate-range nuclear missile force through a dual track approach of counter-deployments and negotiations.

The United States Approach to the INF Negotiations

The negotiating approach the United States and its allies agreed upon was based on five principles:

1. Equality of rights and limits between the United States and the Soviet Union;
2. Limitations on United States and Soviet systems only;
3. Global application of limitations;
4. Unrestricted maintenance of NATO's conventional defense capability; and
5. Effective verifiability of any agreement.

While these principles were specifically designed to meet United States and allied requirements in the context of the INF negotiations, and are fully incorporated in the INF Treaty, they have wider applicability. In addition to these principles, the United States and its NATO allies also made the incorporation into the INF Treaty of constraints on shorter-range INF missiles a fundamental tenet of the United States approach to negotiations.

Equal Rights and Limits

This fundamental principle is grounded in the Charter of the United Nations, which makes provision for the right of collective defense. In concrete terms, this right provides for the United States and its allies to join together in protecting their freedom and independence, including by basing American troops and systems in Europe.

The Soviet Union has long deployed missiles that could strike targets in Europe and Asia. Thus, (so the Soviets claimed) dealing with such systems was essentially an intra-European affair. The most recent example of this type of system was the mobile, accurate, triple-warhead SS-20, deployed in the mid-1970s. The SS-20 could threaten targets throughout Europe, and elsewhere on the periphery of the Soviet Union, including much of Asia. The United States had no comparable force. In addition to its SS-20s, SS-4s, and SS-5s, the Soviet Union also had deployed almost 400 shorter-range INF missile systems (SS-12s and SS-23s), while the United States deployed 108 Pershing I-As until their replacement by Pershing IIs.

In the context of Soviet achievement of strategic parity with the United States, and as the Soviet SS-20 missile force grew, our European allies became concerned that with no comparable United States INF forces on the ground in Europe, Moscow might come to believe (however mistakenly) that American forces could be "decoupled" from the defense of Europe. Consequently, Western European leaders stressed the need for a NATO response to Soviet SS-20 deployments, as much to foreclose a potential perceptual gap as to address a military threat. Well over a year of intensive alliance consultations culminated in NATO's 12 December 1979 "two-track" decision. The first "track" would redress the imbalance of INF through modernization and deployment in Western Europe, starting in 1983, of 572 United States longer-range INF missiles. On the second "track," the United States would call for negotiations with the Soviets to establish global balance in United States and Soviet longer-range INF missiles at the lowest possible level, which was understood to include zero.

A substantial portion of the negotiations was devoted to achieving Soviet recognition of the concept of "equal rights and limits." The Soviets initially refused to negotiate, attempting to impose the condition that NATO must first renounce its modernization "track" and arguing that the United States had no right to deploy INF systems in Europe to help its NATO allies to counter the threat of the SS-20 and similar Soviet systems. Finally, during the summer of 1980, the Soviets agreed to negotiate, and a short set of preliminary talks were held that fall. Formal negotiations with the Soviet Union began in November 1981. From the outset, the United States stressed the principle of equality and proposed the global elimination of all United States and Soviet longer-range INF missile systems. This global "zero option" remained the United States preferred outcome throughout the negotiations. The Soviets called in essence for a "moratorium" on INF deployment in Europe. This would have codified the Soviet missile monopoly that NATO had just rejected.

In March 1983, in an effort to find common ground with the Soviet side, the United States (while continuing to prefer a zero outcome) proposed an interim agreement for equal global limits on long-range INF missile warheads at any number below the planned United States deployment level. Both of these proposals were rejected by the Soviet side, which eventually walked out of the negotiations in November 1983, following the Bundestag approval of deployments to the Federal Republic of Germany and initial Pershing II deployments. Following the extended Soviet walk-out, the United States and the Soviet Union returned to Geneva in March 1985. During the course of these renewed negotiations, the United States continued to stress that any INF agreement had to be based on "equal rights and limits." The Soviets, after renewing their freeze proposal, attempted to define equality as equal reductions.

Eventually, however, the United States position was accepted. Equal limits were agreed, first at one hundred warheads each, and then at zero. The principle of an equal outcome and equal rights (even if one side had to take more reductions than the other) was incorporated in the Treaty.

Exclusion of Third Country Systems

This principle is closely connected to the issue of equal rights and limits for the parties to the Treaty. As part of its argument that the INF issue was an intra-European affair and that Europeans and Americans had no need (or right) to join in a collective approach to counter Soviet INF, the Soviet side for much of the negotiations argued for the inclusion of, or compensation for, British and French systems. The United States insisted that any INF agreement must be bilateral and limited only to United States and Soviet systems.

Behind this argument lay the conviction of the United States and its allies that American INF deployments provided a legitimate counterweight to Soviet INF capable of reaching the European (and Asian) allies of the United States, and that any nuclear weapon negotiations between the United States and the Soviet Union should deal only with the systems of those two countries. The Soviets eventually accepted this principle and thus the Treaty deals only with United States and Soviet INF missile systems.

Global Application of Limitations

The Soviets sought initially to limit any INF agreement to Europe. The United States, by contrast, argued that given the range and mobility of SS-20s, an agreement limited to Europe would not provide real security for our European allies. The United States also stressed the requirement for equal security for Asian as well as European states. Ultimately, the Soviets accepted the validity of this argument. The Treaty's provisions apply on a worldwide basis.

Maintenance of NATO's Conventional Capabilities

This principle is directly related to the question of whether to include dual capable aircraft in the INF negotiations. The Soviets initially sought to include such aircraft in the INF negotiations in a manner that would have decimated United States aircraft in Europe. The United States argued that an agreement should focus on missiles only: the most capable element in the INF force. Moreover, for the United States and our allies, dual capable aircraft play an important role in NATO's conventional defense. In mid-1983, the United States, in an effort to meet Soviet expressed concerns, offered to discuss inclusion of selected INF aircraft in an agreement. The Soviet side, however, continued to propose an outcome that would have effectively undermined the contribution United States aircraft make to NATO's conventional defense. The question was finally resolved when, during the renewed negotiations, the Soviet side changed its position to correspond to the missiles-only approach which the United States preferred. The Treaty, therefore, deals only with ground-launched missiles.

Effective Verification

Effective verification is the keystone of arms control. "Trust but verify" is more than a watchword for the United States; it is also a practical recognition of the problems created by Soviet noncompliance with arms control agreements. As detailed below, the procedures for verification in the INF Treaty are more comprehensive than in any previous agreement. The complex of constraints, inspections, and notifications, coupled with national technical means (NTM) will greatly help to ensure compliance with the Treaty, i.e., that the Soviets eliminate the overt INF inventory declared in the Memorandum of Understanding, and providing the U.S. and its allies with high confidence that the Soviets do not possess a militarily useful covert INF missile force.

Shorter-Range INF Missiles

From the outset of the negotiations in 1981, the United States called for Treaty provisions placing constraints on shorter-range INF missiles. This was necessary because Soviet shorter-range INF missiles could perform some of the same missions as Soviet longer-range INF missiles. Thus, if left unconstrained, Soviet shorter-range INF missiles could undermine the effectiveness and viability of the Treaty.

After some hesitation, the Soviet side agreed with the concerns expressed by the United States and, indeed, included provisions dealing with shorter-range INF missiles in its initial draft INF treaty. However, while the United States remained constant in its view of the need to constrain these systems, when the talks resumed in 1985 the Soviet Union raised objections to including shorter-range missiles in the proposed treaty. The Soviets argued that these missile systems should instead be dealt with in a follow-on negotiation. In time, though, the Soviet side accepted the U.S. view that shorter-range INF missiles had to be limited by an INF Treaty in order that the Treaty would provide real security. Indeed, the sides eventually agreed to eliminate their shorter-range INF systems on the same global basis as their longer-range INF systems.

Treaty Provisions

As for the Treaty, which entered into force on 1 June 1988, it was designed to do six main things:

1. Totally eliminate, within three years, all U.S. and Soviet ground-launched ballistic and cruise missiles, i.e., those missiles with a range between 500 and 5,500 km (about 300-3,300 miles). Shorter-range missiles (500-1,000 km range) were to be eliminated in eighteen months. Intermediate-range missiles (1,000-5,500) were to be eliminated in two phases. The first, lasting twenty-nine months, would bring the sides to equal force levels prior to total elimination at the end of three years. Altogether, over 1,836 Soviet missiles, capable of delivering over 3,000 nuclear warheads, were to be destroyed, along with over 850 United States missiles capable of carrying nuclear warheads;

2. Prohibit production and flight testing of these systems or development of "new types";

3. Institute restrictions on the deployment and movement of INF systems until eliminated, including an extensive process of notifications for and limitations on any movements;

4. Update the data provided in a Memorandum of Understanding on data, which includes a fully itemized declaration of the location, number, and technical specifications of all Treaty-limited systems, support structures and equipment;

5. Provide detailed procedures for the elimination of INF missiles, launchers, support equipment, and unique support structures;

6. Provide a complex, overlapping inspection regime to assist in the verification of compliance to include several kinds of on-site inspection. The Treaty also set up a Special Verification Commission as one means of addressing, as necessary, compliance concerns.

Just as its provisions calling for the elimination of an entire class of nuclear weapons are unique, the Treaty's extensive verification provisions broke new ground. The verification regime, lasting thirteen years and covering nine countries, is the most comprehensive and stringent ever agreed. It consisted of:

(a) "Baseline" inspections, to be conducted shortly after the INF Treaty enters into force to verify the number of missiles and launchers at "declared" facilities (including bases at which missiles are operating, repaired, and stored).

(b) An annual quota of short-notice, on-site inspections of these INF facilities both for the three years during which all INF systems and facilities are eliminated and for ten years afterwards. These inspections will help to verify residual levels until all U.S. and Soviet INF missile systems are eliminated and assure that no such systems are reintroduced.

(c) On-site inspections to verify the elimination of missiles and launchers, and elimination of specific structures at missile bases. Each side will also be permitted to eliminate up to one hundred intermediate-range missiles in the first six months by launching them under restrictive conditions, monitored by on-site observation.

(d) A separate "close-out" inspection to assure that when a declared site is deactivated and removed from the list of declared facilities, INF-associated activity has indeed terminated.

(e) A perimeter portal monitoring regime under which the United States will be able to monitor, for up to thirteen years, production at the key Soviet missile assembly plant at Votkinsk or any other plant where the SS-25 intercontinental-ballistic missile is produced. This monitoring will include the permanent presence of United States inspectors at the Soviet facility. They will be able to weigh and measure Soviet SS-25 canisters and open up eight canisters per year as they leave the plant to ensure the "non-production" of SS-20s, because the first stage of the Soviet SS-25 is outwardly similar to the first stage of the SS-20. The Soviet Union will similarly be permitted to monitor a former Pershing II production facility in Utah.

(f) A permanent flight test ban which, together with national technical means, will preclude the military utility of any covertly-produced INF missile.

To complement this inspection regime, and as a further step in helping to ensure that SS-20 missiles are not covertly deployed with SS-25 missiles, the Soviet Union has agreed to the establishment of a program of enhanced NTM. Six times a year for three years, or until entry into force of a START agreement (whichever comes sooner), the United States can require the Soviet Union to open retractable roofs and display SS-25 missile systems at selected SS-25 bases.

In sum, the verification regime of the INF Treaty provides an extensive network of checks and cross-checks appropriate to a zero level environment where the production, flight testing, indeed the very existence of such missiles is prohibited. It dramatically reduces the possibilities of maintaining a militarily useful covert INF missile force and serves as a deterrent to cheating.

The Future

The INF agreement is of historic proportions. It is not hyperbole to note that never before have two world powers agreed to eliminate an entire category of weaponry, whether the weapons were battleships, bombers, or ballistic missiles. The suggestion that INF missiles are superfluous when compared with vast numbers of strategic systems begs the question of why they were constructed or deployed in the first place, and forgets the deep concern which Soviet INF missiles engendered in Europe and Asia. Consequently, the Treaty has lifted a significant element of threat from the citizens of Western Europe and Asia within the range of those missiles.

Without belaboring the point, it is clear that the elimination of this class of nuclear weapons, regardless of whether it is only one of many classes of nuclear weapons, is a significant step in arms control. But diplomatic history is littered with wasted "significant steps," and the INF Treaty need not be seen as a last step. Rather, it should be seen as an example of the kind of stabilizing and effectively verifiable agreement that improves security to the benefit of all.

Elements of the INF Treaty can provide useful precedents for the emerging conventional stability negotiations, as well as for START. Each of these negotiations, of course, has its own dynamic and requirements. Neither envisages a zero outcome. Nevertheless, recognition of the principle of equal rights and limits can be a useful precedent in other arms control talks. The sides could also draw from procedures in the INF Elimination Protocol or build on aspects of the INF Inspection Protocol in future negotiations.

More generally, the INF Treaty is a positive example of United States and Soviet determination and ability to resolve other controversial issues. The two countries have moved to resolve a security problem long considered intractable, involving key allies both in Europe and Asia. Other issues will not necessarily be easier to negotiate, but at the minimum, an INF Treaty demonstrates that tough problems can be solved. In addition, while our experience with previous nuclear arms control agreements with the Soviet Union has not always been a happy one, successful implementation and full compliance with the INF Treaty will provide an opportunity to establish a different record.

Finally, it remains fundamentally true that improved East-West relations cannot be based solely on arms control. Arms alone do not create insecurity. Arms are as much, if not more, a manifestation of tension as the cause of tension. Progress in arms control cannot, therefore, resolve Washington-Moscow differences if we remain at odds over the rest of the spectrum of our relationship. To be of lasting benefit, movement in arms control must be paralleled by the resolution of problems in other areas such as human rights and regional issues.

Nevertheless, while there is more to be done in these fields as well as in arms control, the successful negotiation of the INF Treaty (and, equally important, its successful implementation) demonstrates and illustrates the point that even though initially separated by major political and security differences, Washington and Moscow can ultimately find the way to agreement. The knowledge that agreement can be achieved in a sensitive area, despite major obstacles, should be among the most important legacies of the INF negotiations and Treaty.

Vignette: Welcome to the Bubble

The secure area in which the INF delegation held its confidential conversations was informally called "the bubble." Such conversations were protected from Soviet electronic eavesdropping. As one might imagine, the delegation spent considerable time in the confines of this room, and various informal protocols developed over the months and years of "bubbling."

A newcomer arrives and takes a convenient empty seat. Shortly thereafter, the INF delegation lawyer, a notably talented woman whose self-confidence could be mistaken for arrogance, enters.

Her first words to the newcomer? "Out. It's my seat."

Welcome to the bubble.

Selected Legal Issues in the Negotiation of the Intermediate Range Nuclear Forces Treaty

Geoffrey M. Levitt

Geoffrey Levitt was a member of the State Department Legal Bureau who was closely engaged in the final stages of the INF negotiations. He provided this article in 1988, when the project to create an INF memoir originated. It has not been previously published.

Anyone who works on arms control treaties for a while quickly understands that they have a characteristic life cycle, featuring a negotiation phase, which usually becomes serious only after the appearance of a deadline, a ratification phase, where the negotiators abase themselves in front of some outside authority in order to secure approval of what has been negotiated, and an implementation phase, where people who had little to no involvement in the first two phases try to figure out what the negotiators, who have all moved on to other jobs, had in mind.

This brief essay will examine selected legal issues of interest that arose in the context of the INF Treaty during the first two phases of the treaty life cycle, negotiation and ratification, because those are the areas of the author's primary experience. As a lawyer, it is a source of some perverse professional pride (and amazement) that a deal whose conceptual outlines were as simple as those of INF (double-global-zero) could yield a set of documents comprising a basic treaty, two protocols, an annex, a memorandum of understanding, several side letters, two basing country agreements, and seven exchanges of notes.

Notwithstanding this voluminous documentation, the first point to keep in mind when looking at legal issues under an arms control treaty is that, unlike in other areas of international endeavor such as extradition law, status of forces, environment, or trade, the bulk of the substantive issues involved in an arms control agreement have no legal content at all, but are basically technical or military. What parameters do you use to define a missile type? What is the best method of destroying missiles, and how fast can it be done? What numbers of which weapons can your military live with? To issues like these, the lawyer can contribute at most perhaps a slightly keener than average drafting sensitivity, but this author can attest from personal experience that there are a lot of non-lawyers involved in the process who think they're pretty good drafters too (and some of them are even right about that judgment).

The silver lining here, however, is that due to the extraordinarily complex nature of the modern arms control agreement (of which the INF Treaty is the prototype) and due to the high political visibility of the arms control treaty process, the scope of what might be called auxiliary legal issues is extremely broad and varied, demanding an acquaintance with many different areas of international and foreign affairs law. To some extent, precisely because of the dearth of legal substance in the core policy issues, the lawyer in the arms control loop ends up focusing on issues that are either too abstract and theoretical, or too specific and specialized, for the policy-level negotiators to feel comfortable with addressing. And these often tend to be the issues that are not only among the most interesting in the entire negotiating process, but whose solution becomes indispensable to the success of that process. A couple of examples will help illustrate.

One factor that helped to complicate INF was that the negotiations were not just between the United States and the Soviet Union, but involved as well five NATO basing countries and two Warsaw Pact basing countries, where missiles were located and where inspections to verify the elimination of those missiles would, therefore, have to be carried out. But these basing countries would not be parties to the INF Treaty. So by what legal authority would U.S. and Soviet inspectors verifying the terms of that treaty be permitted onto their territory? When the Foreign Ministries and parliaments of some of our NATO allies learned that they would be expected to host Soviet inspectors pursuant to a treaty to which they were not even party, they took the position that they could not receive Soviet officials on their territory to carry out official functions without a direct legal relationship between themselves and the Soviet Union. At this point our diplomat-negotiators called for legal help.

In the end, it took a total of only nine international agreements to solve this problem. The United States would have a multilateral agreement with its five allied basing countries, in which the latter would undertake to facilitate the implementation of U.S. obligations toward the Soviets under the main treaty by permitting Soviet inspectors on their territory. Each of the five NATO basing countries would then exchange notes with the USSR, in which they granted direct permission for Soviet inspectors to enter and carry out inspection functions in each of their territories: the direct legal link with the Soviets that they wanted. The United States, in turn, would exchange similar notes with the Warsaw Pact basing countries, who would in turn have a counterpart agreement with the Soviet Union, all in the interests of reciprocity and symmetry. Of course, the Soviets did not want to waste their limited legal resources drafting something on which the U.S. side was doing all the work anyway, so that the text of the agreement between the Soviets and their allied basing countries bears a suspicious resemblance to ours. And if the whole structure seemed a bit overly elaborate to some, any such misgivings were quelled by the fact that it worked.

Of a slightly more mundane, but nonetheless critical nature was the issue of modifying complex technical provisions of the treaty structure after its entry into force. This issue was centered around the two protocols to the basic treaty: one on elimination procedures and the other concerning on-site inspection procedures. Each protocol is long and detailed, and covers types of events that are essentially new in arms control practice: respectively, the destruction of operational weapons systems, and the carrying out of on-site inspections by the other side to monitor this process of destruction, as well as compliance with other provisions of the treaty. The elimination protocol, for instance, provides that "the launcher leveling supports of the SS-20 launcher shall be cut at locations that are not assembly joints into two pieces of approximately equal size, and a portion of its launcher chassis at least 0.78 meters in length shall be cut off aft of the rear axle." Language like this is presumably a long way from what the drafters of the Treaty Clause of the Constitution had in mind when they declared treaties the supreme law of the land, but treaty language it is nonetheless.

But does this mean if it emerges that the best way to disable an SS-20 launcher chassis is to cut off a piece 0.76 meters long instead of 0.78 meters, the United States has to go back and seek the advice and consent of the Senate to an amendment to the INF Treaty? That this same process has to be followed every time the parties want to modify one of the detailed, highly technical, and untested provisions of the inspection or elimination protocols? This would clearly not be feasible. At the same time, the Senate is not about to give the government *carte blanche* to change any terms of a treaty package to which it has given advice and consent after a careful review. So it was manifestly time for creative legal solutions.

The answer worked out in this case was a time-honored one: hand the problem off to a commission.

Step one: include among the tasks assigned to the U.S.-Soviet Special Verification Commission established under Article XIII of the Treaty to "agree upon such measures as may be necessary to improve the viability and effectiveness of this Treaty." Step two: place at the end of each of the two protocols language stipulating that any such measures agreed upon in the Commission pursuant to Article XIII "shall not be deemed amendments to the Treaty." Incidentally, the Soviets, in the process of negotiating this language, displayed an alarming familiarity with our constitutional system of treaty-making.

In the end, having worked out these and innumerable other issues, our negotiators returned to face a Senate advice and consent process at least as arduous as the negotiations they had just completed in Geneva. The lopsidedness of the final Senate vote in favor of the treaty should not mislead anyone as to the severity of the struggle to secure Senate approval. Well over 1,000 written questions on specific treaty provisions, hundreds of hours of open and closed hearings in front of three committees, not to mention endless staff briefings, all topped off by a 180-page counter-treaty memorandum from Senator Helms's office that had to be rebutted practically line-by-line. While at the time all this interest may have struck those of us on the receiving end as quite burdensome, in the cooler light of hindsight it reflected, for the most part, nothing more sinister than a Senate that was taking its constitutional responsibilities very seriously.

Indeed, certain issues that came to light in the advice and consent process ended by providing arguably useful clarifications of important treaty issues. One example is problem of future systems, an issue that in the anti-ballistic-missile (ABM) context has engendered its share of controversy. Given the whole political context of the INF Treaty, its natural focus has been on the elimination of existing types of ground-launched missiles. But of course, there would not be much point in outlawing Pershing IIs and SS-20s if the sides were free to turn around and deploy Pershing IIIs and SS-30s to do the same job. So under the Treaty the sides not only must destroy existing types of missiles, but are also prohibited from producing or possessing any intermediate or shorter range missiles thereafter.

But now comes the interesting part. What types of missiles exactly are subject to this ban? The Treaty provides four basic criteria: The missile in question must be ground-launched; have a range between 500 and 5,500 kilometers; be a ballistic or a cruise missile; and be a weapon-delivery vehicle. This may sound relatively precise at first hearing, but Senate staffers are paid to poke holes in precise-sounding language like this. Of the four criteria, the one that caused the most trouble was that the missile be a weapon-delivery vehicle. "Weapon" turns out to be one of those mercury-like terms that squirts around the table instead of standing still and letting you define it. What, for example, is a missile whose payload is just a transmitter designed to jam enemy communications? Is that a weapon? What if you turn up the volume on that transmitter and fry enemy communications? What if after jamming enemy communications, your missile crashes into them and destroys them physically? In other words, what if ground-launched intermediate range missiles, or devices to perform their functions, are developed in the future based on (to borrow a loaded phrase from the ABM context) "other physical principles?" Are they still covered?

After some deliberation, the administration announced to the Senate that in the context of the treaty definitions, "weapon" meant "any mechanism or device which when directed against a target is designed to damage or destroy it," and that the INF negotiating record demonstrated that both sides had a common understanding that all U.S. and Soviet ground- launched missiles with ranges between 500 and 5,500 kilometers, both present and future, should be subject to the provisions of the Treaty.

For some Senators, however, these administration assurances were not enough. Before they would approve the Treaty, they insisted that we do an exchange of notes with the Soviet Union to enshrine this common understanding on future types of missiles and thus avoid any subsequent doubts or questions. Such an exchange was duly performed in mid-May and the Treaty went forward to Senate approval.

But by far the biggest legal issue in the advice and consent process for the INF treaty was not really an INF issue at all, but a direct descendant of the notorious ABM interpretation dispute. Even to skim the surface of this dispute itself would be far too time-consuming a task for this analysis, and would take it somewhat far afield; in any event, the interpretation dispute, insofar as it affected the INF Treaty, can be summarized briefly as follows. Certain senators, in preparing for the INF ratification debate, put forth the view that the net effect of the administration's position on the interpretation of the ABM Treaty was that "if the Senate is misinformed by Executive Branch officials as to the meaning of the treaty, that is simply too bad." Therefore, according to this argument, the Senate would have no choice but to examine the entire negotiating record of the Treaty, and perhaps even to incorporate that record, as well as administration testimony on the meaning of the Treaty, into its Resolution of Ratification in order to ensure that these sources would be given proper weight in future interpretations of the Treaty.

The administration position was not at all as outlined by these senators. Rather, that position was that authoritative administration representations as to the meaning of a treaty, upon which the Senate relied in approving the treaty, would be binding upon the president in interpreting the treaty in the future. Naturally, we are talking here only about the meaning of the Treaty under U.S. domestic law. For purposes of international law, statements made by one signatory to its own legislative authorities in the course of internal ratification proceedings cannot bind the other party to the treaty after entry into force.

At any rate, this clearly expressed administration view did not prevent the Senate majority leader, supported by the chairman of the Foreign Relations Committee and other influential senators, from demanding access to the entire INF negotiating record. It therefore became necessary to compile this record, which ran to 31 volumes of cables and documents spanning several years of negotiations. Indeed, in order to accommodate this mass of paper, the Senate established an Arms Control Treaty Review Support Office, with full-time staff, consultants, and contractors, all employed, as were a number of Executive Branch officials, in the new sub-industry of producing and reviewing arms control treaty negotiating records.

It is unclear what purpose was served in the final analysis by this unprecedented demand for the delivery of the full negotiating record of a treaty to the Senate for its perusal in the course of the ratification proceedings. Indeed, in its report on the Treaty, the Foreign Relations Committee drew back from the precipice, stating, "Both the administration and the Senate now face the task of ensuring that Senate review of 'negotiating records' does not become an institutionalized procedure." And, with admirable candor, the Committee concluded, "In sum, although internal executive memoranda and other negotiating materials may have been available to members of the Senate, some of whom have sought to assure themselves that this 'record' is consistent with the administration's formal presentation, ...such documents need not have been examined for consistency and should not be deemed material to U.S. interpretation of the INF treaty insofar as they are inconsistent with the Executive Branch's formal presentation of the INF Treaty"[1]

In the end, the Senate adopted a condition to ratification very much along the lines of that recommended by the Foreign Relations Committee, the gist of which is that the United States shall interpret the INF Treaty in accordance with the understanding of the Treaty shared by the Executive Branch and the Senate at the time the Senate gave its advice and consent to ratification, this common understanding being based on the Treaty text and the authoritative representations of the Executive Branch made to the Senate in the course of the ratification proceedings. The United States cannot, according to this condition, adopt a different interpretation except pursuant to Senate advice and consent to a subsequent treaty or protocol, or the enactment of a statute; if a question later arises as to the interpretation of a provision on which no common understanding was reached, it shall be settled in accordance with applicable U.S. law.

The final Senate version was somewhat less sweeping than the original committee recommendation; it stated, for example, that the principles set forth in the condition are "based on" the Treaty Clause of the Constitution, rather than "deriving as a necessary implication" from the Treaty Clause.

President Reagan, in a letter sent to the Senate shortly after the Treaty entered into force, stated that this condition caused him "serious concern" in that it "apparently seeks to alter the law of treaty interpretation" by according to executive branch statements to the Senate primacy over all other sources that international forums or even U.S. courts would take into account, including the intent of the parties, the negotiating record and subsequent practice. "I am compelled to state," concluded the President, "that I cannot accept the proposition that a condition in a resolution of ratification can alter the allocation of rights and duties under the Constitution; nor could I, consistent with my oath of office, accept any diminution claimed to be effected by such a condition in the constitutional powers and responsibilities of the Presidency."[2]

So, in the end, INF closed only a chapter, not the book, in the interbranch confrontation that arose in the wake of the ABM reinterpretation dispute. The next chapter will probably not really open until the START Treaty moves close to completion, a development toward which the Senate has already laid down a marker in the text of the 1988 INF ratification resolution, which provided that START negotiations "shall be conducted with close and detailed consideration of the advice of the Senate ..., and the Senate shall be kept fully apprised of all significant proposals made to the USSR, and, with respect to such negotiations, the judgments and recommendations of the Senate shall be given full and highest consideration and due regard."[3]

Vignette: Rituals

Much of a negotiation is formalized exchange of papers and positions. In semipredictable manner, statements are made; debating points are scored (and recorded for the diplomatic archives). But ritual is not only on glossy paper or the orotund platitudes of formal speeches. It lives in dozens of trivial actions that mark the day-to-day ambience of a negotiation but rarely enter the official record. The mind's eye recalls in a series of frozen tableaus a series of such rituals:

The Russians Are Coming!

The U.S. and Soviet delegations met at each other's diplomatic missions on an alternating basis. The respective establishments were housed on a hill on the outskirts of Geneva with the Soviets closer to Geneva. Thus we were "up the hill" and the Soviets "down the hill." Like mice trapped on a metronome the delegations yo-yoed up and down the hill. As the pace heightened and working groups multiplied, the delegation needed a daily scorecard to tell whether they were coming or going, and who was where.

The Arrival Scene

The United States is the host. The American delegation is arranged at the Mission entry as neatly in delegation rank order as a Kremlin Red Square lineup. Space was reserved for the occasional latecomer to dash into place in line still pulling on a suit jacket and/or adjusting a tie as the Soviet black sedans swing into the Mission courtyard.

The Greeting

In rank order the Soviets emerge from their cars. Who is leading them today? Is there a chance for a responsive dialogue (if not agreement) with their Number Two? Or a "numbalogue" with the Number One? Then the series of handshakes, always each with each down the line of the welcoming delegation with muttered English/Russian pleasantries. And then on into the conference room.

Conference Rooms

The American conference room was standard U.S. government: moderate size; attractively furnished; designed for work. The Soviets' was designed first for show with 20-foot ceilings, crystal chandeliers, and plush drapery. Mercifully the seats in both conference rooms were well cushioned and the discomfort of hours of negotiation was only mental, not physical as well.

The Set-Piece Opening

Always the host ambassador speaks first, welcoming the guests to the room they have visited hundreds of times previously. Always formally as "Mr. Ambassador." Never "Mike" or "Alexi." Politeness is politics. We are adversaries seeking mutually acceptable adjustments to national security, not friends or allies operating from a basis of essential social-political agreement. No one forgets the point.

Always the delegations are arranged in rank order on opposite sides of the table. Sitting in the center, the ambassadors face each other, flanked on the right by the official interpreter and on the left by the ranking military representative. It is a virtually changeless order from week to week, month to month. The ritual naturally sparks the occasional postmeeting question. Where is X? Or Y? Back in Moscow? Does it mean anything?

Setting the Table

Yellow legal pads and number 2 pencils sit before each seat. The Soviets counter with unlined paper and pencils without erasers. The Soviets tended to "borrow" our pads and pencils. Refreshments were also ritual. "Would you like a cup of coffee?" at the start of the meeting. The delegations mingle momentarily at the end of the room pouring juice or coffee. But as the weeks wore on and the hours grew longer, refreshments became nourishment: cookies for breakfast; peanuts for lunch; onion dip for dinner. The United States is inventive and lays out generous plates of "nibblies": sliced fruit; mixed nuts; assorted cookies. The Soviets are consistent with cookies and peanuts. The taste of the peanuts stimulated the delegation to wonder if they had been obtained in barter trade with some Soviet-client African state.

INF Treaty in Perspective

Following are three takes on the INF Treaty—one by the State Department representative on the INF delegation; a second by the Principal Deputy Assistant Secretary for the Politico Military Bureau; and a third by a delegation member—all written in 1988– 1990 specifically for this book project.

The INF Treaty Process from a Geneva Perspective

Leo Reddy

*Leo Reddy served as the State Department representative on the U.S. del-
egation to the INF negotiations in Geneva from March 1985 to December
1987, and then as director of the INF Treaty Ratification Task Force until
the Senate gave its advice and consent on May 27, 1988. This article was
written for the INF memorial project in April 1990 and has not been previously published.*

The guests arriving at the White House on the morning of 8
December 1987 walked briskly from their cars. It was a breezy,
chilly day. The invigorating air added to the sense of expectation.

Everyone was in good spirits as they entered the East Room.
The Soviet retinue was large, since this gathering was a major
event in General Secretary Mikhail Gorbachev's first state visit to
Washington. Mrs. Gorbachev and Mrs. Reagan sat in the middle
of the front row. They were flanked by the senior diplomatic and
military advisors of the U.S. and Soviet governments, who greeted
each other with considerable camaraderie. Leaders from the U.S.
Congress were present. The White House Press Corps was well
represented. TV cameras were banked in the back of the room.

Also arriving were members of the U.S. and Soviet INF delegations who had negotiated the *Treaty Between the United States of
America and the Union of Soviet Socialist Republics on the Elimination of
Their Intermediate-Range and Shorter-Range Missiles.* Each page of the
treaty, which had just been completed in a photo finish of round-
the-clock negotiations in Geneva, had been initialed only the night
before by the chief U.S. INF negotiator, Ambassador Maynard W.
Glitman, and the chief Soviet INF negotiator, Ambassador Alexei
A. Obukhov, on a special U.S. Air Force flight from Geneva.

As soon as the guests were seated, the doors at the front of the East Room opened revealing a long corridor. President Ronald Reagan and General Secretary Mikhail Gorbachev walked alone down this corridor and took their seats at the long, thick mahogany table at the front of the room. Each made relatively brief, good-humored speeches. They signed both the Russian and English versions of the treaty, which had been bound in heavy leather covers, and exchanged pens.

Tucking their respective copies of the signed treaty under their arms, the two leaders smiled and shook hands with a sweeping exuberance, which brought the guests to their feet in an enthusiastic round of applause. Cameras whirred.

The picture of that robust handclasp appeared on television newscasts around the world that evening and many times over the decades. Whatever his views of the merits of the INF Treaty, everyone watching that scene knew he was witnessing an historic event, a major turning point in U.S.-Soviet relations that appeared to symbolize the end of the Cold War between the two military superpowers.

This event also symbolized the central meaning of the treaty, its political significance, and the deep personal involvement of Reagan and Gorbachev. The treaty became a metaphor for the political controversies that swirled around East-West relations in the 1980s: the internal political pressures on NATO governments that accompanied the deployment of U.S. Pershing II and ground-launched cruise missiles in Europe, the ability of the Alliance to cohere in the face of overt military and political pressure from the Soviet Union, the debate over how and whether to "help" a reform-minded, new Soviet leader; the split within the West over whether arms control negotiations should be used merely as a "process" to placate public opinion or as a vehicle to conclude actual agreements; and the concerns in Asia that U.S. foreign policy was too Eurocentric.

The treaty also became caught up in U.S. domestic politics. Differences between progressive and conservative views within Washington over INF negotiating strategy were a mirror image of the perennial, often ideological, altercation within the body politic over how to deal with Soviet communism. Underlying this argument was a more profound struggle over the allocation of national resources, with some believing that a continued high investment in military programs to thwart Soviet military power was indispensable to national security, and others wanting to divert greater resources to domestic economic and social uses. In the background stood another political issue well understood by Americans: the sharing of power between the executive and legislative branches of government, an issue which surfaced with a vengeance during the Treaty ratification process in the U.S. Senate.

As a result of this wholesale politicization, the INF negotiations were, from the very outset, largely open negotiations performed with high drama on a public stage. Options vetted in the Washington interagency process were routinely leaked, as different factions within the government tried to gain public support for their position. Positions of various Allied governments on key issues were generally well known outside the chambers of the North Atlantic Council in Brussels, the inner sanctum of confidential Alliance consultations. Major moves by either side in the negotiations were often announced publicly before they were formally proposed at the negotiating table in Geneva. Even in Geneva, each side routinely held a press backgrounder shortly after making a new proposal in the talks. It was also a time when the U.S. and Allied governments learned, painfully, that Mr. Gorbachev and his new team not only understood "public diplomacy" and image-making, but were besting us at this, our own game.

The overarching political dimension of the negotiations also pervaded the internal discussions within the interagency community in Washington and the U.S. delegation. Although the specific topics for discussion were usually military or technical in nature, consideration of those issues was rarely free of deep-seated differences between agencies over how to manage U.S.-Soviet relations. As a result, discourse over seemingly obscure points could quickly become rancorous—especially if the discussion involved even the suggestion of a change in the U.S. position to move the negotiations forward. "Technical" details in the Treaty could (and often did) become political, both during the Treaty negotiations and the ratification debate.

The ultimate expression of the INF Treaty as a political instrument became its critical importance to the political futures both of President Gorbachev and President Reagan, as well as that of then Vice President George H.W. Bush. This is not to say that the Treaty was significant only in political terms, and not also in military terms. It would, when fully implemented, eliminate all U.S. and Soviet ground-launched missiles with ranges between 500 and 5,500 kilometers (300 to 3,400 miles). Although these forces represented well under ten percent of the nuclear arsenals of the two superpowers, this Treaty represented the first time the United States and the USSR agreed to reduce (rather than merely to limit) their nuclear forces. And an unprecedented regime of on-site inspection and comprehensive data exchange embodied in the Treaty promises far into the future to increase mutual confidence and reduce the risks of military miscalculation.

Yet, understanding the full significance of the INF Treaty requires grasping its political dimensions. They are what give the INF Treaty its *raison d'être* and historic significance. Therefore, in an effort to put the INF Treaty in perspective, this paper will focus primarily on interaction between the process of negotiations and the contemporaneous political dynamics.

The politics of the INF negotiations were marked by continuous testing: of the strength of collective security commitments, of the courage and resolve of government leaders, of Gorbachev's ability to bring the Soviet military into line, and of Reagan's willingness to override the opposition of Republican conservatives to an arms control deal with Gorbachev.

The Origins of the Negotiations

The process of testing began in 1977, when the Soviets started replacing ageing SS-4 and SS-5s with SS-20 missiles. This new missile was far more capable than its predecessors. A triple-warhead, road-mobile, solid-fuel system with a range of nearly 5,000 kilometers, the SS-20 was more accurate and practically invulnerable to attack. West German Chancellor Helmut Schmidt, in a highly-publicized speech in London late in 1977, raised the alarm over this threatening weapons system, warning that, "In Europe this magnifies the significance of the disparities between East and West as regards nuclear tactical and conventional forces." As a Western response,

Schmidt called for either a negotiated reduction of forces or for a massive NATO buildup.

Many in Washington did not share Schmidt's concern over the SS-20, viewing it as a routine modernization program. But there was no mistaking his political message: he was elevating the SS-20 deployment to the level of a Soviet politico-military challenge, requiring a staunch NATO (especially U.S.) response. Partly as a result of Schmidt's political challenge and partly because the U.S. military perceived this as an opportunity to deploy a new generation of U.S. intermediate-range missiles, the United States decided to mount a military response. Both the United States and its allies recognized, however, that U.S. deployment of INF missiles in Europe would encounter stiff resistance from left-of-center parties and pacifist groups in Western Europe.

Building on Schmidt's two alternatives, NATO decided to pursue both a deployment path and a negotiating path in NATO's "two-track" decision of 12 December 1979. This opened the way to U.S. and NATO military authorities to develop a plan to deploy 464 U.S. ground-launched cruise missiles (GLCM) with a range of 2,500 kilometers and 108 Pershing II ballistic missiles with a range of 1,800 kilometers. This NATO decision also set the stage for political ferment which nearly toppled friendly Allied governments.

An Alliance under Pressure

In 1981 the combination of President Ronald Reagan's hard-line anticommunist views and former President Carter's repeated warning in the 1980 Presidential campaign that Reagan would lead the nation into a dangerous military course aroused fears in Europe over an escalation of East-West tension. The proclivity of the President to engage in tough anti-Soviet rhetoric and of Secretary of Defense Caspar Weinberger and Secretary of State Al Haig to speculate publicly on war-fighting scenarios in Europe (including the notion of a winnable nuclear war) added to those fears.

Public opinion polls in Europe, at the time, reflected growing opposition to U.S. missile deployments. Many Europeans were concerned that these deployments would increase the risks of a nuclear exchange. Others believed the Reagan administration was seeking a pretext for nuclear war–fighting in Europe. As a result of this rising tide of discontent, pressure grew within the Alliance to begin work on the negotiating track. The year was drawing to a close with no appearance of serious interest within the Reagan administration in arms control negotiations. The administration appeared to be concentrating its energies exclusively on the largest military buildup in the nation's peacetime history, of which INF was only one element.

Somewhat belatedly, the President tried to respond to European apprehensions by outlining a comprehensive position on arms control at the National Press Club on 18 November 1981. As the centerpiece of his presentation, the President announced his famous "zero-zero" proposal: the United States would refrain from deploying new INF missiles in Europe if the Soviet Union would dismantle its existing INF force of 250 SS-20 missiles and 350 SS-4 and SS-5 missiles. The fact that the President had finally come out with a comprehensive policy on arms control was greeted with considerable relief and gave hope to European publics that the INF negotiating track would have sane actual substance. Public opinion both in Europe and America reacted positively to the fact that the President was sending his negotiators to Geneva with something in hand. The President's proposal that a whole class of nuclear missiles be eliminated and thus "substantially reduce the dread threat of nuclear war which hangs over the people of Europe" struck a responsive note with pacifist groups.

Knowledgeable observers were aware that the President had enunciated a position which was patently nonnegotiable. Brezhnev and Gromyko would have scant interest in a scenario in which they would scrap the entire deployed Soviet INF missile force in return for a U.S. commitment not to deploy a nonexistent U.S. INF missile force. For a time, however, the President had appeared to calm jitters in Europe. In the bargain, he had inadvertently demonstrated that public opinion does not distinguish between negotiable and nonnegotiable proposals in arms control. Any proposal is welcome, theatrical or real, if it appears to add stimulus to the negotiations. This lesson became more important as the negotiations wore on.

In any case, the favorable public reception for "zero-zero" was especially good news for the leaders of the five NATO countries which had agreed to serve as the "basing" countries for U.S. INF deployments: Great Britain, the Federal Republic of Germany, Belgium, the Netherlands, and Italy. INF deployments had already become a burning political issue in all of these countries, and opposition groups to U.S. deployments were numerous and well-organized. On 30 November 1981, U.S.-Soviet negotiations on INF began in Geneva with Paul Nitze as the Chief U.S. Representative and Yuli Kvitsinsky as the Chief Soviet Representative. The fact that Nitze was a distinguished American with long experience in national security affairs helped to bolster public confidence in the talks.

On that same day, 30 November, Ambassador Nitze tabled the "zero-zero" plan as a formal U.S. proposal in Geneva. The Soviet delegation responded with a counterproposal that dramatized the gulf between the positions of the two sides. The Soviets proposed that "NATO" reduce its INF forces, missiles, and aircraft to 300, leaving this figure as the INF ceiling for both sides in Europe. This position was also plausible publicly, since it called for equality between NATO and the Soviet Union in intermediate-range nuclear forces in Europe.

Again, however, knowledgeable observers recognized that this approach would be wholly unacceptable to the United States and NATO. First, in discussing "NATO" forces, the Soviets were referring to the nuclear forces of Great Britain and France, who were not even represented at the talks in Geneva. If Britain and France were to accept the Soviet proposal, their forces alone would meet the collective ceiling of 300 missiles and aircraft. In other words, acceptance of the Soviet proposal would have automatically excluded any U.S. INF deployments in Europe, and would curtail existing deployments of U.S. dual-capable aircraft, including those based on carriers stationed in the waters around Europe. Moreover, the Soviet proposal would not affect SS-20s based in the Asian territory of the USSR.

These observers would have missed the critical point. The Soviet proposal (like the original U.S. proposal) was not advanced with any serious expectation that it would include elements acceptable to the other side. Rather, it was designed quite explicitly for its public appeal and its divisive attractiveness in Europe. The argument that the Soviet Union faced a threat from three Western nuclear powers and should thus enjoy parity with them collectively would sound reasonable to Western opinion. The targeting of Allied nuclear forces in this proposal underlined the Soviet intention to focus on public opinion in Western Europe and to exacerbate internal divisions within Europe. Both Britain and France were engaged in significant, and costly, nuclear force modernization programs that were controversial within their own countries.

Predictably, given the incompatible positions of the two sides, the talks wore on inconclusively. As the climate of U.S.-Soviet relations worsened and public opinion became restive with the ostensible lack of progress in Geneva, Ambassadors Nitze and Kvitsinsky attempted to break the deadlock. During a renowned "walk in the woods" in the Jura Mountains above the Swiss town of Nyon, the two worked out a comprehensive approach under which the United States and the Soviet Union would have had equal numbers of INF launchers and aircraft, and the Soviets would freeze SS-20 deployments.

This was a classic example of two experienced, respected negotiators working on margins of formal sessions to hammer out an informal compromise package which involved significant concessions from both sides. Under the "walk in the woods" formula, the Soviet Union would have to reduce its existing SS-20 force from about 250 to seventy-five, cease further SS-20 deployments in its Asian territory, limit its intermediate-range nuclear-capable bombers, and drop its demand for inclusion of British and French nuclear forces in the agreement. For its part, the United States would replace the "zero-zero" approach with limited deployments by each side, forego plans to deploy the Pershing II in its Pershing PII modernization program, and reduce the number of its land-based, dual-capable aircraft stationed in Europe.

This was a workmanlike solution, which would have left both sides with their essential political and military interests in the matter intact. It was also a bold solution, precipitating the two governments towards a denouement more rapidly than either had anticipated. However, this promising gambit by Nitze and Kvitsinsky fizzled within a few months.

In Washington, Nitze was criticized for offering this formula to his counterpart without instructions, for abandoning Pershing II deployments, and for including aircraft. More importantly, the domestic politics and timing of this solution were all wrong. A stunning diplomatic breakthrough on INF in mid-1982 would precipitate a resurgence of detente, undermining the rationale for the massive U.S. military buildup and changing the administration's priorities. Especially, given the fact that the administration was pursuing a rhetorically hard line against the Soviets at that time, a sudden rush to an arms control agreement would be deeply divisive within the Republican Party.

While we are not privy to Moscow's innermost deliberations on this matter, subsequent events made it clear that Moscow essentially decided to postpone a diplomatic solution, which would require major concessions on their part, and to fight out this issue on the streets of Europe in a battle for public opinion. Moscow must have calculated that a better course would be to allow the debate in the West over U.S. INF deployments to fester. At best, public opposition to stationing Pershing II and GLCMS would be so intense that the Americans would be blocked from making these deployments altogether; and conservative governments, especially in Britain and the Federal Republic, might fall in the bargain. At worst, U.S. deployments would be plagued by public protest at each step of the way, and even if INF missile modernization in Europe succeeded, a precedent of political upheaval would be established which would deter future modernization programs of this kind.

If these were Moscow's calculations (and post Cold War documents imply such), they were nearly correct. While the Soviets in Geneva rejected any negotiated outcome in 1982-83, massive protests broke out all over Europe, and the future of the governments in the five Allied basing countries did, in fact, appear to hang in the balance at times. Nonetheless, government leaders held the line, the Alliance maintained its cohesion, and U.S. INF deployments began in November 1983. Ambassador Kvitsinsky led his delegation out of the INF talks on 23 November.

This entire episode is a case study in the close interaction between politics, military power, and diplomacy. If the United States had had its druthers, it would have preferred to modernize its INF forces in Europe as a routine military activity without the encumbrances of a negotiating track. But Allied leaders in Europe correctly sensed that this track was vital to their own political requirements. Had the United States rejected negotiations and attempted to deploy Pershing IIs and GLCMS without this political cover, the vigorous public opposition to deployments would probably have succeeded in blocking them. This would not only have undermined incumbent governments in London, Bonn, The Hague, Brussels, and Rome, it could have unraveled the postwar collective security system in Europe.

For both Washington and Moscow, therefore, the negotiations were a political necessity, but not necessarily a forum for resolving the INF issue. The overarching U.S. requirement was to proceed with INF modernization, and Moscow estimated that it could prevent those deployments politically without resorting to cutbacks in the SS-20 program. What sustained the negotiations, in addition to the ingenuity of the negotiators, was the need for both sides to demonstrate seriousness of purpose to public opinion. This required the periodic exchange of proposals, each accompanied by public fanfare. Yet, with the exception of the remarkable "walk in the woods" formula, the proposals from both sides were half measures which did not reflect the underlying reality.

The reality was that the United States simply did not have negotiating leverage because it had no weapons systems to trade against proposed Soviet reductions. And the political climate seemed to be running in the Soviets' favor. There was little actual inducement for the Soviet Union to give something for nothing, especially when they stood to gain mightily both in military and political terms if deep fissures within NATO over nuclear modernization ultimately blocked U.S. deployments.

Moreover, this Soviet game plan bore some fruit from the Soviet standpoint. The missile deployment issue did create deep scars in NATO. The United States was left appearing to public opinion as the aggressor, while the Soviet Union was unencumbered by any arms control agreement to postpone its own SS-20 deployments. Certainly the political groundwork was laid for blocking future generations of new U.S. nuclear weapons systems in Europe. From the political perspective, however, the Soviets sacrificed some of these hard-won gains when they walked out of Geneva. It was a maladroit step, which created greater sympathy for the United States and NATO. The Soviets compounded this error by walking out of the negotiations on conventional force reductions in Vienna as well.

By the time the Soviets returned to the negotiating table in Geneva in March 1985, they were relieved to be back. Their effort to block U.S. INF deployments through political and public pressure had failed. However, they were now facing a qualitatively different situation. Conservative governments in Western Europe had strengthened their position, partly because of their steadfastness over the INF issue. Public opinion had come to accept the Pershing II and GLCM deployments, which were proceeding inexorably and on time. The United States was also pleased to be back at the negotiating table, especially now that it had real negotiating leverage.

A New Soviet Leader Makes the Difference

Although the Soviets returned to Geneva more prepared to bargain on INF, they retained their penchant for striking positions designed to appeal to public opinion in the West and to create fissures within the Alliance. Their public villain in 1985, however, was no longer INF deployments, but a new target, "Star Wars," the President's Strategic Defense Initiative (SDI) program. SDI had stirred a major controversy in the United States where many questioned its feasibility, desirability, and cost, and in Europe, where "Star Wars" reinforced the impression of a trigger-happy President fixated on military-technology solutions to world problems.

The Soviets were determined to subordinate their strategic objectives in Geneva to an all-out effort to block the SDI program. When Secretary of State Shultz and Foreign Minister Gromyko met early in 1985 to work out the terms of reference for the arms control negotiations, Gromyko insisted on a close interrelationship between the negotiations on defense and space (D&S) issues, which would focus on SDI, the negotiations on INF, and on strategic arms reductions (START). This interrelationship would give the Soviets leverage to link progress on INF and START to progress on SDI issues in the D&S talks.

Shultz reluctantly agreed to this infelicitous arrangement as the price for resuming the arms control process. All three negotiations were placed under a single umbrella, the "Nuclear and Space Talks" (NST). Ambassador Max M. Kampelman served both as head of the overall NST delegation and the D&S delegation, with Soviet veteran negotiator on strategic arms Viktor Karpov as his counterpart heading the Soviet NST delegation. The U.S. INF delegation within this framework was headed by Ambassador Glitman, who had served as Ambassador Nitze's deputy in the 1981–83 INF talks, and the Soviet delegation by Ambassador Obukhov, a senior Soviet arms control expert.

The new general secretary of the Communist Party, Mikhail Gorbachev, reinforced this Soviet concentration on the SDI program soon after he assumed power in March 1985. Vociferous opposition to the U.S. "Star Wars" program marked Gorbachev's earliest statements on foreign and defense policy. In the early rounds in Geneva, the Soviets echoed Gorbachev, trying among other things to minimize the frequency of meetings of the START and INF fora and to maximize the number of meetings of the overall NST delegation, which had no independent substantive area for negotiation.

This Soviet posturing on "Star Wars," both publicly and at the negotiating table, effectively stalled any progress on INF in the first six months of the Geneva talks. Both sides were essentially repeating positions held over from the 1981–83 INF talks. In the meantime, Gorbachev was gaining substantial mileage from his public incantations against "Star Wars." Public opinion polls in Western Europe began to show even at that early stage in Gorbachev's incumbency that publics viewed him as "more of a man of peace" than the U.S. President.

Gorbachev's associates were quick to build upon this favorable public image of their new leader. They began to hold press conferences in Moscow where hitherto anonymous Soviet military figures took questions and answers. *Glasnost* suddenly made news from Russia more abundant and credible. Gorbachev displayed his own charisma and self-confidence in more open exchanges with the press and with visiting officials. He also made clear that he would play a direct, personal role in arms control matters.

Typically, the first break in the Soviet INF position came from Gorbachev personally, and was enunciated in public before taking the form of a formal, written proposal in Geneva. In October 1985, in his first visit to the West in his new capacity, Gorbachev traveled to Great Britain and France. His interlocutors were impressed with his candor, constructiveness, and pragmatic approach to problem solving. They were also impressed with how well he was received by public opinion.

The most striking thing about these visits to London and Paris, however, was that Gorbachev used them to change the Soviet position on UK and French nuclear forces in INF. He stated publicly that they were "off the ledger" in the INF negotiations. To INF-watchers, this was a dramatic change in the Soviet position. The inclusion of third-country nuclear forces in the INF agreement was more than a question of principle; it was an article of faith in the Soviet position in the 1981-83 talks. Gorbachev was also signaling that from the potpourri of arms control possibilities (strategic, defense and space, conventional, chemical, nonproliferation, nuclear testing), INF was the most promising area in which to test the waters.

In what became customary in Geneva, the U.S. delegation waited to see when the Soviet delegation would put one of Gorbachev's publicly stated positions on the negotiating table as a formal Soviet proposal. Starting with the Soviet position on British and French nuclear forces, the time gap was often considerable. The U.S. delegation pressed the Soviet delegation daily for some indication of a formal change in the Soviet position on this issue. Since Gorbachev's ability to sustain his power was potentially tenuous in those early days, there was much speculation on the U.S. side over the meaning of these delays. Was Gorbachev having difficulty gaining Politburo support for moves on arms control? Was there an Old Guard in the Foreign Ministry loyal to Gromyko which was resisting change? Were Soviet military leaders dragging their feet? Was the military supporting Gorbachev or opposing him?

When, some weeks after Gorbachev's public statements in Great Britain and France, the Soviet delegation did alter its position on third country nuclear forces, there was a sense that this important move on the Soviet side was linked to internal shakeups in both the Foreign Ministry and the General Staff. Whatever was happening behind the scenes, the United States was interested in exploring the limits of Gorbachev's flexibility. It responded to Gorbachev's move on British and French nuclear forces with a proposal for an "interim" INF agreement, i.e., something short of "zero- zero." The U.S. proposed a limit of 140 Pershing II and GLCM launchers and reductions of Soviet SS-20 missile launchers in Europe to the same number.

The idea of an "interim" agreement seemed to catch hold. In November 1985, President Reagan and General Secretary Gorbachev met for the first time in Geneva. Their communiqué included a commitment to progress on arms control, including "the idea of an interim agreement." Yet something more profound had happened at the Geneva summit. Ronald Reagan and Mikhail Gorbachev discovered that they could communicate and could understand each other's political agendas. It was that discovery which opened the path to the INF Treaty.

The Political Imperatives of Reagan and Gorbachev

From the time of his earliest pronouncements on *perestroika*, Gorbachev took the position that reductions in Soviet military expenditures were central to his economic reforms. He and his followers had clearly concluded that the Soviet economy was in dire straits and that extraordinary measures were required to reverse its fortunes. He made clear that sweeping reform of the Party and the government bureaucracy were needed concomitants of change. He also moved swiftly to place his own appointees in charge of the armed forces.

In promulgating both *glasnost* and *perestroika*, Gorbachev presented himself as a reformer. His survival in power would depend upon the success of these reforms. They were not achievable, however, without much improved relations with the West, particularly the United States. In the absence of sweeping arms control agreements with the United States, he could not justify reducing the Soviet armed forces by amounts large enough to affect the overall Soviet economy. Without the personal prestige and influence which derive from playing the role of well-liked and respected world statesman, Gorbachev would have less leverage in securing his power base at home. He was also less likely to obtain critical technology, commerce, and credits from the West as long as the Soviet Union was overtly threatening its neighbors with nuclear weapons.

A major arms control agreement, especially if it involved nuclear weapons and could be the basis for frequent meetings with U.S. leaders, would be well tailored to satisfy all of Gorbachev's objectives. Gorbachev was well aware of the strong resistance in some quarters in the United States to reducing defense spending or to concluding an arms control agreement with Moscow. The best way to accelerate progress would be a series of bold moves on the arms control front which would capture the imagination of Western publics and add pressure on Washington to be responsive.

Any arms control agreement with the United States would meet Gorbachev's political desiderata. As the public reaction to the "zero-zero" option had demonstrated, the public does not make nice distinctions between arms control plans. Most people are pleased to see any kind of movement on nuclear arms control. Gorbachev could have chosen to focus on INF for any number of reasons: progress there would appeal to popular opinion both in Europe and the United States; INF was less organically linked to "Star Wars" than was START and thus could be split off more easily for separate consideration; INF was relatively less complex than START and could thus be advanced more rapidly; it was easier to pressure the United States through its allies for progress in INF than it was in START, where Allied interests were not as directly involved; the substantive positions of the sides were closer together in INF than in other arms control fields; and the Soviet military would need to be asked for fewer sacrifices to achieve an INF agreement than they would for a strategic or conventional force reductions agreement.

The fusion between Gorbachev's political imperatives and an INF Treaty was thus plain to see. The political imperatives underlying President Reagan's quest for an arms control agreement with the new Soviet leader were less dramatic than in the case of Gorbachev, but were quite tangible nonetheless. In 1985, U.S. concern was growing over the burgeoning federal budget deficit, which was soaring over the $200 billion mark. Defense spending was contributing heavily to that deficit. The President had established national priorities in his first administration—a major defense buildup accompanied by a cut in taxes—which could be financed only through strong economic growth. Yet an unexpected recession in 1981 reduced expected federal revenues and plunged the Reagan presidency into a position of indebtedness from which it would never recover.

Indeed, the Reagan defense "boom" was over by 1985; defense spending had tapered off and was starting a gradual decline as a percentage of GNP. The choices for reducing the deficit were limited and politically unattractive to the White House: raise taxes, cut domestic programs further, or reverse the defense buildup. Pressures were growing in Congress to single out the defense budget to bear the greatest burden. For example, the *Gramm-Rudman-Hollings Budget Deficit Reduction Act* required that the Pentagon bear 50 percent of the balance needed to reach prescribed annual deficit reduction targets.

The savings accruing from an INF agreement would be insignificant in this context, but would still shield the President and his party against charges that they had endorsed runaway defense spending in flagrant disregard of budgetary realities. They could argue that the main rationale for the defense buildup, to restore America's military strength in order to bring the Soviets to the negotiating table, had been successful. In other words, the strategy of negotiating from positions of strength had worked. (Indeed, this is precisely the way Vice President Bush used the INF Treaty in his successful campaign for the presidency in 1988. The Treaty nailed down the peace plank for the Republican Party.)

If an arms control success could illustrate the validity of the "peace through strength" thesis, then that same thesis could be applied to other areas as well. It would be imprudent, for example, to cut back unilaterally on strategic modernization programs or on the SDI program until a START agreement were concluded, or on the next generation of tanks or tactical fighters until a conventional accord had been reached. Thus, a successful INF agreement could simultaneously placate criticism that the administration was not serious about arms control and preserve the rationale for continuing with the essential elements of the President's military buildup program, including SDI.

On a more subjective level, one could also argue that the 1986 Iran-Contra affair strengthened the President's interest in arms control, primarily to divert public attention. It is difficult to establish any clear cause-and-effect relationship in this case. Another explanation of the President's growing interest in INF was that he was becoming increasingly conscious of his historical legacy and wanted to be remembered as a man of peace. Whatever their respective motivations, once the President and the General Secretary concluded that they wanted to proceed towards an INF agreement and were willing to provide the kind of discipline and leadership within their respective governments to obtain it, the various pieces of this complex document began to fall into place.

In January 1986, just three months after his meeting with President Reagan in Geneva, Gorbachev publicly announced his willingness to accept a "zero" option for European-based U.S. and Soviet INF missiles, which would be eliminated over a five to eight year period. At the October 1986 Reagan-Gorbachev meeting in Reykjavik, Gorbachev agreed for the first time to reduce Soviet SS-20 deployments in Asia to an interim equal global limit of 100 per side outside of Europe. Interestingly, this triggered a strong negative reaction from Japan, China, and Australia, which rejected what they viewed as a differentiated U.S. and Soviet approach between European and Asian security. They raised this concern at political levels with the Soviets, which led to Gorbachev's July 1987 statement to an Indonesian journalist that he would agree to the total, global elimination of all ground-launched INF missiles, including the SS-20 force stationed in the Asian territory of the Soviet Union.

In spring 1987, Gorbachev led another major departure from the Soviets' traditional opposition to reducing their shorter-range INF missiles, the SS-12s and SS-23s with ranges of up to 900 kilometers and 500 kilometers respectively. He publicly offered a "second zero": namely, the elimination of all shorter-range missiles with ranges between 500 and 1,000 kilometers. Under this formula, the Soviets would eliminate the SS-12 and SS-23 missiles. The U.S. would destroy the Pershing IA, which was no longer deployed in Europe as a U.S. system, and the Pershing IB, which was still to be developed. Although this offer appeared to be strongly biased in the U.S. favor, it succeeded in creating considerable political controversy among our European allies. They worried that by lowering the threshold of the Treaty, a ban on shorter-range missiles was a potentially dangerous step towards total denuclearization. Some were concerned that a ban could later inhibit (which ultimately it did) the deployment of modernized short-range missiles with ranges under 500 kilometers, such as the follow-on version of the U.S. Lance missile.

Gorbachev's "second zero" proposal also brought into focus another politically volatile issue: the Federal Republic of Germany's Pershing IA missile system. Modernization of this force had been a subject of vigorous debate within Bonn for years. The Soviets argued that, since these missiles were armed with U.S. warheads and fell within the 500-1,000 kilometer range limitation, they should also be eliminated. The United States replied that since U.S. warheads for these missiles were provided under a long-established program of cooperation between the United States and the Federal Republic, and since the launchers belonged to a third party, these systems should be excluded under the Treaty. Quite apart from the various lines of argument, the Soviets succeeded in portraying the FRG's PIA missile force as a potential obstacle to the Treaty. Chancellor Kohl responded to this successful political squeeze play by announcing that Germany would dismantle its Pershing IA force, but outside the context of the Treaty.

The two leaders, for their own internal political reasons, thus set the basic parameters of the INF Treaty: global double zero, i.e., the world-wide elimination of all ground-launched missiles of both intermediate range (1,000-5,000 kilometers) and shorter-range (500-1,000 kilometers). Once these parameters had been established, a complex task of wrapping up a detailed treaty text remained. The only question then was not whether the INF Treaty would be ready for signature, but when.

Finishing Up

The final few months of work on the Treaty were challenging and hectic, but took place among foreign ministers, ambassadors, and experts largely out of public view. The bulk of the work was devoted to ironing out the details of complex counting rules and verification provisions. This work broke a great deal of new ground in the world of arms control negotiations, but was largely the domain of arms control and military specialists. The President occasionally had to enter the fray to resolve interagency differences over remaining issues (a notable example was his decision to overrule the Pentagon's desire to exclude conventionally-armed INF-range cruise missiles from the Treaty, by siding with the argument that such a provision would be unverifiable.) Presumably, Mr. Gorbachev may have entered the debate within the Kremlin occasionally as well, on critical details related to verification. But these details were not dealt with as political issues.

The most important final political decision which both leaders took to secure the INF Treaty was relatively simple, but essential: setting the date for the summit meeting in Washington at which the Treaty would be signed. During a trip to Washington by Foreign Minister Shevardnadze at the end of September, the starting date for the summit was set as 7 December 1987. Subsequently, observers with a memory for history noted that it would be inauspicious to sign a landmark treaty on the anniversary of Pearl Harbor, and the summit date was switched to 8 December. Without that deadline, the negotiations in Geneva would probably have continued for several more months.

Only a month before the summit, one hundred bracketed passages remained in the Treaty text, and a wealth of detailed Treaty implementation procedures had to be set aside for resolution after Treaty signature. Without the pressure of the Summit deadline, the delegations in Geneva and their backstopping committees in Washington and Moscow would doubtless have moved forward at a more measured pace. This experience demonstrates once again that one of the most important powers which a chief executive has is the power to set deadlines.

Without underlying political imperatives on both sides and personal involvement at leadership levels, arms control negotiations become a cottage industry for specialists. The Mutual and Balanced Force Reductions in Vienna (1972-89) were a classic case in point. There was nothing inherently wrong with the forum, the format, the substantive content, or the competence of the negotiators in Vienna. The problem was simply that there was no single time at which the leaders of the major participating countries all believed that an actual conventional force reductions agreement was in their own interest. If INF had not met the respective agendas and timetables of both Presidents Reagan and Gorbachev, the INF talks would have suffered the same fate as MBFR, a "process" of negotiations not intended to produce a concrete outcome.

The INF Treaty was achievable because of a rare confluence of events that brought the interests of the two nations and their leaders together at roughly the same time. The result was quite remarkable. The treaty itself, in bulk alone, surpasses any previous agreements of this kind. Its text, including protocols and appendices, far exceeds in length all of the arms control and disarmament agreements concluded since World War II combined. In substance, it is the first treaty actually to reduce nuclear arms and contains verification provisions so intrusive that they shatter a tradition, many centuries long, of the inviolable secrecy of military installations. The INF Treaty is a fitting benchmark for the dramatic turn of events that drew the Cold War to a close.

The Endgame in Washington

Roger Harrison

Roger Harrison was the Principal Deputy Assistant Secretary for the Politico-Military Bureau in the Department of State during the final stages of the INF negotiations. The article has not been previously published.

Elsewhere in this volume the point is made that it is difficult to determine precisely when a negotiating endgame begins. I disagree. The endgame of any negotiation begins when the bureaucracies charged with conducting it are given unequivocal notice that negotiations are concluded when the political leadership wishes it. Until that notice is given, intra-governmental disagreements, and the resultant lack of negotiating flexibility, will usually dictate a glacial negotiating pace. Once a clear decision has been taken on both sides to conclude, bureaucracies can perform with admirable efficiency.

By this measure, the INF endgame began on 18 September 1987, when, at the conclusion of their meetings in Washington, Secretary of State Shultz and Foreign Minister Shevardnadze announced that the Treaty would be signed at a Reagan/Gorbachev Summit before the end of the year.

This announcement put a formal end to a debate about the advisability of the Treaty which had never quite died out in Washington, even after the administration was formally committed to achieving one. The debate had been like glue in the bureaucratic gears.

But a series of Gorbachev concessions through the early part of 1987 made clear that the Soviets were determined to conclude the Treaty on terms proposed by the United States. Gorbachev accepted the U.S. position on "double-global-zero," that is, the argument that all missile systems in the intermediate range wherever stationed would be destroyed. Indeed, he had gone beyond that position by agreeing to destroy his shorter range missiles (between 500-1,000 km), for which there was no Western equivalent. The resulting reductions would be highly asymmetrical in favor of the United States, a position the United States had maintained from the beginning, and the Soviets had long rejected. There was also agreement that destruction would be preceded by a wide-ranging exchange of information about the numbers and locations of existing stockpiles. Finally, there was agreement that compliance with the Treaty would be monitored by verification measures of unprecedented intrusiveness, including on-site inspection of facilities associated with intermediate range missiles.

In short, Gorbachev's acceptance of the Reagan administration's desiderata for arms control in general, and the INF Treaty in particular, made a treaty inevitable. The Shultz/Shevardnadze announcement formalized this inevitability and added the additional element of time pressure. With both governments committed, the cost of postponement into 1988 would have been unacceptably high. No official on either side could ignore the consequences of being seen to contribute to such an unhappy outcome. Accordingly, the question from mid-September on was not whether or even when a treaty would be signed, but how agreement in principle would be translated into exact and detailed Treaty language.

The task of completing the Treaty fell largely to the negotiating team and, in Washington to the INF Interagency Group (IG) and its subordinate Working Group (WG).

Within the overall Reagan NSC system, IGs had been envisioned as Assistant-Secretary-level policy making bodies. The time demands of an intensive IG schedule, however, meant that by mid-1987, IG participants were, for the most part, deputy assistant secretaries. All concerned agencies were represented: the Office of the Secretary of Defense, the Joints Chiefs of Staff, the Department of Energy, the Arms Control Agency, the Director of Central Intelligence, and the National Security Council Staff. Other agencies would be added for particular issues; for example, domestic law enforcement agencies took an active role on issues involving the presence of Soviet inspectors in or near sensitive U.S. facilities as part of the on-site inspection regime.

Delegation cables reporting on the course of the negotiations and seeking guidance in part provided the formal grist for the IG mill. These cables usually represented a consensus position of the agencies represented on the delegation. But each delegation rep had back channel communication to his home agency, and the recommendations made in these channels sometimes differed from the delegations consensus advice. In addition, the IG benefited from Working Group and agency studies on particularly complex or technical issues.

Sessions of the IG were preceded by meetings of its Working Group, whose composition mirrored that of the IG, but at the action officer level. This group's chief function was to define the issues for the subsequent IG meetings, as well as to give IG participants a sense of other agency positions. The period between WG and IG meetings was the occasion for intense lobbying efforts, as coalitions formed for the debate to come. The IG meetings usually began in late afternoon, after the WG results had been digested and the results of the day's negotiating session in Geneva were known. When the IG meetings ended, ACDA staffers, toiling late into the evening, prepared the guidance cable to the delegation. Meanwhile, IG participants were responsible for ensuring that the IG consensus was acceptable to their agency; this was usually the case, because IG reps understood their agency interest, and because overruling the IG meant involving principals (whose time was always in short supply) with no guarantee of a more acceptable outcome. The NSC staff exercised a final control to ensure that the guidance cable was, in fact, acceptable to all concerned agencies.

The IG resolved perhaps eighty percent of the issues presented to it, without recourse to higher authority. Those issues which remained disagreed at the IG level were forwarded to the White House for decision, or remanded to the under-secretary-level Special Action Group (SAC-G) or, in the most important cases, forwarded to the NSC for presidential decision. At first, agencies forwarded closely argued rationales with their positions; later, as time became more pressing, the NSC staff representative (who attended IG meetings) took on the added task of representing agency positions directly to higher authority.

It should also be noted that some key issues, including the

politically most sensitive, were never brought to the IG, but rather taken immediately in hand by the President and his key advisers. Still, the IG was the center of the action: the boiler room of the INF endgame.

The IG's success was the more remarkable given the very different perspective with agency players brought to the process. Every nuance of opinion, from the most ideological to the most pragmatic was represented, but *generally* (and what follows is a generalization) agencies adopted more or less consistent approaches reflecting their own particular concerns.

The Joint Chiefs of Staff, for example, tended to look closely at the practical implications of various measures, particularly those involving verification and elimination. The Chiefs understood that they would be ultimately responsible for implementing such measures, however impractical, expensive, or environmentally objectionable they might be. For example, while agencies agreed on the benefits of intrusive verification measures to lessen the chances of any possible Soviet cheating, the Chiefs were forced to balance this benefit against the possible negative effect of such measures on U.S. operating flexibility and the need to protect sensitive U.S. programs unconnected to INF. As well, the Chiefs had to pay close attention to the effect of INF provisions on other weapons programs, including some so highly classified that they were unknown to other agency representatives.

In sum, since the burden of implementation would fall largely on the military services, the Chiefs tended to be the pragmatists of the interagency process. They could not afford to sacrifice practicality for ideology. At the same time, the role of the JCS in the negotiating process was of key importance. All U.S. players recognized that no agreement would be ratified by Congress unless it had the Chiefs' unreserved support.

The Intelligence Community (IC), like the JCS, tended to take a pragmatic view, but here the concern was somewhat different—chiefly that the IC not be held by the Treaty to be responsible for monitoring Soviet activities which could not effectively be monitored. The rule was simple: "Do not create Treaty limitations which cannot be monitored." The monitoring agencies were vigilant in ensuring that the rule was upheld. Moreover, the IC, like the JCS, had to balance between the desire for more intrusive measures against the need to protect both sources and methods, and its own sensitive programs unrelated to INF.

The IC was very active on issues involving its expertise/interest: as a matter of course, it abstained on strictly "policy" issues where its equities were not involved. The same attitude was true of other agencies, which, like the director of central intelligence, tended to have relatively narrow and pragmatic concerns. The Department of Energy, for example, had a clear interest in protecting security interests at many potential inspection sites, and the FBI, which joined IG discussions on questions involving the presence of Soviet inspectors on U.S. territory, did so from the perspective of that bureau's responsibility to guard against Soviet use of their inspection corps for purposes of espionage.

The interests of the remaining agency players were more broadly focused, and occasionally more diffuse. The Arms Control and Disarmament Agency (ACDA), for example, had formal responsibility for preparing guidance cables to the delegation based on IG decisions, but this was an administrative rather than a substantive function. For the rest, ACDA tended to be influential in the process not because it represented a clear organizational interest, but because of the quality of its representative, whose experience and expertise made him perhaps the most universally respected of IG participants. Indeed, the lack of any clear ACDA organizational focus in the negotiation allowed its representative to serve as a key broker in IG debates often suggesting solutions which satisfied the minimal interests of all agencies and allowed the process to move forward.

The role of the State Department (DOS) representative was affected by the organizational requirement both to chair IG meetings and to represent an agency point of view. In the role of chairman, the Department of State's representative was required to be above the battle: a moderator and neutral broker. In his agency role, he was charged with representing DOS equities. Those two roles sometimes coexisted uncomfortably. DOS's organizational interests, on the other hand, were clear. They were focused first on the need to keep Allied governments and public opinion firmly behind the U.S.

position, and secondly on the integrity and credibility of the negotiating process. DOS was always aware that the INF Treaty was only one aspect of the broader relationship with the Soviet Union: a relationship which could be affected for better or worse by the both the conduct and outcome of the negotiations.

The Office of the Secretary of Defense (OSD) tended to represent the negotiating verities which had been advocated by the Reagan administration from the beginning: tough verification measures, skepticism about the need for reciprocity, and insistence on greatly asymmetrical Soviet reductions. But OSD was not blind to the problems which overly intrusive verification posed for U.S. security interests or the potential limits to the benefits of any verification regime, no matter how intrusive. Indeed, there was a widespread assumption, at OSD and elsewhere, that the Soviets would never allow inspectors to see a violation, whatever the Treaty provisions might say. Given this fact, it was sometimes argued (though not by OSD reps) that the United States should dispense with all "cooperative" verification measures such as on-site inspection, and rely instead solely on national technical means for verification.

Finally, the representative of the National Security Council staff played a key role in the IG. He was charged with reminding IG members when they strayed from the president's announced policies, or from previous presidential decisions. As mentioned above, NSC reps also gradually took on the function of recorder, charged with accurately reflecting agency disputes for White House resolution.

Aside from differing agency viewpoints, other inputs affected debate in the IG. Among these, of course, were the recommendations of the chief negotiator. When the ambassador chose to take a strong stand, and especially when he was supported by a united delegation in Geneva, Washington agencies were reluctant to overrule him. Another was the climate of public debate in Washington, and here leaks played an important role. Bureaucratic players tend to be rendered particularly cautious by the knowledge that whatever they suggest might be broadcast to the world the next day in the columns of the *Washington Post*.

An even greater influence on the intra-administration process was the specter of the congressional ratification debate. At least since the SALT II experience, no administration can take Senate ratification of an arms control treaty for granted, nor should this be the case. Still, one effect is to put a premium on multiple safeguards, in part to ensure against legitimate grounds for objection from a properly attentive and concerned Senate, but also in part to avoid providing raw material (however inconsequential) for the sort of demagogy which many feared would be an element of the ratification process.

The IG's job proved formidable, in some measure because participants were dealing with issues unprecedented in the annals of arms control, or indeed of relations between adversary nations. Never before had two nations agreed to destroy as formidable an arsenal as that covered by the INF Treaty. Never before had a treaty included verification provisions remotely as extensive or intrusive as those included there. Never before had nations agreed to exchange sensitive military information to the same extent. Each step beyond precedent involved complex negotiations in Geneva and in Washington—negotiations which took on added significance because of the assumption (both within the administration and on Capitol Hill) that verification provisions agreed in INF would become precedents for the far more important negotiations on strategic arms reductions.

The result of all these factors: the novel nature of the issues, the pressures of a semi-public negotiation, the differing agency viewpoints and specter of a difficult ratification debate, was an intra-administration negotiation of Byzantine complexity. Even relatively straightforward issues often turned out to be both complex and politically fraught. The key endgame issues are recounted elsewhere in this volume. For our purposes, it will suffice to focus on one problem: to make the point that the complexity of modern arms control treaties has changed the nature of the "game" to one in which, arguably, the treaty making process no longer ends with signature and ratification.

A case in point is the INF Treaty's novel treatment of verification. More stringent verification had been a key demand of the Reagan administration from the outset, a demand usually summarized under the slogan, "anywhere, anytime challenge inspection." But "anywhere, anytime" was always a better slogan than a program. No country could allow a literal anywhere/anytime regime to be applied to its sensitive military and national security facilities. On the U.S. side, for example, merely identifying and preparing for inspection all of the potentially sensitive sites would involve enormous (some argued incalculable) trouble and expense. Nevertheless, the need for an intrusive inspection regime and high levels of verification certainty was a both a military and a political requirement in the United States: one which, by the time of the endgame, the Soviet Union had come to accept.

It was also clear by that time that such a regime would involve a significant presence of U.S. inspectors on Soviet territory, and vice versa. In the Treaty, that presence takes two forms: on the one hand, inspection teams enter the country to conduct short-notice inspections at "formally declared" INF sites, i.e., sites which each country had declared in the data exchange which accompanied Treaty signature. Inspectors also are present at Soviet elimination sites to witness destruction of Treaty-limited missiles. Finally, the two sides agreed to establish "permanent portal monitoring (PPM)," i.e., teams of inspectors permanently installed at the portals of one of the other side's production facilities.

The need for PPM arose because of the similarity of the SS-20 and the intercontinental range SS-25, which is not covered by the Treaty. The Soviet missile production plant at Votkinsk, which had produced SS-20s, was now producing SS-25s. The question was how the United States could be certain the SS-25 infrastructure, including this plant, was not being used to produce and maintain a clandestine SS-20 force. The answer was PPM, giving the United States a right directly to observe what emerged from the Votkinsk plant. Of course, this sort of intrusive inspection was not cost free. The Soviets demanded reciprocity, leading (after considerable haggling) to establishment of a Soviet PPM team at the portal of a Magna, Utah facility which had (but no longer) produced a stage of the Pershing missile.

Both on-site inspection and PPM will now doubtless be features of any future arms control regime with Moscow and both add enormously to the complexity of the resultant treaties. This complexity arises in part from the need to protect U.S. personnel in an adversary country, as well as to protect sensitive U.S. programs against the espionage potential of inspectors in the United States. But there is also a list of technical issues which sometimes seemed endless. The problem is relatively simply stated: how to provide sufficient access to inspectors to ensure against possible violations, without allowing access to other, unrelated national security information. Implementation was another matter.

For example, the sides agreed on installation of "imaging" devices at their PPM sites. From the U.S. perspective, the need for such devices arose because of Soviet claims that SS-25s emerging from Votkinsk could not safely be removed from their canisters. (The U.S. side would have the right to "pop the tops" of selected canisters; but the need for greater certainty dictated imaging of the canisters, to ensure that SS-20s were not concealed in the longer SS-25 canisters.) With agreement in principle on imaging, the Treaty was signed and ratified, but it was only beginning of the issue. The question which then arose was how much imaging was enough, i.e., what were the precise parameters which would allow an imaging device to perform its Treaty function of detecting illegal missiles, without permitting the inspecting side to use imaging to collect intelligence about, for example, the other side's missile technology. The Special Verification Commission (SVC), established by the Treaty to oversee implementation, continued to labor over that and other technical issues throughout its existence.

What lessons can be drawn, then, from Washington's experience with the INF endgame? Most were lessons often learned in past negotiations, but at least one is potentially new and not unique to INF: it is that open covenants, openly arrived at, have become the norm. That delights all true democrats, but it also poses difficulties for negotiators. For example, bluffs and feints are tactics no longer readily available to U.S. negotiators because of the virtual certainty that such tactics will be revealed to the world in the press before they can be deployed. Nor can negotiators easily explore novel solutions, as they might if their discussions were confidential (Ambassador Nitze's famous "walk in the woods" demonstrates that even the most confidential exchanges will not long remain so). And finally, publicity ensures that negotiating positions will be chosen with one eye on their public relations value. The result is the sort of one-ups-man-ship which characterized the final stages of the INF process, albeit in this case leading on to a fortunate conclusion.

Still another lesson, which is as old as negotiations between nations, is that the clearly expressed political will to reach agreement on both sides is vital to success. Without this impetus, negotiations deteriorate into stalemate at the table and fruitless haggling at home. Bureaucracies, left to their own devices, fulfill predictions of universal entropy. A corollary is that the old saw about not negotiating against deadlines is not necessarily true. George Shultz was candid in acknowledging that one reason for his monthly meetings with Shevardnadze during the endgame was to provide the sort of "forcing event" necessary to get the bureaucracies moving. Setting a date, as Shultz and Shevardnadze did in September 1987, can be a very effective way of imposing the will of political leaders on squabbling officials. Not surprisingly, it was the right wing that inveighed against this process, not because they feared a hastily written Treaty, but because they hoped delay would make it impossible for President Reagan to conclude a START Treaty before the end of his term.

But perhaps the most interesting lesson of the INF endgame experience is not one which has been taught quite so clearly before—I mean the lesson that modern arms control, in all its complexity, may have outgrown the traditional treaty-making process. Illustratively, had the INF delegations been required to decide *all* issues (including, for example, the exact technical configuration of the imaging devices at Votkinsk and Magna) *before* ratification, the negotiation would still be in progress, and the hundreds of Soviet missiles already destroyed would still be ready on their launchers. The upcoming START Treaty, with far more inclusive provisions for on-site inspection and permanent portal monitoring will doubtless require what is, in effect, an ongoing negotiating forum between the two sides after Treaty ratification (as, arguably, the SVC became for INF). Combine this circumstance with the recent agreement between Moscow and Washington to put in place some verification provisions before a START Treaty is concluded, and the result may be that treaty-making as process, in which signature and ratification set the parameters for what is in effect a continuing dialogue between the super powers on their security relationship.

Vignette: A Meeting

Teams are arrayed on opposite sides of the long immaculate table. The centered ambassadors face one another. The initial cups of coffee have been drawn from steaming samovars, pencils fiddled with, note takers are poised. Prepared statements and talking points are readied for deployment. The preliminary niceties regarding weather or whatever exchanged.

Hundreds of meetings either full plenary session, subgroups, working groups lie behind. Unknown numbers are ahead. Official reporting has trapped them all for the "Ultimate Graduate Student" who in the year 20xx will begin to track his way through the labyrinth of documented words. Beyond the serious substance there are other memories:

The Notes

Encouraged by the ambassador, the U.S. delegation regularly passed him notes and comment. "Keep those cards and letters coming" was his philosophy. A few quickly jotted words to point out a flawed Soviet argument or reinforce a U.S. position were the usual content as the United States pressed daily for movement. This group participation, unspoken as it was, always seemed to irritate the Soviets who, without ever saying so, gave the impression that we were coaching unfairly from the sidelines. (The Soviet side never passed such notes to their ambassador.) Of course, all notes were not serious. "Is his nose growing?" "Here we go again." "Pizza tonight?" were also exchanged.

The Expert

We were deeply engaged in one of the more technical issues of the negotiation, i.e., deciding how to determine whether some future newly developed cruise missile would fall under the Treaty provisions. The Soviet position was simple: if tested below 500 km, it is permitted. The United States was pursuing a complex, detailed technical criteria with extensive engineering rationale. The Soviets resisted and professed not to understand. The United States unveiled a PhD-credentialed engineer to provide a comprehensive technical explanation. He was persuasive, even brilliant in clarity, able at least to convince the U.S. delegation that they knew what he was talking about. The Soviets sat stolidly. The answer is still *"nyet."* So much for technical virtuosity.

The Interpreter

Far more than a translating machine, the U.S. interpreters were vital elements of the negotiating team. In contrast, the Soviet interpreters sometimes appeared to be still in training, minor league AA players suddenly given a World Series slot, and could be subject to rough correction by the Soviet ambassador ("That's not what I said.") Deep into the end game, the delegations are anticipating a mini Summit between ranking officials from Washington (Ambassador Kampelman) and Moscow (Deputy Foreign Minister Vorontsov). U.S. and Soviet delegations are attempting to resolve/clarify outstanding issues. The Soviets are pressing a point and Ambassador Glitman is fending them off while scoring rebuttal arguments to reinforce the U.S. view. In a moment of silence, the U.S. interpreter hears a whispered Russian exchange "Drop it for now. We'll get it past Kampelman tomorrow." Forewarned, they didn't.

INF Endgame:
Another Perspective

David T. Jones

David Jones was a member of the INF delegation. The article was written during a sabbatical in 1988-89 and not previously published.

"ENDGAME: The last stages of a chess game,
when the forces on both sides have been greatly reduced
and the basic power relationship has been established."

— *Webster's New International Dictionary,*
Second Edition, Unabridged

Every negotiation has an "endgame," even if it is defined as no more than discussion of the final elements of an agreement prior to successful completion. Thus agreements on Cultural and Educational Exchange or Science and Technology Cooperation would each have their own "endgame." If, however, we conceive of the "endgame" as a period of tension and pressure building to a climactic conclusion, U.S. bilateral arms control negotiations with the Soviets over the past twenty-five years have epitomized such a genre.

Indeed, each of the major strategic arms control agreements has had its own apocalyptic stories. Reportedly final SALT I language was being composed as the combined U.S. delegation flew from Geneva to Vienna. In SALT II, the letter outlining Soviet "Backfire" bomber commitments was altered the night before signature, after the copies of the agreement had been dispatched by courier to NATO Allies in Brussels. Changes were telegraphed to the U.S. Mission at NATO and a revised Backfire letter substituted before distribution.

It is sometimes asked why there is frequently such a negotiating intensity at the conclusion of an agreement. Some, living neatly patterned lives, are simply puzzled that problems are not pre-identified and time allotted for them, including of course a measured amount of time reserved to handle the unexpected "black swans." Their observation carries the implicit criticism that those doing the negotiating are inefficient, lack foresight, or do not practice sound management techniques. They are politely skeptical at the explanations of negotiators who suggest that negotiating with an adversary is less predictable than negotiating with a friend or ally and, fail to acknowledge an application of Parkinson's Law, that "work expands to fill the time available in which to do it."

Others are more hostile. They assume that if a job is completed against a tight deadline, there must be mistakes: errors of commission or omission. These are individuals who take for granted an athlete's ability to act in fractions of a second, a race driver's ability to perform flawlessly for hours at 150 mph, or a pilot's skill in making hundreds of "no fault" landings, but assume that diplomats with years or even decades of experience must be making major mistakes even if they have hours or days in which to reach decisions. Presumably these critics, more familiar with words than deeds, project their own shortcomings onto diplomatic projects.

In some aspects, the INF Treaty "endgame" followed traditional negotiating patterns. A great deal of negotiating, language drafting, and text preparation had to be completed in a shorter rather than a longer time. Over this work hung the anticipation of a U.S.-Soviet Summit meeting, the timing of which was contingent both upon a successfully completed Treaty and forcing the pace toward its completion. That is to say, without a completed INF Treaty, the rationale for a Summit was slight and consequently no date was set until the sides were confident that the remaining issues, whether large or small, could be resolved. Consequently, after the Summit date was determined, the impetus for Soviet, as well as for U.S. negotiators to complete the agreement was very high. There are no foregone conclusions either in life or diplomacy, and an INF "failure" was always possible, but each side was aware that only a major substantive shortcoming, clearly understandable to publics and foreign governments, could explain an incomplete Treaty.

Background to the Endgame

At the beginning of 1987, only a very sanguine or exceptionally pre-scient observer (and none were writing for the record) would have predicted an INF agreement by the end of 1987. Following substan-tive advances in INF at the October 1986 Reykjavik Summit, the Soviets had re-linked an INF agreement to satisfactory solutions to their Strategic Defense Initiative (SDI) concerns—a move which appeared to be a return on their part to a negotiating dead end in which we had previously been trapped. This strategic deadlock had no internal time limit demanding resolution.

At the same time, the U.S. arms control community had plunged into its own dead end: an attempt to determine just what a nuclear free world as hypothesized at the Reykjavik Summit might look like. The investigation was pursued seriously, at a minimum as an intellectual effort on a topic which had not been comprehensively examined in many years. Some of the results were "blue sky" think pieces, concluding for example that war, even between great pow-ers, would be less catastrophic and that a "no nukes" world would enhance the status of currently secondary or tertiary powers. Other studies for which the Department of Defense was responsible were designed to determine how, without vastly increasing defense ex-penditures, the U.S. could continue to meet its military commit-ments.

In the early part of 1987, working beneath the strategic dead-lock of the Soviet INF-SDI linkage, the INF negotiations were still reacting substantively to the Reykjavik Summit developments. The U.S. and Soviets had concluded that an INF Treaty, while eliminat-ing all INF missiles from a still to be defined "Europe," would per-mit each side to retain a global total of 100 INF warheads outside Europe. There was distinct satisfaction with the parameters of such an agreement in many quarters. The Soviets had, after all, already accepted the basic U.S. requirements of "equality" (each side would have equal numbers of INF warheads following agreement) and "globality" (the agreement would apply worldwide). The Soviets were committed to asymmetrical reductions and had made no fur-ther fuss over their long standing desire to include UK and French INF systems in the Treaty, or to be compensated for them in some manner. The Soviets were even committing themselves to "effective verification," although what this was to mean in the language of specific provisions was still totally undetermined.

In mid-January, the U.S. tabled a proposal which reflected the Reykjavik agreement and recommended completing reductions by the end of 1991. We stressed that there could be no connection between any INF agreement and other issues, i.e., no linkage between INF and SDI. Additional focus was given to shorter-range INF (SRINF) systems (500–1,000 km range) reflecting NATO's concern that an INF agreement that eliminated the SS-20 could be effectively circumvented by a buildup of Soviet systems just below the INF range threshold. Such perfectly legal systems could strike most of the targets threatened by the SS-20. Consequently, the United States proposed:

1. To limit SRINF to global totals at the existing Soviet level;
2. To ban development of systems with ranges between the U.S. Pershing II and the Soviet SS-12 ; and
3. To begin follow on negotiations on additional SRINF constraints and/or reductions within six months after reaching any INF agreement.

As part of the mosaic of verification measures, the U.S. specifically mentioned that there must be on-site verification of destruction of INF systems and subsequent monitoring of facilities, including on-site inspection, following elimination of systems.

Despite significant satisfaction with the essentials of the Reykjavik accords, there were problems. Effectively monitoring the numbers of a residual force of Soviet INF missiles would be very difficult. The "cheating scenarios" possible with such a force suggested verification problems that only a highly intrusive inspection system could overcome. U.S. planners were grappling with methods for limiting geographic areas into which Soviet INF missiles could deploy, "tagging" the remaining permitted missiles with a tamperproof label to assure that a "covert" missile could not be hidden under a false number, and creating limited and monitored entry and exit points from the deployment areas. The more cumbersome the inspection system and the more cautious the intelligence specialists became over their ability to monitor Treaty provisions with high confidence, the more dubious Senate ratification appeared.

Simultaneously, Asian allies, particularly Japan, were notably unenthusiastic. They had not been pleased with the substance of the Reykjavik Summit and made their position clear to Ambassador Rowny during his post-Summit tour of Far-Eastern capitals. Despite U.S. arguments stressing the dramatic anticipated reductions in the SS-20 force based in Soviet Asia, they argued that an agreement eliminating INF missiles in Europe while a threat remained in Asia discriminated against them. While accepting at face value U.S. assurances that an INF agreement leaving a hundred-warhead residual force was only a first step and that our ultimate goal was worldwide elimination of INF systems, Japanese quickly pointed out the Soviet ability to shift their Asian-based SS-20s to threaten Europe again and noted the monitoring/inspection weaknesses inherent in attempting to verify the levels of a residual force.

Gorbachev Reverses the Field

On 28 February, the Soviets flip-flopped again. Gorbachev announced that the Soviets recognized that an INF agreement could be concluded separately from SDI/START.

On 3 March, President Reagan exploited this development by announcing that the United States would begin to table a new INF Treaty draft incorporating basic elements of agreement, and on 4 March the U.S delegation in Geneva began this process. The timing was only partly fortuitous. Clearly a draft Treaty cannot be written from scratch in less than a week. Quite to the contrary, the United States had been painstakingly struggling through the interagency process since October-November 1985 to devise a new draft Treaty and resolve internal differences over substantive points, such as the fate of the conventionally armed cruise missile and the concept of a commission to investigate compliance problems (what ultimately became the Treaty-mandated Special Verification Commission). Over the months of wrangling, however, a document had slowly emerged that stressed U.S. verification concerns. Thus, while incorporating the Reykjavik Summit conclusions, the draft Treaty required *inter alia*:

- **Noninterference with National Technical Means** (NTM) with no encryption of missile test flight data and a ban on concealment measures that impede verification (attacking a long standing SALT II problem);
- **Reciprocal exchange of comprehensive data** on Treaty-limited systems, facilities, and support equipment with regular, required data updating;
- **Specialized procedures to destroy, dismantle, or convert Long Range INF** (LRINF) systems, including on-site inspection to verify such actions; and
- **Specified areas and facilities for treaty-limited items** with a prohibition against their location elsewhere.

The Soviets took this extensive presentation on board with the negotiating "round" ending in late March 1986. The conclusion of the round, however, had left the impression that the Soviets were now seeking to separate SRINF from an initial INF agreement: a move which would allow the Soviets a virtual SRINF monopoly and freedom to increase such a force, effectively giving them the ability to circumvent any agreement reducing or eliminating LRINF systems.

Zero SRINF?

Secretary Shultz met in Moscow in mid-April with Gorbachev and Foreign Minister Shevardnadze. They reinforced agreement on the Reykjavik formula, and emphasized that inspection "must contain provisions for very strict and intrusive verification." The sides also agreed that there must be global limits on SRINF, and the United States emphasized that such limits should be based on "equality." Upon reporting these developments to NATO Allies, Secretary Shultz also noted the Soviet commitment to withdraw SRINF in East Germany and Czechoslovakia, and that Moscow intended to propose reducing SRINF to zero in one year.

While withdrawal of SRINF systems in East Germany and Czechoslovakia was not surprising (they had been deployed there to "compensate" for U.S. LRINF deployments), the prospective "zero" proposal brought NATO to attention. The longstanding NATO requirement for collateral constraints on SRINF was a prudent move, particularly as it provided a preemptive defense against potential critics. It was quite a different story, however, to consider the total elimination of this class of system. Although the U.S. had no deployed systems in this range band (our Pershing I missiles had been withdrawn to the U.S. and stockpiled), NATO was considering deployment of a "Pershing Ib" (essentially the first stage of the PII). The discussion had been underway for years, but in a back-burner, take-one-problem-at-a-time manner while deployment of U.S. LRINF was being implemented. While the Alliance mulled over the Gorbachev proposal, the U.S. made it clear that it was willing to reject a global zero for SRINF; but (and this was a major "but") it would not do so merely to preserve the option to deploy a new SRINF system. Thus an Alliance decision to reject any prospective Soviet "zero offer" on SRINF would be, in effect, a decision to deploy the PIb. There were advantages and disadvantages to either accepting zero SRINF or accepting PIb deployments, and they were debated extensively.

But, in the final analysis, the U.S. was not prepared to bear alone the burden of rejecting an ostensibly attractive Soviet arms control proposal for no evident benefit (the Soviets, after all, had several hundred SRINF systems including the highly regarded SS-23 just in the early stages of deployment). Left unresolved was the question of Pershing IA missiles owned by the FRG, but armed with U.S.-controlled nuclear warheads: a topic the Soviets had not yet raised.

The Alliance mulled over the decision for two months before supporting, in its 12 June 1987 NATO Ministerial communiqué, a call to eliminate all SRINF. Simultaneously, the ministers reemphasized the basic U.S.-NATO negotiating position that all ground-based LRINF missiles should also be eliminated. This objective was reemphasized in the Nuclear Planning Group Ministerial in Stavanger, Norway, but carefully couched as a "goal" rather than a requirement for INF agreement.

On to Global Zero

Although agreed at the Reykjavik Summit and enshrined in both U.S. and Soviet draft treaty texts, many were still unenthusiastic about a residual, Asia-aimed Soviet INF force. Thus, the pursuit of global zero continued on both European and Asian fronts. The European INF element was straightforward: epitomized, for example, by the June NATO Ministerial communiqué and other Alliance statements. U.S. INF negotiator Ambassador Maynard Glitman repeatedly seized opportunities to remind his counterparts that the still-to-be-negotiated "Inspection Protocol" for the treaty would be greatly facilitated if global zero was the working hypothesis for a verification regime.

Simultaneously, however, U.S. diplomats built on Asian concern over the Soviet residual force: a concern that had not dissipated over the months following Reykjavik. U.S. representatives noted that if Asians found the residual Soviet INF force offensive and/or discriminatory, their quarrel was not with us. The U.S., after all, had no objection to global elimination of INF missiles; it had been our original proposal and remained our objective. The U.S. understood the point even if the Soviets did not, and perhaps the Asians should argue their case directly with Moscow. Perhaps the Soviets believed we were exaggerating when we noted Asian concerns; but, in any event, the party most concerned is the best advocate.

Clearly, the Soviets were also rethinking their position during this period. The question of how much inspection would be necessary to verify a residual INF force was surely a problem. The Japanese had pressed their views through standard diplomatic channels. Likewise, the Chinese, in at least one nontraditional channel, made their views clear. At the UN-sponsored 6-13 June 1987 Dagomys conference on the Black Sea, the PRC UN ambassador emphasized Beijing's view that all LRINF should be eliminated. As this view was expressed in the presence of U.S. Ambassador Edward Rowny and ranking Soviet representatives such as Chervov and Karpov, it was clearly meant to be included in Soviet calculations. Rowny subsequently pressed the point further with the Soviets in Dagomys and again in Moscow. One cannot identify a specific "straw" which determined the Soviet decision, but on 23 July 1987, in an interview granted to the Indonesian paper *Merkda*, Gorbachev announced his commitment to eliminate the Soviet LRINF residual force and all SRINF ("operational and tactical missiles" in the Soviet parlance): both conditional, of course, on reciprocal action by the United States.

Back to FRG Pershing Missiles.

Earlier largely unmentioned by Moscow, and consequently not raised by the U.S., the Soviets now focused on the FRG Pershing IA force. Presumably the Soviets now felt that they could not leave Bonn holding the only ground-launched nuclear missile force in this range band in Europe. During August, the Soviets hammered on Bonn to give up its Pershings. The Soviets now termed FRG PIAs as "the main barrier" to an INF agreement and demanded that the INF Treaty address them. The U.S. handled this Soviet charge as it had responded to similar ones in the past: the INF Treaty was a bilateral agreement between the United States and the Soviets. It would not address systems owned by third states. Thus, FRG-owned systems, as was the case for UK and French nuclear forces, were outside the bounds of any bilateral agreement. The U.S. technical case, however, was weakened by the fact that while the FRG had indeed owned the seventy-two PIAs for many years, their nuclear warheads (in contrast to the UK and French forces) were U.S.-owned and controlled.

Indeed, the Soviets were willing to permit the FRG to retain the missiles—if the U.S. removed the nuclear warheads. The public perception was growing that Bonn was standing in the way of an INF Treaty for the sake of seventy-two essentially obsolete shorter-range missiles for which a long-postponed FRG decision on modernization had stymied the Bonn government. German domestic politics were divided on the topic with substantial ambivalence on the utility of the systems outside the conservative wing of the CDU/CSU. Unable to generate European support for its desire to retain the systems, and fearing the consequent isolation if publics concluded that its position had caused the agreement to fail, Bonn moved on 26 August to dismantle the roadblock. Chancellor Kohl announced that the FRG would eliminate its PIAs, if the United States and Soviets both eliminated their LRINF and SRINF missiles.

This, however, was not to be the end of it. As the summer came to a close in mid-September, Secretary Shultz and Soviet Foreign Minister Shevardnadze again met in Washington. Again FRG Pershing IAs entered into the conversations, and the Soviets sought to incorporate references to these systems in the INF Treaty. The United States rejected specific Soviet requirements, noting that

Chancellor Kohl had resolved the issue and that it was inappropriate to refer to bilateral programs. The Soviets, however, insisted on assurances that elimination of the U.S-supplied nuclear warheads be reflected in some manner in the Treaty. Although not resolved at the September ministerial, a solution eventually emerged (and was embedded in the Elimination Protocol). The sides would complete their formal elimination programs at least fifteen days before the end of the scheduled, official three-year elimination period. Such a cushion was wise in any event, in order to assure that procedural glitches, e.g., inclement weather, did not create technical treaty violations. The fifteen-day "cushion" will now specifically be used to withdraw to the U.S. "reentry vehicles which, by unilateral decision, have been released from existing programs of cooperation," where they will be eliminated immediately according to Treaty procedures. This mechanism permitted the United States to adhere strictly to the FRG statement that it would eliminate its PIAs only after U.S. and Soviet systems were eliminated, to take care of any residual elements of an officially lapsed program of cooperation within Treaty timelines, and still to exclude any reference to third parties from the Treaty.

Otherwise, ministers' injunction to their respective INF delegations on 18 September was to "complete promptly" an INF treaty which the President and Gorbachev would sign at a Summit meeting in the fall. Still no date was set. It had been a warm summer; it was to be a long hot fall.

The Endgame Begins

One element of the endgame is simply determining when it begins. From the preceding observations, an observer could suggest a number of points following which it became clear that there would be an INF agreement. An argument could be made for the Reykjavik Summit itself, where the Soviets met classic U.S. requirements for equal force levels, global limits on INF missiles, and made a commitment (although notably nonspecific) to comprehensive verification. Perhaps a stronger case can be made that following Gorbachev's acceptance of "global zero," the original U.S.-NATO negotiating position from the inception of negotiations, an agreement was inevitable. In the end, however, the 18 September commitment to a Summit in autumn 1987 made it clear that both sides anticipated agreement. At that juncture, U.S. negotiators in Geneva and the support structure in Washington moved into even higher gear to address the remaining issues and bring the Treaty to completion.

It is useful to recall that an endgame need not deal with the most vital negotiating issues. For INF, these had already been decided with basic agreement *inter alia* global zero, for both SRINF and LRINF to be implemented over a relatively brief time frame, conceptual agreement to a detailed inspection regime during and after elimination of INF systems, exclusion of UK and French forces, exclusion of aircraft, and the fate of FRG PIAs. Perhaps only one point addressed during this period (the similarity between stages of the SS-25 and the SS-20) would qualify as a "treaty-stopper," because it was not identified as an issue until late in the endgame negotiations. Thus the endgame was not primarily devoted to cosmic issues. The problems addressed were instead important, detailed, specific problems; they were important more because they were the last remaining issues than because they were the most critical to the negotiations. Indeed, at one juncture in the final weeks, the INF delegation combed the Treaty for unresolved points creating a list of issues (either 99 or 105 depending on the version of the list). Subsequently, critics suggested that because this number of "issues" remained at a late date, solving them must have been done with unseemly (and thus mistake prone) haste. Of course the reality of this list of issues was that, in many instances, it was the same issue repeated in different parts of the text of the Treaty or protocols, or a set of interconnected issues, where resolution of one would mean resolution of the problem set.

In managing the endgame action there were two primary U.S. elements: the interagency group (IG) process in Washington and the INF negotiating team in Geneva. All major Washington agencies concerned with arms control (Departments of State and Defense, Arms Control and Disarmament Agency, Joint Chiefs of Staff, CIA) were represented in both the Washington IG process and the Geneva delegation.

Washington

The concept of the IG is simple, its execution complex. The bureau-cratics of power sharing placed the Arms Control and Disarmament Agency officially in charge of the INF negotiating text and the drafting and transmission of guidance to the Geneva delegation. The Department of State, however, and its Politico-Military Bureau in particular provided the chairmen for the INF Working Groups (WG) and Interagency Group (IG), which reviewed studies and passed on requests for guidance on specific problems. These topics were either proposed by the INF Geneva delegation or suggested by one or another agency in Washington. Problems arose and were ad-dressed first by specific INF WGs. Unresolved problems were sent to the INF IG. Issues still unresolved at the IG were incorporated into decision papers with each agency viewpoint listed and sent to the NSC for resolution. As the pace quickened, it became custom-ary for the INF IG to meet daily, often in late afternoon following efforts by individual agencies during the day to resolve what could be resolved and clarify differences on what could not be agreed.

Geneva

Each Washington agency represented in the IG was also represented in Geneva. The Head of Delegation, Ambassador Glitman, a career foreign service office, in effect represented the President. His depu-ty, Ambassador John Woodworth, also represented the Department of Defense. There were separate representatives for State, ACDA, JCS, and CIA. Each representative privately reported developments and personal views to his agency via "back channels" (telegrams seen only by the agency he represented) to complement the official reporting. These individuals were in the frequently difficult posi-tion of having, on the one hand, to interpret their agency positions to the entire delegation and, on the other hand, to sell the official delegation position to their individual agencies. Not infrequently, the Washington position of a specific agency was at variance with the position taken by the INF delegation, which could not make a recommendation to Washington without unanimity (Ambassador Glitman could, however, make a "personal" recommendation). Thus, the agency representative had to choose between his agency's position and the consensus of the delegation. The impetus in Geneva was to gain an internal consensus to give the delegation's views greater weight in the IG discussion in Washington. During the final months of the negotiations, the U.S. delegation was substantially reinforced with experts from Washington, many of whom had been involved with the negotiations for years.

The Opening

Immediately following the conclusion of the September Shultz-Shevardnadze meeting in Washington, the U.S. and Soviet delegations began an article-by-article review of the draft text. This review, despite daily and frequently morning and afternoon meetings of full delegations, moved slowly. In general, the "Treaty" text consisted of broader, more general language agreements while the Inspection Protocol, the Elimination Protocol, and the MOU on data provided specific language.

The Final Two Weeks

Following are a selection of issues which were examined and resolved in the final two weeks of the negotiations. It does not pretend to be a diplomatic history, which would require detailed recourse to diplomatic archives which will presumably remain confidential for many years. Thus the selection is a "personal" one, an attempt to give a representative selection of important issues which had technical aspects, but hopefully not in overly detailed form. Each of the major documents composing the INF Treaty had specialized issues as illustrated below.

The Treaty

Stages

The "stages" issue reminds one of the complexities of the famous nineteenth century Schleswig-Holstein question, in which it was claimed that only three individuals knew the "answer," and one went insane. In short, LRINF missiles are created from sections or "stages," which are first produced and then assembled. For technical reasons, the stages of the U.S. Pershing II missile are shipped from production facilities individually, and assembled in the field. Consequently, it would be logical to account and inspect for individual stages of U.S. PII missiles. The Soviet SS-20 on the other hand, although manufactured in stages, is immediately packed into a canister from which normally it is never removed. Consequently, the Soviets argued that their missiles should be accounted for only as entities, and that "stages" of SS-20s did not exist. Initially, the U.S. believed this was a tactical argument assumed by the Soviets to restrict the size of an item being inspected to that of a fully assembled missile. That was indeed one reason for this odd argument. A deeper, and potentially disastrous further reason, however, emerged only later, during U.S. efforts to assure that manufacturing of SS-20s would halt, and that inspection would ensure that all elements of the SS-20 would be eliminated. To make this result certain, the U.S. required that all production of SS-20s and their "stages" be banned. The Soviets resisted furiously and gradually it became apparent that the first stage of the (to be banned) SS-20 was very close (indeed virtually indistinguishable) from the first stage of the Soviets' new strategic missile, the SS-25.

The issue was then posed: how to assure that the *second* stage of the SS-25 was not also identical to that of the SS-20, so that there would be no covert production of the SS-20 under the guise of the SS-25? Likewise, how could we assure the elimination of all elements of the SS-20, without also prohibiting production of the first stage of the SS-25? The answers came slowly and haltingly.

The initial breakthrough was agreement that each side could produce a stage that was "outwardly similar but not interchangeable" with a stage of a banned missile. First, it was necessary to clarify and limit such description. The Soviets wanted a broad, permissive interpretation; the U.S. a very carefully delimited one. Following the 23-24 November Ministerial meeting in Geneva between Secretary Shultz and FM Shevardnadze, the Soviets moved in several directions; they

- Sought a **direct exchange of commitments** permitting them to produce the first stage of the Soviets new strategic missile, the SS-25 which was "outwardly similar" to the first stage of the

SS-20 while the United States would be permitted to build the "P1C" (the second state of the PII).

- Subsequently sought to **widen the exception** to permit them to produce an "outwardly similar" stage of the SS-20 for missiles other than the SS-25 (while claiming they did not intend to do so).
- sought a U.S. commitment that they could build the SS-25 in its **existing configuration.**

The U.S. insisted that the agreement to permit production of an "outwardly similar" stage of the SS-20 applied only for the SS-25. To reassure the Soviets that we were not attempting to capture a key element of their ICBM force under an INF agreement, on 2-3 December, the United States outlined a hypothetical oral statement to the effect that if the technical data supplied by the Soviets on the stages of the SS-25 was accurate and verified by the United States during the course of the inspection regime, we would not object to its production. On 4-5 December, the Soviets agreed that an "outwardly similar" stage would be produced for only one missile (the SS-25) and took note of the U.S. oral assurances.

A good deal of specific work was necessary to turn such a paper commitment into procedures that could be monitored under an inspection regime. It was necessary to secure the measurements of both stages of the SS-20 and the first two stages of the SS-25, and to be able to measure both of them for ourselves. Then it would be necessary to devise a regime that would assure that SS-20s were not being secretly produced in the production facility and brought out labeled as "SS-25s." One approach would have been to regularly inspect the interior of the production facility. Neither side, however, wanted such a regime, fearing the compromise of technical information. The result, consequently, was the "portal monitoring" system (detailed below in the discussion of the Inspection Protocol) with an interlocking mesh of weighing, measuring, x-raying, or opening selected SS-25 canisters as they were sent from the Votkinsk production facility.

Testing SLCM, ALCM, and SLBM from Land

Eliminating testing is a key element of any inspection regime for an agreement involving total elimination. If a missile cannot be tested, no new missile development is operationally feasible and, over time, confidence in the reliability of existing missiles declines. Consequently, the United States sought prohibitions on testing ground-based INF range missiles. There was, however, a problem. The United States also frequently tested (or wished the flexibility to test) its sea-launched and air-launched cruise missiles and sea-launched ballistic missiles from the ground. Such tests were cheaper and more efficient and had been U.S. practice for years. Unfortunately, our practice occasionally was to test such systems from launchers which if not "mobile" to the degree that they were integral parts of a vehicle, were certainly transportable, i.e., they could quickly be loaded on the back of a flat bed truck. How then to assure that the U.S. testing program could continue, while the Soviets could not create a covert GLCM force while claiming they were simply testing a SLCM/ALCM? After considerable exploration of the best choice of words, the sides agreed a cruise missile would not be a GLCM if "it is test launched at a test site from a fixed land-based launcher which is used solely for test purposes and which is distinguishable from GLCM launchers." Thus, the deciding factor has become the fixed nature of the launcher and its perceptible difference from the prohibited GLCM launcher.

Enhanced National Technical Means (NTM)

One of the innovations of the INF Treaty was formalized agreement to improve the effectiveness of U.S. NTM. The Soviets are well aware of U.S. "spy satellites," although unaware of their specific capabilities. The INF text was already a major improvement over SALT II, which had prohibited only "deliberate" interference with NTM, making any arguments over any Soviet concealment an issue of intent rather than fact.

The evolution of enhanced NTM in INF grew from the U.S. concern that SS-20 missiles could be hidden among SS-25 missiles at SS-25 bases, particularly those which had been recently converted from being SS-20 bases. The Soviets opposed on-site inspection of such facilities as they were strategic forces, not covered by any INF agreement. The conclusion was a carefully negotiated compromise, permitting the United States to require, on six hour notice, the Soviets to open the roofs of fixed structures and display missiles and launchers in the open without concealment for six hours. Such a demand can be made six times a year for three years, or until a START agreement is reached: whichever comes first. Technically the language also applies to the United States, so if we deploy a road-mobile strategic missile, i.e., "Midgetman," prior to July 1991, it would be subject to the same requirements.

Nailing down non-circumvention

In law, "non-circumvention," that is, the requirement not to act in a manner contrary to the purpose of the agreement, is implicit. Thus a "non-circumvention" clause in a treaty is more a political matter and its explicit language designed to provide the potential to object to actions only distantly related to any specific element of the treaty. Such a frustrating struggle regularly absorbed negotiating time where semantics became substance. The Soviets sought language which would permit them to object to U.S. or NATO-related conventional or nuclear force activities, such as deployments, modernizations, or cooperative efforts with allies, which they could hypothesize as circumventing the INF agreement. Obviously the United States would not accept language akin to that in the SALT II Treaty, which the Soviets had used to protest various U.S. activities in Europe. After much wrangling, the United States and Soviets agreed on an English language formulation that "the parties...shall not assume any international obligations or undertakings which would conflict with its provisions."

This formulation, however, was only the beginning of the issue. The most vexing problem came in translating the English into Russian. The Soviets persistently sought a Russian translation of "undertakings" which would equate with "actions." Such a translation would provide them opportunity to object to virtually any U.S. activity involving the defense of NATO, e.g., additional deployment of F-111 aircraft, development of a tactical air to surface missile, or U.S.-UK cooperation on the British Trident program. Over the final weeks there was a steady reading of Russian dictionaries and considerable cross discussion between interpreters. Arcane definitions were examined and mutual suspicion of motives became as important as lexicography. The issue was resolved as one of the final items on 6 December when the United States accepted a Russian phrase translating "undertakings" as "any international acts." "Acts" in this phrase would mean formalized arrangements, such as the 1971 Helsinki Final Act for CSCE.

Memorandum of Understanding

Numbers, Numbers, Numbers—The Data Dilemma

The acceptability of data has been an endlessly contentious element in U.S.-Soviet negotiations. Information on numbers and technical details for U.S. systems is as easily obtainable as copies of the Department of Defense budget or JANES, whereas information on comparable Soviet systems is a state secret, with U.S. estimates developed over time from multiple intelligence sources. Multilateral NATO-Warsaw Pact negotiations in Vienna on conventional force reductions spent more than a decade disputing the accuracy of Soviet information on Warsaw Pact forces. In SALT II, the Soviets never supplied data but reached agreement by not objecting to the accuracy of U.S. supplied information on their forces. In the INF negotiations, however, the United States took a different approach, arguing that each side must be responsible for the accuracy of its own information. Such a decision was designed to stymie potential critics of any Treaty, who otherwise would attempt to claim either that the Soviets had never agreed with U.S. figures on their forces, or that the United States was responsible for confirming Soviet figures. Nevertheless, it was clear that figures on Soviet systems, no matter the source, would have to closely coincide with U.S. estimates. If, for example, the Soviets claimed to have fewer missiles than we believed they had, no agreement would be possible.

The Soviets vigorously resisted the timing and content of a data exchange. The reticence may have been partly psychological: it seemed as hard for the Soviets to exchange such information with capitalists as it would be for a strongly religious individual to curse in public. The Soviets probably would have been happiest with a data exchange on the day the Treaty was officially signed. As it was, exchange of data was spasmodic, halting, and frequently interrupted. Constant pressure was required in Geneva and with intervention in Washington and Moscow to push the exchange of information. Eventually the United States was informed by ostensibly surprised Moscow officials that the last elements of the required data had been transmitted to Geneva somewhat earlier. Indeed, the ranking Soviet official in Moscow expressed surprise that it had not been supplied. Thus stimulated, the Soviets hastily provided the remaining required data on 2 December.

Many individual arguments over the type and presentation of data in the MOU were optical. The Soviets were clearly concerned over the impression that they were giving up much more than the United States. This attitude was demonstrated, for example, in the category of "systems tested, but not deployed." The Soviets had developed and extensively tested a GLCM, 84 of which were in pre-deployment storage. The United States had rather casually investigated the possibility of a "PIb," which was essentially one stage of the PII. At the time of the treaty, nothing which could be attributed as being a PIb was in the inventory; there was nothing even that could be used to take a photograph! The Soviets, however, for symmetry's sake, insisted on listing the PIb although all categories of information in the MOU on deployment are filled with "NONE." The case was similar for listing production facilities for INF systems. Initially the Soviets sought to list only Votkinsk and Magna, Utah, the facilities at which there would be perimeter-portal monitoring: a perfect symmetry. The United States wanted all production facilities, past and present, to be listed, even though they were not open to inspection or currently in use. A compromise was struck with the listing of production facilities other than those for the SS-4 and SS-5.

Smile for the Camera: Photographs

A clear photograph of each type of system or support facility to be eliminated was to be a specific element of the data package. This U.S. requirement generated many hours of argument, initially concentrated on the manner and detail in which the photograph was to be taken. At first we attempted to specify distances, type of camera, type of film, etc. to avoid being "taken" and getting unusable photos. This level of specificity ultimately collapsed as what is an "appropriate distance" from a missile might only get you the picture of a wall of a missile shelter. Finally we reached a rule of reason agreement that the photos should be mutually acceptable concerning size and clarity. And indeed, some of the photographs exchanged on both sides were remarkable. Obviously done in something of a hurry, the photos of the U.S. launch pad shelters apparently were taken in the rain, and included at least one miserable looking soldier with a "what is this all about" look holding a measuring pole to determine dimensions of the facility. Similarly, the photograph of the PIb was an old publicity photo as no PIb existed to be photographed.

Less amusing was the protracted ordeal involved in obtaining a photograph of the SS-20 outside its canister. Recognizing as we did the key nature of the SS-20, the political realities behind the agreement would have made it impossible to agree to destroy something we had never seen. The Soviets were indifferent to this reality, insisting that such a photograph did not exist because the SS-20 never appeared outside its canister. Indeed, it was probably difficult to secure a photograph of a "naked" SS-20 as it was rare and possibly dangerous for one to be removed from its canister after having been inserted. Nevertheless, such a contention was also an adjunct of the Soviet position that SS-20 "stages" did not exist and that all SS-20s should be accounted for as entities. Soviet negotiators in Geneva insisted until the end of the negotiations that we would never see such a photograph. Equally strongly, the U.S. negotiators insisted that the MOU requirements demanded such a photo, and that it was required to confirm measurement data. The issue was settled between ranking U.S. and Soviet officials in Washington, when we were assured on 5 December that Moscow would supply an SS-20 photograph. The required photograph was supplied before Treaty signature on 8 December and subsequently replaced by a better "glossy" copy. Even so, it lacked a picture of the reentry vehicle, which also had to be supplied separately.

Site Diagrams

Any agreement permitting inspection of an INF site had to have limits of some sort. Where did the base end? What about activities that had no connection with INF, but happened to be on the same facility? How much detail should a diagram of the site demonstrate? Ostensibly these appear straightforward points, but due to the massive numbers of sites involved (over one hundred facilities and missile operating bases), the prevalence of multiple use facilities in the NATO basing countries, and the time constraints, this requirement produced one of the less satisfactory negotiating efforts.

The issue was not joined until after the 23-24 November Geneva Ministerial. First, the Soviets argued that no site diagrams were necessary until inspectors arrived at the facility. Moreover, the United States initially preferred a "broad" diagram showing extensive detail of a facility vice the Soviet preference for a sketchier diagram. Obtaining information from capitals on the details of the sites was akin to pulling teeth. Such detailed information is not stored in file drawers or computers, as someone might imagine. Lack of this type of data bank might best be illustrated by the fact that the initial map coordinates we supplied for the facility at Magna, Utah would have placed it in the Great Salt Lake. Eventually the problem was addressed on a facility-by-facility basis in an *ad hoc* working group, first by exchanging sample diagrams and discussing requirements. The United States subsequently agreed to construct site diagrams with limited detail. At one point, the Soviets attempted to refuse to provide site diagrams for their GLCM facility, as we had no site diagrams for the PIb— facility (because it didn't exist).

Although completed in time for Treaty signature (with diagrams for two Soviet launcher production facilities provided on 8 December), in retrospect, no one was satisfied with the accuracy of the diagrams. These were not gross errors, such as forgetting entire facilities or any intimation of deliberate concealment of information, but the niggling errors in accuracy that dismay those concerned with precision, e.g., the "north arrow" pointing in the wrong direction. During a subsequent review of the diagrams in Geneva shortly prior to Treaty ratification, many U.S. diagrams, and virtually all of the Soviet diagrams, were revised to correct such mistakes.

Elimination Protocol

Eliminating Soviet SS-20 Launchers

The U.S. and Soviet launchers were very different. The United States essentially attached a flat bed trailer to a tractor with the missile on the flatbed. To eliminate the launcher, one could detach the flatbed from the tractor and cut it into pieces. The Soviet launcher, however, was an integral, inseparable combination of tractor and launch vehicle. Cutting the "launcher" into sections would mean cutting the drive train for the vehicle, thus rendering the vehicle into junk. The United States urged such a solution while the Soviets countered that the United States would lose virtually nothing (a cheap flatbed trailer) while they would lose an expensive heavy-duty transport vehicle. If the United States persisted, the Soviets would insist that the United States destroy its tractors as well (tractors which were indistinguishable from U.S. tractors for many other vehicles). The Soviets put it bluntly. "You want to drive something away; we want to drive something away." Thus the elimination negotiation focused on how to alter (and thereby "eliminate") the SS-20 missile transport vehicle so that it would be forever incapable of serving as a launcher for the SS-20. Some unsung genius determined that cutting off a substantial portion of the end of the vehicle would make it impossible for equipment to be reattached that could erect the missile. The final arguments were ones of inches (where to make the cut) thus stimulating in compromise the curious final formulation that "a portion of the transporter vehicle chassis, at least 0.78 meters in length, shall be cut off aft of the rear axle."

Why No Front Ends?

On 2-3 December, the Soviets informed us that none of their non deployed missiles had "front sections" (a portion of the missile that in effect holds the warhead). Moreover, they claimed, some of their deployed SS-23s did not have "front sections" either. The United States explored this curious development in depth to assure that the Soviet usage of "front section" was not a semantic difference relating to nuclear warheads. In extended sessions on 3-4 December, the Soviets insisted that some of the systems had been produced and sent directly into storage without front sections. The final agreement on 5 December was that each side would destroy one front section for each deployed missile.

Launcher Training Vehicles: Another Oddity

When learning to handle a system, frequently troops do not train with real equipment but use mockups or equipment "simulators" that replicate the reality. In the Soviet case, launcher training vehicles were close copies of SS-20 launchers. The Soviets admitted this point in a plenary statement on 2 November, and all subsequent elimination protocol discussions assumed their elimination. Nevertheless, on 5 December, the Soviets declared they would not eliminate their launcher driver training vehicles, contending that they were not unique vehicles. The United States responded on 6 December that it would reopen the previously agreed Elimination Protocol and destroy no training vehicles unless the Soviets reversed position. Later on 6 December, following a slight revision of the elimination procedures, the Soviets agreed to eliminate their launcher driver training vehicles and listed sixty-five such vehicles in the MOU.

Inspection Protocol

What Happened to "Anywhere, Anytime" Inspections?

One theoretical inspection concept is that, on very short notice, inspectors can go to any location and examine the site for Treaty violations. This concept was shorthanded in the negotiations to "anywhere, anytime" inspections. Originally, the United States (particularly prior to Soviet acceptance of global zero) believed that such an inspection regime was necessary to assure compliance. With agreement to zero-zero, however, U.S. agencies became more wary of "anywhere, anytime." It would clearly have opened a wide variety of U.S. facilities, indeed any building large enough to conceal a Treaty-limited item, to Soviet inspectors. Inherently these facilities would have included stealth production facilities, ICBM missile silos, SLCM/ALCM factories, and even top secret facilities such as the National Security Agency and CIA Headquarters. Consequently, the inspection regime was designed to concentrate only on those facilities identified with INF activities as specified in the data MOU. Such a regime was a critical element in the last stages of the negotiations when they were nearing completion.

Nevertheless, in mid-November, the INF negotiators received new guidance from Washington which could be interpreted as suggesting a return to "anywhere/anytime." As part of a special negotiating mission, NSC representative Colonel Robert Linhard arrived in Geneva to outline what satirically became known as the "Froot Loops" plan. A modified "anywhere/anytime" plan was under consideration. Such a proposal would have each side construct a secret list of facilities the other side could not visit, e.g., stealth production facilities. Everything else would be fair game for inspection. If, for example, Soviet inspectors arrived and stated their desire to visit a particular facility on the "secret list," its presence on that list would be identified to the Soviets and the inspection denied. If, however, it was not a facility on the "secret list" (a "Froot Loops" breakfast cereal factory was the illustration given), after consultation with the private owners of the factory, the Soviets would be permitted to visit. The proposal begged any number of questions: What limits would be placed on facilities on the "secret list"? How would an open society such as the United States keep such a list secret over the long (or any) term? Assuming such a list would become public, would we dare list some of our most secret facilities, laboratories, "safe houses," and such? The proposal was made to the chief Soviet negotiator present at the session (Yuli M. Vorontsov) who rejected it out of hand. Subsequent speculation suggested that it was a proposal designed to fail, advanced only to satisfy last gasp supporters of "anywhere/anytime" inspections within the USG and to build a firebreak against prospective criticism from the Senate that we had not done enough to secure still more intrusive inspection.

How Big an Item Do You Inspect For (Other Than at Votkinsk and Magna)?

Late on the evening of 6 December, the negotiating teams addressed for the last time the size of the item for which an inspector could inspect. The Soviets continued to contend that since the U.S. missiles were transported in "stages," the Soviets should be able to inspect for items the size of individual stages. In contrast, since their missiles were moved as assembled systems, the United States should inspect only for items the size of complete missiles. To accept such a position would mean creating a loophole that would permit the Soviets to conceal the "stages" of their missiles and, perhaps, assemble them elsewhere. Thus the United States insisted upon reciprocity: each side inspecting for items the size of the smallest missile stage necessary to assure that a Treaty-limited missile was not present. The final discussion featured a theatrical walkout by the United States, followed by a corridor reconciliation when the Soviets suddenly professed to discover that they had misunderstood the U.S. position.

Creating a "Perimeter-Portal" Inspection Regime

The United States had dropped its insistence for on-site monitoring of production facilities in light of the agreement for global zero. However, there was a partial resurgence of the concept, necessitated by the discovery that the first stage of the Soviet SS-25 was "outwardly similar" to the first stage of the SS-20. Therefore, the negotiators sought to design on short notice a system which not only would assure that no SS-20s could be shipped from the Votkinsk factory, but also guarantee the safety and effectiveness of U.S. inspectors to be permanently stationed in Votkinsk.

One key element was the random opening of SS-25 containers. Following the 23-24 November Ministerial, the Soviets attempted to argue that we had agreed to open only one of every thirty SS-25 containers—a totally inaccurate contention and a proposal which would have had no random aspect to it and consequently be easy to evade. Instead the United States argued for twelve random inspections per year. The Soviet haggled, and the outcome of the horse-trading was eight random inspections per year.

Another special problem was measuring the SS-25 stages to determine that they were not SS-20 stages, once the United States had "popped the top" on the SS-25 canister to be inspected. Initially the Soviets were sanguine about such measurements suggesting we could just "put a stick in." Clearly this was a political rather than a technical judgment, as the Soviets then attempted to reverse field claiming that any mechanical probe could damage the SS-25. Considerable discussion followed with the United States enjoined to find a technical solution that would permit "no hands" measuring. The solution ultimately reflected U.S. creativity with range-finding equipment to be employed from outside the opened canister.

Although the United States was the demandeur for the detailed provisions of the portal regime, we managed to secure virtually our maximum original proposals including *inter alia*, permanent provision of utilities; provision of site construction material and site preparation; communications both telephonic and radio; size limitations on structures; types of sensors and equipment to be installed; assured access to and noninterference with sensors; and limits on numbers of exits from the site, size of the "portal," and maximum distance between road and rail lines out of the portal. Likewise, the ultimate size of the cadre stationed at the portal (thirty) was closer to the original U.S. proposal than the Soviet counter-offer.

Point of Entry for inspections in East Germany

Each INF basing country in Europe has a specific "point of entry" for inspection teams. This point was designed to be a convenient, politically noncontroversial airport whose chief characteristics were proximity to the INF facilities to be inspected and good technical capability to handle the aircraft carrying the inspecting teams. Consequently, the United States proposed Leipzig in the GDR, and made it clear that we could not accept Berlin. Nevertheless, after delaying designating POEs for Warsaw Pact basing countries past the 23-24 November ministerial, the Soviets eventually designated Schoenfeld, airfield for Berlin, as the POE for the GDR. They contended that the GDR was a sovereign country and free to designate its own point of entry, that NATO allies had used Schoenfeld for its CDE-related inspections, and that Schoenfeld was not part of the Berlin regime.

Here the INF delegation lacked technical expertise. Berlin had a more than forty-year history of entangled legalities whose experts could split any hair at least four ways. The delegation referred the issue to Washington, simply repeating to the Soviets that it was mischievous to insert Berlin into an INF treaty and that accepting Berlin as a POE would create a permanent prejudicial exception in the Berlin agreements. Similar messages were given at high level outside Washington and Berlin-associated allies such as the UK and France were energized to make comparable demarches. The United States was inclined to compromise on this point, however, and by 6 December had constructed a complex scheme involving automobiles and aircraft. Nevertheless, upon hearing this presentation, the Soviets waved it aside and accepted Leipzig (Schkeuditz Airport) as the GDR POE. Apparently the Soviets under pressure from GDR leadership had agreed to carry the POE/Berlin issue as far as possible before yielding the point. Still, we were concerned that we had not heard the last of the issue, as the Treaty permitted any party to change its POE unilaterally upon five months advance notification (Inspection Protocol, Article IV, paragraph 5).

The Basing Country Agreements

A unique and largely unexamined aspect of the INF Treaty was the involved noninvolvement of both NATO and Warsaw Pact INF "basing countries." Although the INF Treaty was a bilateral agreement affecting only U.S. and Soviet weapons systems, these systems frequently were deployed outside the United States and USSR. Yet so long as states are sovereign, whether or not that status frequently has appeared *pro forma* in the East, neither principal could commit its partnered basing countries to the terms of a bilateral agreement. Thus the United States feared that Washington and Moscow could come to an agreement, but Czech or GDR authorities could make a mockery of the accord by refusing to permit inspection of Soviet basing sites. Likewise, Moscow professed concern that NATO nations might tire of the weight of inspections over the years, perhaps, for example, barring Soviet inspectors after all U.S. INF systems were removed.

The negotiators, and consequently the United States and its NATO partners, did not address this issue until relatively late in the negotiating process. It was quickly decided that we did not want individual basing countries negotiating separate access agreements with the Soviets, a process that would have been an open invitation to play one off against another. Nor did we want the basing countries at the negotiating table *en masse* to attempt to work out a corporate agreement. Nor, for their part, did the basing countries wish to be up front, directly opposed to the Soviets in a negotiation (and responsible subsequently for enforcing it, perhaps against Soviet pressure). The result was a carefully constructed scenario in which the United States negotiated an agreement with its basing country allies (satisfactory to the Soviets) that would assure their detailed commitment to the terms of the INF treaty. Simultaneously, the Soviets secured Czech and East German agreement to specific diplomatic notes directed to the United States assuring that Prague and Berlin accepted the applicability of INF inspections on their territory.

Unsurprisingly the Soviets had no special difficult securing appropriate assurances from its Warsaw Pact allies. The United States, however, had a considerably more tedious "chicken herding" exercise before all basing country allies reached agreement. Lawyerly disagreement over how best to protect sovereignty contended with how to assure compliance with Treaty provisions. Such points became increasingly heated, particularly between Washington and London. The basing country allies met repeatedly in Washington over language debated both by local embassy representatives acting on instructions, and on occasion reinforced by national experts flying in from capitals. In Geneva, in the final weeks, the United States set up a small subgroup of State Department personnel to work out the details: a process which somewhat amused (and occasionally bored) the Soviet representative who apparently believed this exercise was very much a sideshow.

What Can We Learn from the INF Endgame?

Learning from any endgame implies of course that the negotiators have gotten there; and we must recall that while every completed negotiation has an endgame, many negotiations never conclude in agreement. Negotiations are directed at many objectives, and agreement is only one possible goal. History has seen negotiations deliberately designed to fail, to serve as the official pretext for war, or simply as a public relations exercise to convince casual observers that "something is being done" (the protracted MBFR negotiations were more designed to placate arms control and "Mansfield Amendment" audiences than to reduce conventional forces in central Europe.) Obviously, however, we did reach INF agreement and that fact suggests some general, as well as some specific conclusions:

The Soviets Were Increasingly Serious about Arms Control

This apparent "given" is more obvious today than it was in 1987 with the blizzard of Gorbachev's current disarmament proposals having become the arms control equivalent of *Playboy's* playmate of the month. Each was attractive, colorful, appealing and, in contrast to the magazine, perhaps even attainable! Gorbachev's serious and professional approach to a global concern was in stark contrast to the post war history of the Soviet Union where Moscow's arms control proposals were normally a haystack of propaganda with (perhaps) a needle of substance. This observation is not to suggest that Gorbachev operated under a mantle of selfless altruism indifferent to national interest but only that his perception of Soviet national interest appeared closer to U.S./NATO's traditional security and arms control objectives than traditionally was true. The INF Treaty should not be regarded as proof that any or all possible agreements with Moscow can or should be concluded but only that the parameters for agreement are wider. The public perception that Moscow is a serious actor in arms control negotiations was becoming more important to Moscow's international image. To preserve this image will require its negotiators to present serious responses to reasonable Western proposals—unless they wish to forfeit the more responsible negotiating image they have been cultivating. An expectation that your negotiating partner will be serious and reliable (whether or not you agree) is an important component of any negotiation and vital in the endgame.

Better Appreciation of U.S./Western Requirements

Slowly Moscow came to recognize that East-West arms control agreements must meet Western standards for public and parliamentary review. For decades, even sophisticated negotiators appeared to believe that that Senate ratification was a charade, and that U.S. negotiators used the specter of ratification as a negotiating technique rather than reflecting a reality. This view has not entirely faded, but post-INF ratification, Moscow appeared ready to acknowledge that the Executive branch does not negotiate in a vacuum. Indeed, noting the increasing interest the Supreme Soviet paid to previously off limits issues, we may find Moscow's negotiators making reciprocal claims that its legislators are getting out of hand: and expect that such a statement will be taken seriously rather than greeted with a hoarse/horse laugh.

More Favorable Ground Rules for the West

Many of the INF provisions both major and minor will put the United States and NATO in more favorable positions for future endgame negotiations. While every negotiation ostensibly starts with a *tabula rasa*, negotiators quite humanly tend to use those formulae which have been previously agreed, at least as a starting point. If there are lines of discussion that have repeatedly failed, most negotiators will avoid spending much time pressing them. Over time these become negotiating parameters within which diplomats seek the possible. In this regard, the INF Treaty was akin to a single athlete simultaneously smashing the four minute mile, the twenty-six-foot broad jump and the sixteen-foot pole vault. Negotiating absolutes were broken and the parameters of the possible expanded to as yet unexplored limits. It is clear, for example, that asymmetrical reductions, equal limits, global applicability and intrusive on-site inspections as overall principles will help Western negotiators throughout most future arms control negotiations. Other INF Treaty precedents such as highly detailed data breakdown, substantial geographic separation of shorter-range missiles and launchers, early elimination of these systems (when the United States had none deployed), acceptance of highly detailed procedures which frequently both assured elimination of Soviet systems while saving vital, expensive components of U.S. systems and procedures for enhancing the effectiveness of NTMs are just a few of the provisions which will bolster the interest of our future negotiators.

The foregoing were more "cosmic" observations; the following are more specific.

A Hectic Conclusion Is Inevitable

Much as the diplomat would prefer a neat, all-ends-tied-up conclusion for a major agreement, the history of SALT I, SALT II, and
now INF suggests that negotiations will drag on absent a "forcing
event," specifically a head of state Summit. It is not just human, it
is diplomatic, to withhold concessions as long as possible, in hopes
that the other side will accept your initial arguments or first fall-
backs on key substantive positions. Substantive concessions are a
national resource that no negotiator spends lightly. The longer the
delay, the more likely it becomes that the time crunch at the end
will be intense. That being recognized, the corollary must be that
as much as possible should be done to delay announcement of a
forcing event until the overwhelming mass of the detailed drafting work, let alone the primary substantive decisions, are complete.
INF's conclusion was traditionally hectic, but that was primarily
because of the discovery of the major problem associated with the
"outwardly similar" nature of the first stages of the SS-20 and SS-
25. This required complex additional Treaty language and negotiation of a new type of inspection (perimeter-portal monitoring).
If this point had not been resolved, however, it would have been
regarded as a major verification loophole and could have resulted
in the Senate rejecting the Treaty.

Reciprocity Is the Name of the Game

Optical balance in form and substance is imperative. In instance
after instance, Moscow demanded arrangements that were substantively meaningless but conveyed the optical impression that
the United States had made concessions equal to those granted by
Moscow. The nonexistent U.S. PIb was balanced against the Soviet
GLCM as a system "developed but not deployed." To match the
vital perimeter-portal facility to examine SS-25s exiting Votkinsk, a
meaningless parallel was devised for Magna, Utah, where there is
no comparable production. Negotiators should accept and exploit
this yearning for optical equivalence by devising packages with
"balance," even if there is no obvious equivalent. Moscow will demand such balance in any event and we gain negotiating credibility
for our position by taking their needs into account.

High Tech Is the Way to Go

Diplomacy is surprisingly low tech. Although communications between capitals is by high speed, coded electronics and jet plane,
the diplomat producing this material often is a long step behind
the cutting edge of existing technology. For example, meetings
are recorded with pen and paper; it is regarded as a breach of eti-
quette to tape record a session. Although many officers are familiar with word processors, a surprising number of senior officers
drafted messages in longhand or dictated to secretaries. In the INF
endgame, however, the U.S. delegation benefited from what was,
by diplomatic standards, high tech: secure word processors; high
speed Xerox equipment; classified telephone lines to Washington;
high speed distribution of messages within the Washington community. The Soviets had nothing comparable, burdened as they
were with antiquated reproduction equipment and virtually no
word processors. As a consequence, the United States dominated
the drafting process as our superior equipment permitted far greater speed and flexibility. Proper exploitation of advanced technology proved critical to success at a point when both workloads and
fatigue were building. Such technology, however, is barely first
generation for diplomacy. Needed are elements such as electronic
filing and sophisticated data bases that will permit rapid retrieval
of statements on specific subjects instead of frantic paper scrambles
of the "Where did I see that?" nature. Of course if you have nothing
to say, saying it faster is feckless. But a thoughtful blend of modern communication and word processing equipment can serve as a
force multiplier for a diplomatic team.

A United Delegation Is Imperative

It is impossible to manage an endgame if the negotiators on the
U.S. team are at odds. This does not mean that we should expect
some sort of halcyon atmosphere of sweetness and light to prevail.
Strong personalities operating under pressure can be expected to
disagree; even vigorously disagree. But the imperative should be
to resolve problems, not simply to be mouthpieces for Washington
agencies. The delegation that hangs together affects the results of
the debate in Washington. A divided delegation is little better than
a mail drop for decisions from Washington.

A Strong Ambassador Is Equally Imperative

The negotiating ambassador must be above agency disputes, regardless of his agency or origin. His leadership must be more than "first among equals." Without having to belabor official ratification of his leadership, he must have it recognized by force of intellect; competence; personality or what have you. Successful negotiating teams are not commanded; they are led.

Washington Must Be Organized to Take Expeditious Decisions

Only toward the end of the negotiating process, did Washington adopt the bureaucratic management style that led to decisions on difficult issues rather than delay/hope they go away. The implicit requirement of the Summit was the "forcing event" required to stimulate daily IG meetings to address draft guidance, react to proposals from the Geneva delegation, formulate alternative agency positions when necessary, and transmit these alternatives to the NSC for decision.

Vignette: It's in the Bag

It was time for formal delegation photos, the day for officially recording on film the group photos of those present in Geneva for the negotiating round. The photo would join the long line of round-by-round photos that had marked U.S.-Soviet nuclear negotiations in the 1980s. Later in the session, the Soviets would join the Americans for the ritualized, rictus-like smiles that characterize such official photographs. Some Soviets, apparently unwilling to be photographed for intelligence agency biographic files, never appeared.

Substantive issues were still unresolved and pressure was rising for agreement. The Soviets were due to arrive momentarily for joint photos.

A final photo. A last blast from the flashgun.

But no. "Wait a minute," said the executive secretary, moving swiftly to a previously unnoticed box. He opened it and distributed scores of paper bags with eyeholes marked "INF." A now semihysterical delegation could hardly get the bags over their heads. "If we make it, we'll use the first photo. If not, the second." Like NFL fans, the INF delegation was now able to become anonymous. The ultimate question for the delegation, "Will we succeed?" had become a tension-defusing joke.

From then on, the Treaty was "in the bag." And both photos hang on many walls.

How the Treaty Would Operate

Following are two articles that analyze the prospective operation of the INF Treaty: a review of the Treaty verification provisions and an assessment of the "elimination" procedures for equipment to be destroyed. Both were prepared during 1988-89; neither has been published previously.

INF Verification:
Making the Treaty Work

David T. Jones

The INF Treaty is more about verification than arms control. Although eliminating the threat of Soviet INF missiles was important, it is vital to be able to confirm that this threat remains eliminated. Long standing and bitter post World War II experience with Soviet ability to thwart the spirit of an agreement while observing the letter of it (if they did not simply break the agreement directly) had left the U.S. and NATO allies far more cautious than merely "once burnt, twice shy." The caution incorporated in U.S. negotiating instructions was the diplomatic equivalent of ordering negotiators to don asbestos suits if the Soviets offered to light their cigarettes. President Reagan's repeated injunction to "trust but verify" was a reflection of basic U.S. attitudes toward the Treaty. As an illustration of this visceral attitude, and the consequent substantive emphasis during much of the negotiations, the Treaty's Inspection Protocol is longer than the basic Treaty text, and the article in the basic text addressing verification issues (Articles XI) is the longest of the Treaty. In the final year of the INF talks, U.S. negotiators spent far more time and energy attempting to ensure that the Soviets would honor the agreement (or that we would be able to determine quickly that it had been broken) than on any other topic.

The conclusion of the INF Treaty was widely regarded as a negotiating *tour de force*. The inspection and verification provisions incorporated in the Treaty were unprecedented in their scope and detail. They met every U.S. negotiating criterion and broke new ground throughout, As well as requiring the elimination of every INF system and support facility, the Treaty also bans all production and testing of INF systems. However, because the mobility of INF missiles presented unique verification challenges, the United States

sought (and achieved) agreement to a wide variety of location restrictions designed to enhance our ability to monitor Treaty-limited
missiles while permitting routine training until these missiles are
eliminated. The location restrictions require that all Treaty-limited
missiles and launchers must be at declared bases or support facilities, in deployment areas surrounding operational bases or in transit between permitted locations. The interlocking web of provisions
to monitor compliance with these requirements includes a variety
of innovative mechanisms such as:

- A network of on-site inspections over a thirteen year period,
  covering every aspect of elimination of the systems. These inspections included "baseline" inspections to assure that all
  Treaty-limited items (missiles, launchers, etc.) were accounted
  for; "elimination" inspections to assure that such items are either destroyed or unable to serve INF roles; "close-out" inspections to confirm that an INF facility (base, storage area, etc.) is
  no longer performing this function; and a sliding scale of "quota" inspections permitting rapid access to active (or closed) INF
  facilities to help assure continued compliance with Treaty provisions.
- A "portal monitoring" inspection team permanently stationed
  at the Soviet missile assembly facility in Votkinsk, which previously built SS-20s, to assure through weighing, measuring,
  x-raying, and opening shipping containers that the Soviets are
  not producing forbidden SS-20 INF missiles under the guise of
  permitted SS-25 strategic ICBMs.
- Agreed upon lists of inspectors totaling up to 400 whose rights
  of access, type of equipment, and range of activities during inspections have been incorporated in the Treaty and its Protocols.
- "Reciprocal measures" to facilitate U.S. satellite photography to
  determine that Soviet missiles bases for the road-mobile SS-25
  missiles do not conceal a hidden force of SS-20s.

Remarkable as these Treaty provisions were in both scope and detail, they certainly did not complete the structure devised to implement INF Treaty inspections. Indeed, the Treaty was akin to a
new house which was well designed and carefully constructed but

which lacked many of the little touches that turns a "house" into a "home." To recognize this point is not to fault the negotiators. Indeed, the negotiators anticipated in the texts of the Treaty and protocols that these would be living documents, subject to elaboration and revision, and thus made provision for either formal amendment or mutually agreed measures "to improve the viability and effectiveness" of the Treaty or its inspection and elimination protocols. In some instances, they recognized the requirement to extrapolate and expand specific elements of their work, e.g., a requirement to agree on characteristics and methods of use for equipment to be used by inspectors within thirty days after entry into force of the Treaty.

In other areas, there were either errors that needed correction (both Soviet and U.S. site diagrams depicting individual INF facilities had a number of small mistakes such as incorrect North-South arrows or measurement scales) or procedures that were going to require elaboration. Such, however, were no longer the province of the U.S. INF negotiating team, the majority of whom initially were directed toward securing Senate ratification and subsequently to a wide variety of non-INF assignments. INF was to transition from its negotiators and ratifiers to its "implementers," slowly moving from a politico-diplomatic forum to one which while recognizing the political implication of any problem essentially stressed procedural-technical points. In contrast, the Soviets, who had no concerns about securing ratification from a then rubber stamp legislative system, switched their key INF negotiators into the implementation process.

The organizations primarily concerned with INF implementation are the On-Site Inspection Agency (OSIA), the agency essentially concerned with the day-to-day mechanics of the Treaty, the Special Verification Commission (SVC) supposedly designed to focus on "big picture" problems, and the Nuclear Risk Reduction Center (NRRC), which handles INF-related communications. It is a reflection of the operation of U.S. domestic politics that the three major organizations for implementing the Treaty were allotted to different bureaucratic agencies: Defense Department (OSIA); Arms Control and Disarmament Agency (SVC); and State Department (NRRC) (The Soviets essentially combined all three operations). As bureaucratic responsibilities evolved through mid-1989 following the ritualistic restructuring which characterizes every new administration, the principal interagency group involved with implementing the INF Treaty was the Arms Control Policy Coordinating Committee (PCC) with high-ranking representatives from, *inter alia*, Defense, State, the Intelligence Community, and ACDA. Supporting the PCC was a Subcommittee for INF Implementation chaired by the National Security Council, with the same agencies represented, but also including officials from the OSIA and NRRC. In response to any new treaty implementation issues, this subcommittee formulates policy guidance for the SVC and OSIA, after of course negotiating the labyrinth of interagency clearance.

On-Site Inspection Agency (OSIA)

On 15 January, even before formal presentation of the INF Treaty to the Senate, White House directive established the OSIA. It was designated as a field operating agency of DOD reporting to an executive committee consisting of the Under Secretary of Defense for Policy, the Under Secretary of Defense for Acquisition, and the Chairman of the JCS. Consequently, DOD provides the OSIA with operational guidance, administrative and logistic support, and the policy guidance formulated in the PCC subcommittee on INF implementation. The Director of OSIA is appointed by the Secretary of Defense (with State Department concurrence) and approved by the president. After an interagency tussle, an ACDA representative was designated as principal deputy with other deputies from State and the FBI.

There was a relentless logic in subordinating the OSIA to the Defense Department. Inspection procedures were going to require men, money, and equipment. Neither the tiny Arms Control and Disarmament Agency (ACDA) nor the perennially short-funded State Department had appropriate resources or technical expertise to manage an operation of such scope and magnitude. OSIA was unprecedented. There was no "school solution" to prepare an organization that would have to operate across 19 time zones, conduct 133 inspections to identify over 5,300 accountable items, and simultaneously play host to 31 Soviet inspections in 60 days (the "baseline" inspections)—as well as preparing a permanent presence of U.S. inspectors for the "portal" inspection at Votkinsk. Creating even more pressure was the initial projection that the Treaty would be ratified by the beginning of March 1988, a bare two months after submission to the Senate; and overriding all was the attendant blare of publicity associated with every aspect of the Treaty, marked by critics poised to exploit any discrepancy and a concomitant requirement to "get it right the first time."

While not an invasion of Normandy or an Apollo space shot, the organization and first year operation of OSIA deserves at least an appreciative nod of recognition for sustained bureaucratic skill. While solving the variety of bureaucratic and administrative tangles endemic to "start up" of any organization, OSIA and the SVC also fleshed out inspection procedures with their Soviet counterparts. That it did so without the errors and bungling frequently reported by the media in other areas is a tribute to both U.S. and Soviet administrations, each of which devoted sufficient resources and assigned competent personnel committed to flexible problem solving. That this success went virtually unremarked by media, and is unknown outside the circle of INF aficionados in both Europe and the United States, illustrates the philosophy that "good news is no news."

Institutionally OSIA began with the traditional small "band of brothers," led by the former Defense Attaché in Paris, and assistant Army Attaché in Moscow, Brigadier General Roland La Joie, a highly regarded army officer with extensive experience in Soviet affairs. There was also a ten-person cadre to coordinate procurement, airlift, budgeting, accounting, and logistics. Such a staff proved grossly inadequate, and OSIA eventually evolved to approximately 200 military and civilian personnel. Throughout the first six months, OSIA labored to thrash its way through thickets of logistic, planning, and personnel administrative problems, and to locate the resources to solve such problems. Initially housed in antiquated quarters normally occupied by the Coast Guard at "Buzzards Point" in Washington, where communications and operations were often a patchwork of the shared and borrowed, OSIA moved in mid-1989 to state of the art facilities on the outskirts of Dulles Airport, better reflecting the high tech, high touch demands of Treaty implementation. Financially OSIA proved to be a rare bureaucratic bargain. Although authorized for as much as $82.9 million (which would have included massive commercial aircraft rentals), OSIA eventually spent only $19.9 million during FY 1988 as use of Defense Department Military Airlift Command aircraft permitted substantial savings.

Although there were endless organizational problems, the most pressing administrative hurdles included creating the framework for inspection teams and arranging the portal monitoring facility at Votkinsk.

Short-notice Inspection Teams

These ten man teams are the heart of the INF inspection process. Drawn from a cadre of 200, their observations form the basis for official comment on the Treaty through the factual "inspection report" concluding each inspection. Yet these inspection teams had to be created from scratch. Prior to the INF Treaty, the United States had no corps of trained inspectors, nor any need for them. As a group, OSIA needed Russian linguists, Treaty experts, intelligence specialists, and individual technical experts on each type of missile. There was no role for the casual bystander. Rather than creating a bloated staff to deal with the initial requirement for 133 "baseline" inspections in the initial sixty days, OSIA elected to train a cadre of temporary duty personnel loaned primarily from military and intelligence agencies. Led by carefully selected team chiefs, who were frequently former military attaches in Moscow or had other intensive experience with Soviet military procedures, the observers were given detailed training in the provisions of the INF Treaty and intelligence collection techniques.

It was also clear that as well as monitoring compliance with the Treaty, we sought to exploit fully the opportunity to collect intelligence of Soviets systems and procedures that no Western representative had ever seen "up close and personal." A corollary to our planning to inspect Soviet facilities was to prepare our facilities both in the United States and basing countries (UK, FRG, Italy, Belgium, and the Netherlands) for inspection by Soviets. Did local commanders understand what was permitted and prohibited? Could a career-long focus on protecting classified material be selectively modified to accord with new legal obligations in a manner that left all smiling rather than gnashing their teeth? Consequently, following academic instruction, the United States scheduled mock inspections against all its INF facilities using full-scale inspection teams and Treaty-agreed procedures which were later judged "worth their weight in gold" not only for honing inspection techniques but for developing rapport between escorts and local commanders.

There is an aphorism that if you train hard you have an easy fight. This proved the case for INF inspections. If glasnost in East-West relations had been hinted with the signing of the INF Treaty, it took a long step toward institutionalization with the first year of Treaty inspections. Although Soviet sites were often extremely isolated, sometimes requiring six or seven-hour rides at high speed over indifferent roads following air flights to the nearest airport, Soviet base commanders were cordial and accommodating beyond what had been thought possible. For their part, Soviet inspectors were thorough and businesslike on inspections and "never met a camera they didn't like" when provided a media opportunity. It was a time for pragmatics rather than dramatics. During the baseline inspections, for example, a U.S. missile was found to weigh three tons less than officially stated in the Treaty's Data MOU. Soviet inspectors waited patiently while U.S. personnel scouted up sufficient ancillary equipment to bring weight up to required levels. Site diagrams remained occasionally inaccurate (the arrow pointing north, did not; a measurement scale was wrong).

There was a high degree of harmony during all baseline and quota inspections (each side performed its full complement of twenty quota inspections). Most infractions proved trivial (a Soviet inspector arrived in England with a visa for the United States rather than the UK and thus did not participate), some were less so. A U.S. inspection team, for example, discovered a local Soviet unit welding the ends of SS-23 launch vehicles back on to the chassis from which they that had just been carefully removed. This procedure, which appeared stimulated by local "initiative" to make a better heavy duty flatbed truck rather than to recreate an SS-23 launcher, was subsequently rectified. The conclusion, however, was recognition that both sides had devised institutionalized procedures that were sufficiently flexible to identify and register significant problems, as well as minor ambiguities, without transforming them into political confrontation.

Portal Monitoring

The "Votkinsk Machine Building Plant" in the Udmurt Soviet Socialist Republic is as close to the middle of nowhere as a U.S. citizen is likely to get. Built on the outskirts of Votkinsk, a city of approximately 100,000 previously most noted as the birthplace of Tchaikovsky (who left at age eight), the Votkinsk SS-25 missile assembly facility features a Berlin wall style perimeter which must be negotiated on cross-country skis during the winter. It was OSIA's responsibility to arrange in cooperation with the Soviets for construction of Treaty-mandated facilities at the site and associated housing which would make the U.S. permanent presence at Votkinsk more than the equivalent of a concentration camp existence for the thirty man inspection team.

Starting with a site survey prior to Treaty ratification (reciprocally the Soviets visited Magna, Utah), OSIA personnel determined requirements for the Votkinsk facility, including arranging for special flights to deliver required equipment. U.S. inspectors were on the ground at Votkinsk by mid-June 1988, shortly after Treaty signature, to refine plans for the layout of the monitoring system and to assure the Soviets understood U.S. requirements. Initially the U.S. inspectors made due with low tech equipment (tape measures, flashlights, surveillance cameras at exits, and Polaroid cameras) but by November 1988, we had installed a more sophisticated monitoring system (with the exception of the CARGOSCAN x-ray discussed below) including infrared break-beam profilers for dimensional screening of vehicles, TV cameras with lighting, induction loops, and semaphore gates. The United States intended to rely heavily on contractors to establish and man the Votkinsk portal inspection operation, but initial funding constraints forced OSIA to assume the burden for several months. Subsequently, however, approximately twenty of the thirty inspectors were supplied by a contractor (Hughes Technical Services Corp). For approximately twenty-five million dollars spread over five years, Hughes agreed to install, operate, and maintain the technical on-site inspection equipment for monitoring shipments exiting Votkinsk.

Initial experience suggests that portal monitoring will be a long dull process, as both rail and road traffic out of the Votkinsk facility is low, and only exiting rail cars have been large enough to contain an SS-20 (and thus trigger the Treaty inspection provisions). During the first year, the Soviets trans-shipped seventy-eight SS-25 missiles and, during the course of the year, the United States used all eight of its authorized container inspections.

Special Verification Commission

In stark contrast to OSIA, the Special Verification Commission (SVC) was the orphan of the INF Treaty. In comparison with the intensity and detail with which the Treaty's inspection provisions and its Inspection Protocol were negotiated, the Treaty provides only the sketchiest outline for the role and functions of the SVC. Article XIII, paragraph one, of the Treaty reads as follows:

> To promote the objectives and implementation of the provisions of this Treaty, the Parties hereby establish the Special Verification Commission. The Parties agree that, if either Party so requests, they shall meet within the framework of the Special Verification Commission to:
> (a) resolve questions relating to compliance with the obligations assumed; and
> (b) agree upon such measures as may be necessary to improve the viability and effectiveness of this Treaty.

Thus, in juxtaposition to the detail and specificity of the remainder of the Treaty, its associated protocols and data MOU, the SVC is the epitome of imprecision:
"... meet within the [undefined] framework ... questions relating to compliance ... agree upon measures as may be necessary to improve the *viability and effectiveness* ..." [emphasis added].
Nor was this vagueness accidental. Instead it was a conscious position by U.S. decision makers based on internal compromises stemming from the U.S. experience with the Special Consultative Commission (SCC) created in accordance with the provisions of the SALT I Treaty.

The Legacy of the SCC

The extended operation of the SCC (established by a U.S.-Soviet MOU in December 1972) moved ultimately from attempts to resolve ambiguities in interpretation of the SALT I Treaty (and the never ratified SALT II agreement) to pure political confrontation. The body was designed to meet on an agreed schedule and address a specific agenda. Thus, the SCC addressed, but did not resolve, a wide variety of U.S. charges of Soviet noncompliance with arms control agreements, particularly the ABM Treaty, SALT I, and SALT II. Particularly irritating to the United States was Soviet refusal to hold special meetings to deal with fresh problems as they arose. American institutional frustration steadily increased with Defense Secretary Weinberger reportedly referring to the SCC as a "black hole" in which the United States pressed fruitlessly for redress of Soviet wrongdoing. In this view, the SCC (or anything similar) was worthless, merely a mechanism for the Soviets to evade justice, and thus should not be included in any INF Treaty. INF related issues should be handled in normal diplomatic channels or through media statements. Initially, this view prevailed in constructing the U.S. INF negotiating position.

Critics of the Reagan administration, however, contended that the SCC had provided a limited, but useful tool to register U.S. concerns in previous years. They argued that the Soviets eventually responded to U.S. SCC complaints, not always directly and never with a *mea culpa*, but usually in a way which resolved the point under contention. Instead, critics charged, the United States was at fault for politicizing the SCC and transforming it into a propaganda forum, which vitiated its utility in resolving those substantive and procedural Treaty compliance problems which could be handled in an essentially technical meeting.

Another sizeable body of opinion, while no less frustrated by Soviet intransigence in the SCC and the history of Soviet noncompliance in arms control, believed that some SCC-like structure was necessary for the INF Treaty. Technical and substantive points, other than the inspection/verification concerns to be dealt with by an on-site inspection agency, would inevitably arise, and a number of "blanks" remained to be filled in Treaty provisions. Inspection team members were designed to function as eyes and ears, not negotiators. Additionally, work-a-day diplomats would lack the background and the time to hammer out solutions to such questions. Nor could complex technical points be handled by competing press releases (not the most subtle of negotiating mechanisms).

Creating the SVC

For their part, the Soviets were straightforward. They required a body in which compliance disputes could be addressed. They proposed simply extrapolating the organization and terms of reference for the SCC into the INF Treaty. The United States rejected this proposal, itemizing our problems with the SCC, but it became clear that some formalized body would be necessary. The Soviets offered a face saving device: change the name! The United States focused on addressing specific procedural irritants: the preset agenda and schedule of meetings. As ultimately constituted, the U.S. hardliners (although hardly totally pleased) saw something of a victory in the creation of the final form of the SVC. They anticipated that by eliminating scheduled, every six months, meetings, there would be virtually no meetings, or at least none that the United States did not call, to bring the Soviets to task for Treaty shortcomings. Moreover, they anticipated no formalized structure for the SVC and few, if any, issues that it would need to address.

During the Senate ratification debate, Democratic senators were skeptical. The Senate Foreign Relations Committee (SFRC) report on the Treaty noted its undefined nature, citing criticisms by former SCC Commissioner Sidney Graybeal and Sec-Def Harold Brown. The report implied that the SCC and SVC operations should be combined both to coordinate arms control compliance concerns more effectively and benefit from SCC experience on the topic. Senators indicated that the SCC was under-utilized and that the projected public nature of the SVC could be duplicated by the SCC through amendment of SCC rules. Indeed, the administration was fooling no one through its maneuvers and rationalizations to justify an SVC: the SCC was politically unacceptable to the administration. The SFRC report tweaks the administration a bit on the point only to indicate that the Senate was not "born yesterday," but it was not willing to make an issue of precisely how to address future compliance problems; perhaps it was concerned that such a focus would stimulate doubts over the likelihood the Soviets would honor the Treaty. Such a compliance debate, after all, would be akin to arguing over which marriage counselor to consult prior to the nuptials.

The SVC Reality Has Been Different

Throughout the Senate ratification debate, the SVC stayed on the backburner. In contrast to the massive administrative and substantive efforts of the OSIA, planning for the SVC was honored by its absence. No U.S. SVC representative was named, and other agency representation was distinctly an afterthought. Indeed, even when the United States was informed that the Soviets intended to call an SVC meeting immediately after the Treaty entered into force, the United States delayed naming its chairman, and did not designate one until after the Moscow Summit at which the Treaty was signed. Likewise, argument over the U.S. SVC Deputy continued until virtually the day discussions began. In line with this beginning, the operation of the U.S. SVC retains a distinctly *ad hoc* character. Other than the U.S. representative and a secretary, there is no full time permanent staff. Similar to the OSIA, however, the U.S. SVC representative receives his instructions from the PCC subcommittee on INF Implementation, and the United States has not had to meet the Soviets without instructions as occasionally was the case for the SCC.

For each session, the United States sent a full interagency team with a panoply of experts, including legal and scientific personnel. The Soviets have matched this representation; in fact the full range of Soviet expertise necessitated comparable U.S. technical support. Again, in contrast to the United States approach, the Soviets drew heavily from the ranks of their former INF delegation.

Most obviously during its first year of operation, the SVC was not a sometime affair. First, the blithe assumption that (because there were no scheduled meetings) the United States would control the pace and timing of SVC sessions was simply wrong. The Treaty provisions are reciprocal, and thus the Soviets have been quite capable of calling meetings, or making it clear they wanted to meet.

Consequently, the SVC held four extended sessions in Geneva, each averaging about six weeks, of which three were called by the Soviets. Indeed, during the first year of INF Treaty implementation, the SVC met longer and more frequently with the Soviets than any other U.S.-Soviet bilateral negotiation. During the first year of Treaty implementation, the SVC addressed many points that needed elaboration and resolution but which will not be repeated. Nevertheless, the precedent appears set for extensive and detailed discussion in the SVC.

During its first year of operation, little was heard from the SVC despite these extended, intensive negotiations. The results of these negotiations were closely held, as the commitment to openness differentiating the SVC from the SCC applied only to "documents representing agreements" and not to work in progress, or even sub-elements of such work. Thus, for the "mountain" of effort, there was only a public "mouse": a house keeping document stating how the SVC would perform its function, and an elaboration of a U.S.-Soviet agreed minute prior to Treaty ratification, providing more procedural detail on measuring items exiting thru the "portal" inspection facility at the Votkinsk SS-25 assembly plant.

A massive "work in progress," however, providing elaboration of many individual aspects of the Inspection Protocol, was grinding through the SVC. This "Memorandum of Agreement" provides for a range of instruction, such as the physical characteristics of tape measures, flashlights, and cameras which inspectors can bring with them on inspections or the procedures to be followed when meeting inspectors, processing their persons and luggage, etc. at the airport point of entry. Many of these procedures were easily agreed and followed rule of reason principles. The sides agreed that OSIA and Soviet inspectors would adopt such procedures, despite the absence of official announcement.

The most knotty problem, however, dealt with the provision for "imaging" items exiting from the Votkinsk SS-25 production facility and tied up agreement on the MOA for over six months. The provision for "imaging" (essentially x-ray) originates with the extensive "end game" INF negotiations in 1987 to devise provisions assuring the United States that the Votkinsk facility would not be able to produce SS-20s and ship them disguised as SS-25s. Since the SS-20 and SS-25 first stages were effectively identical, the key to such an assurance was being able to measure the SS-25 second stage. Initially highly reluctant to open SS-25 containers for direct physical inspection, the Soviets suggested "imaging" as one mechanism to measure the SS-25 stages. Although after intensive negotiation the sides eventually agreed upon eight random openings per year, the provision for "imaging" remained in the Inspection Protocol with the Soviets leaving it up to U.S. technological ingenuity to devise a "non damaging" system. Never loath to tackle a technological challenge, the United States devised such a system. Labeled CARGOSCAN, the proposed system is akin to a massive airport x-ray machine which takes a vertical picture of the contents of a container passed in front of it. It is large, complex, expensive, and, because of the sophisticated computer software necessary to operate it, possibly open to undesirable technology transfer to the Soviets. For their part, the Soviets, perhaps concerned over the potential for U.S. intelligence collection derived from x-ray of their missiles, recanted and offered to open every SS-25 canister exiting Votkinsk: a proposal which had it been offered in November 1987 would have been accepted with alacrity by the U.S. negotiators. Additionally, the Soviets apparently were suspicious that the imaging could somehow undetectably damage the missile ("fry" the electronic components) in ways only the clever Americans could accomplish.

Violations

This massive inspection and monitoring process slowly distilled into the regular report on Soviet Noncompliance with Arms Control Agreements; and there have been instances of Soviet noncompliance with the INF Treaty. These Treaty violations were identified through a combination of National Technical Means and on-site inspections. They fell into several categories:

Transits of missiles on launchers between missile bases and other facilities

Although the Soviets properly notified these transits, the Treaty requires that the missile be separated from the launcher during a transit. It is of course more complicated and inconvenient to separate the two, but separation makes a covert missile force harder to create and sustain. During the negotiations, the Soviets agreed to this element of the Treaty without significant debate (or possibly real thought over the potential inconvenience) and may have hoped quietly to ignore the point. The Soviets subsequently changed their practice to comply with Treaty provisions.

Failure to list all Treaty-limited items or to have them at the proper locations

These problems appear to have been the consequence of disorganization rather than designed deception. The Soviets corrected their errors. Interestingly enough, the United States was also guilty of comparable technical errors including finding unannounced Treaty-limited items at INF facilities.

The point is two-fold. First, noncompliance is unacceptable by either side. Such errors must be corrected to sustain the confidence of the negotiating parties. Second, some noncompliance in any complex contract (and the Treaty is ultimately a complex contract on a limited category of arms control) can be anticipated, and is understandably more an illustration of the need to master new procedures than a threat to the provisions of the Treaty.

What Next?

Expand the OSIA

The first year of operation for both OSIA and SVC has provided both a clear indication that the INF Treaty can be appropriately monitored and a clear warning that more must be done to prepare for monitoring and inspecting the various arms control agreements (START, chemical weapons, Conventional Forces in Europe). Although predictions of whether, let alone when, an arms control agreement will be completed are for the daring rather than the diplomat, there is clearly an impetus to complete rather than defer such agreements. It is obvious that an on-site inspection element will be a component of any forthcoming arms control treaty. The contemporary success of monitoring and inspection for the INF Treaty could lead to a blithe assumption that additional monitoring responsibilities can be easily assumed. This is not the case—or at least not with current resources.

The OSIA is the obvious organization to pick up the cudgels of future requirements for on-site inspections. It has not, however, been designated for such responsibilities and if negotiations drag on (as they are often wont to do), with the waning of INF Treaty monitoring requirements in mid 1991, OSIA could be effectively a skeleton force at the time when other arms control agreements are reaching completion. It was possible to create OSIA for INF monitoring with more than a bit of *ad-hoc-ery* as, while the inspection provisions were unprecedented, the numbers of accountable items (5,366) and initial range of inspections (117) were not unmanageable. A START agreement will involve vastly more types of systems and bases and the long term retention of residual forces will demand even more careful and extensive monitoring. One illustration of this point is the estimate of 2,500 locations in the Soviet Union open to a strategic arms reduction agreement vice the approximately 120 INF Treaty locations. Likewise, the projected requirement for a conventional forces agreement to account for and eliminate not hundreds but tens of thousands of items (together with monitoring residual conventional forces) will provide a significant challenge to any monitoring organization. As both a START and CFE agreement could well be operating at the same time (together with the continuing although diminished monitoring requirements for the INF Treaty), the demands on an OSIA-type organization could be enormous.

The conclusion is obvious. The United States (and in the context of a CFE agreement, our NATO allies as well) must begin active planning for OSIA to monitor each of the projected arms control agreements. Some of these negotiations ultimately may prove to be dead letters, becoming negotiations of drift rather than decision, but, nevertheless, the planning needs to be centralized and specific and be done now. This includes expanding the cadre of Russian linguists, identifying and training an enlarged pool of inspectors with special skills as necessary (metallurgy, production line engineers), defining contracts, and identifying contractors beyond Hughes and Sandia laboratories, assuring that Military Airlift Command assets can perform a substantially larger inspection support mission without detracting from its military requirements, etc.

As well as devising such a personnel database, OSIA could be charged with verifying the technical data and site diagrams where trivial errors plagued and embarrassed the post-ratification verification process. It should supervise trial elimination procedures for prospective treaty items and test inspection equipment and techniques. Moreover, rather than waiting until all the provisions of an agreement are complete, OSIA should plan for and conduct mock exercises and inspections in the context of various proposals as they are made. Moreover, U.S. agencies should be informed of the costs and resources which their proposals (or competing Soviet proposals) would entail: a process completely lacking during the INF negotiations, where negotiators were wholly innocent of consequent costs. It cannot be expected that inspection will be done "on the cheap" (not even to mention the costs of national technical means of inspection) but an internal estimate of cost effectiveness should be part of verification proposals.

Combine SVC and SCC

The administration needs to end the ideological angst distorting its view of the SCC and SVC. Most of the unresolved SCC arguments are now dry bones whose political utility approaches zero as the Soviets profess sweet reason on more important topics in other fora or offer *mea culpas* to U.S. charges such as the Krasnoyarsk radar. The remaining points are as likely to be resolved as the United States is to obtain repayment of WWII war loans.

Efficiency suggests the organs be combined and that the SVC be permitted to benefit from the degree of structure and bureaucratic continuity that marks the SCC. De facto, the SVC is developing structure and precedent, if only to deal with the overweening reality of having to anticipate meeting with the Soviets for months on end. At the same time, the SCC continues to wither on the vine with little substance to address. It should not be beyond the politico-legal expertise available to collapse the SCC into the SVC with the SVC assuming (but in effect indefinitely tabling) the existing SCC agenda of irresolvable/irreconcilable issues.

Swords into Plowshares:
The Elimination Protocol

Ronald J. Bartek

Ronald Bartek was a State Department member of the INF negotiating team. The article was provided in 1989 for an INF Memoir and has not been previously published.

When a group of U.S. congressmen visited an INF elimination facility not far from Kiev in August 1989, they watched attentively as Soviet technicians disassembled an SS-20 launcher and, with plasma torches making short work of heavy metal, cut up the launcher components precisely as prescribed in the Treaty's Elimination Protocol and under the watchful eyes of ten U.S. inspectors. One of the congressmen summed up the day's activities for his own colleagues and the group of newly-elected deputies of the Supreme Soviet hosting the visit by proclaiming in rather reverent tones, "We have just watched these Soviet technicians eliminate a launcher that used to fire a missile that could fly 5,000 kilometers with three warheads that were each some ten times more powerful than the one that destroyed Hiroshima; not a bad day's work."

The Elimination Protocol contains specific procedures to be followed in eliminating each item subject to the Treaty. Naturally, the evolution of this protocol (as it was painstakingly worked out by the two negotiating teams) reflected many of the same conflicts of approaches and positions that were evidenced in the development of the main body of the Treaty text. It also reflected the great numerical differences between the material assets the two sides would have to eliminate: a factor which exerted considerable influence on the Soviet approach to negotiating the Treaty in general, and the Elimination Protocol in particular.

The Treaty's Memorandum of Understanding lists 1,752 Soviet missiles—more than twice as many as the 859 U.S. missiles listed. It lists three times as many Soviet launchers (845 versus 283) along with more than 400 additional Soviet missile support vehicles compared to zero for the United States. Such figures documented the asymmetric reductions to be taken by the Soviets and indicated the magnitude of relative costs involved, while establishing a precedent that would call for much more of the same in subsequent negotiations, like those regarding conventional forces in Europe. These numerical realities often seemed to drive the Soviets toward "practical" solutions in the INF negotiations (especially in terms of the Elimination Protocol) and, later, toward cost-saving arrangements in the implementation of the Treaty.

The most notable case in which such a "practical" Soviet approach came to bear on elimination procedures involved the vehicles subject to the Treaty. The Soviets were eventually to be required to eliminate almost 1,300 vehicles (launchers and support vehicles such as missile transporters), compared to only 283 for the United States. Furthermore, throughout most of the negotiations, the United States insisted on vehicle elimination procedures that would have exacerbated this situation in a way that proved unacceptable to the Soviets. All the U.S. vehicles involved (Pershing and cruise missile launchers) were "trailers" drawn by detachable, German-produced ten-ton "tractors" that were widely used for other purposes. The U.S.-proposed definition for a "launcher" captured only the "trailer," which housed the erector-launcher mechanism that elevated and fired the missile; the "tractor" would be exempt from elimination. The United States argued for this approach on the grounds that the "trailer" included all the launcher mechanisms, and elimination of such "tractors" would not be verifiable (given the large number of identical vehicles being used in other capacities). The U.S. approach called for cutting the "trailers" and components of their erector-launcher mechanisms in half, while the "tractors" could drive away unscathed.

The vast majority of the Soviet vehicles, meanwhile, were of fully integrated designs—the "tractor" portion could not be detached. Also, the Soviets reported that, because of the manner in which these integrated vehicles were balanced and their transmissions were constructed, cutting the "trailer" portions in half would render the remainder of the vehicles "useless pieces of junk." The Soviet negotiators made it clear that they could not accept an outcome that found the United States driving away 283 perfectly serviceable and versatile vehicles from its launchers while the Soviets reduced 1,300 vehicles to rubble. At one point, the Soviet negotiators even indicated willingness to cut their vehicles in half if the United States were to do the same with both its tractors and trailers, but the U.S. position on this matter had been embedded in concrete.

As the U.S. and Soviet negotiators pored over the details of these vehicles in search of a solution, it became clear that, not only could the Soviet vehicles not be cut in half without rendering them absolutely useless, the vehicle chassis had to remain intact, back to and including the rearmost axles, in order to avoid the same result. Once the U.S. negotiators realized the Soviet vehicles could, at best, be cut aft of the last axle, they focused their attention on that portion of each type of vehicle. Fortunately, the rearmost portions of the Soviet vehicles contained the equipment and structures most important to the support, erection and launching of missiles. The negotiators, therefore, explored how much of the rear of each type of vehicle could be cut off and removed, and U.S. engineers and analysts studied each type of vehicle to determine how much would have to be cut off to preclude its use as a Treaty-limited vehicle (as well as the possibility that removed portions might be welded back on effectively).

After a great deal of very tough negotiating, the sides agreed, as part of a broader package and in addition to cutting in half all components of the erector-launcher mechanisms, on specific lengths to be cut from each type of Soviet vehicle. The U.S. side had concluded that these agreed lengths were sufficient to preclude restoration as Treaty-limited items, and the Soviets would be able to salvage a large number of vehicles useful for other purposes. The U.S. side could have accepted the same approach to eliminating its launcher trailers, but decided, having already exempted its tractors, to cut its trailers in half and scrap them.

The broader package within which the vehicle question was finally agreed involved another issue over which the two sides had long argued—how to destroy ground-launched cruise missiles

(GLCMs). The Soviets had insisted from the beginning that U.S. GLCMs and all their parts, including "internals," be completely destroyed. The U.S. side argued for GLCM elimination procedures that would permit retention of the sophisticated (and expensive) internal workings of these missiles (guidance packages, engines, and rocket boosters). The U.S. negotiators further argued that procedures requiring destruction of such internal missile components would be impossible to verify. They pointed, too, to the precedent of the elimination procedures for other "air-breathing systems" (aircraft), established in the SALT negotiations. These procedures called for cutting airframes, wings, and tail sections but did not require destruction of engines and internal instrumentation. The U.S. side additionally emphasized that GLCM "internals" could be useful in a number of non-Treaty-limited projects, such as reconnaissance drones.

Ultimately, the U.S. ambassador proposed a package of "practical solutions" in which the Soviets would accept the U.S.-proposed elimination procedures permitting retention of GLCM engines and guidance packages, while the U.S. side would accept the vehicle elimination procedures permitting the Soviets to retain usable truck chassis. The Soviets accepted this package in the final days of the negotiations with General Medvedev, the Soviet negotiator who delivered the acceptance, displaying a good deal of anger over the solution (he had led the fight against retention of GLCM parts, arguing that such retention was tantamount to conversion of GLCMs to their sea- and air-launched variants).

Another issue in which numerical asymmetries came together with the Soviet propensity for practical solutions involved the missile support structures (buildings) subject to elimination under the treaty. The original U.S. position had called for elimination of such buildings by destruction or modification, and had listed the SS-20 single-bay launch garages and multi-bay support vehicle garages on the Soviet side, along with Pershing II and GLCM launcher shelters and support vehicle garages on the U.S. side. In fact, the U.S. Intelligence Community had long insisted that all the buildings on the Soviet INF missile bases should be torn down (with no option to modify them), but the Washington interagency process decided against this approach, mostly because its reciprocal requirements would have resulted in unacceptable effects on U.S. military facilities in Europe. The U.S. side had originally proposed the modification option to preserve structures for deployment of shorter-range INF missiles. Even after the agreement ("double zero") was made to eliminate shorter-range as well as longer-range INF missiles, the United States had an interest in preserving some of these structures for deployment of systems not bound by the Treaty (multiple launch rocket systems, for example).

The ultimate solution in this matter (agreed by both sides and based primarily on a Soviet proposal) was that only those buildings from which INF missiles could be launched would have to be destroyed. At the time the Soviets proposed that solution, they had about 450 such structures (SS-20 launch garages) while the United States had only one (a Pershing II launch shelter). Exempt from this solution were about 150 rather inexpensive SS-20 support vehicle shelters that did not house launchers on the Soviet side and from which missiles could not be launched, and, on the U.S. side, Pershing II shelters that did house launchers, along with the very expensive, hardened shelters for GLCM launchers. NATO forces would, therefore, be able to make use of these structures for non-Treaty-limited purposes with no requirement to modify them so that they could not accommodate an INF launcher.

Once it became clear that the two sides would be required to eliminate their entire INF arsenals, the Soviets (with 1,752 missiles to destroy) began to express concern about their ability to do so within the three-year period proposed by the United States. In fact, they said they could not agree to that time limit until they were certain that missile elimination procedures could be agreed that would enable them to comply with it. At a meeting of the two Foreign Ministers in the middle of 1987, it was decided to send missile technology experts from the two capitals to supplement the Geneva delegations and explore the destruction methods that would have to be employed in order for the Soviets to meet a three-year deadline. As a result of discussion among these experts and subsequent negotiations, the two sides agreed on two methods (explosive demolition and static firing). The Soviets proposed a third method—launching missiles to destruction, but the U.S. side balked at this proposal. The Soviets argued that they would not be able to meet the deadline without this third method. A Rocket Forces general serving on the Soviet delegation of missile technology experts also explained that, "After all, the natural death of a missile is to be launched." U.S. officials were concerned that a provision permitting launch to destruction might be used to circumvent the ban on missile testing. The resolution was to permit launching as a means of destruction but only under strict conditions and to a limited extent (for example, only 100 launches each could be conducted, prelaunch inspection by the other side was required, and no test data could be collected).

One particular episode in these deliberations on missile elimination procedures illustrated a constant and important aspect of the Soviet negotiating mentality throughout the INF talks: the absolute requirement for reciprocity. It appeared to the U.S. negotiators that the absolute nature of this requirement was based not so much on substantive concerns, as on the compelling drive to have the Soviet Union be seen as the equal to the United States in all matters. The illustration of this principle in this particular case came in regard to the missile elimination method known as static firing, referred to in the text of the Elimination Protocol simply as "burning." Static firing involved securing a missile stage to a fixed stand, igniting the rocket motor, allowing the fuel to burn at the normal rate, and destroying the missile parts that remained. The U.S. side knew from the outset of the expert discussions on missile elimination that static firing would be the principle method used to eliminate Pershing missiles, and proposed that it be considered by the Soviet side for eliminating its ballistic missiles as well. However, after the Soviet side formally proposed that static firing, among several other methods, be permitted under the Treaty, Washington instructed the U.S. delegation to reject that method for Soviet use while retaining it for the United States (there was concern in some Washington circles that the Soviets might collect valuable test data from static firing of missiles).

Soviet reaction to the U.S. rejection of Soviet use of a method that the United States intended to use and had earlier suggested for Soviet consideration was predictable: the Soviet delegation "went ballistic." First in the Elimination Protocol working group and then at the ambassadorial level, the Soviets adamantly protested this nonreciprocal approach in very strong terms. However, even while the Soviet side argued forcefully to protect its right to the static firing method, the U.S. negotiators knew that it was highly unlikely the Soviets would ever make use of the method (discussions among the missile technology experts had revealed that static firing for Soviet ballistic missiles would raise serious safety concerns). The sides eventually agreed to permit static firing for both Parties under conditions that prohibited data collection. Despite the Soviets' neuralgic reaction in this matter, and their forceful insistence on protecting their reciprocal rights, they did not eliminate a single missile through static firing.

Another constant and important Soviet theme in the INF negotiations, in this case a substantive one, was Moscow's persistent attempt to subject the Pershing I missiles of the Federal Republic of Germany to the INF Treaty. The Elimination Protocol, as it transpired, was the document in which the resolution of this issue, at least in terms of its effect on the INF Treaty, was reflected. The Soviets had long insisted that the FRG Pershing missiles be counted directly in the U.S. INF inventory, but the United States, of course, refused.

Knowing that the Germans owned these Pershing I missiles and launchers but that the United States controlled the reentry vehicles (which contained the warheads) for these missiles, the Soviets had proposed language for the Elimination Protocol laying out elaborate procedures for eliminating warheads. The Soviet proposal would have required withdrawal of the German Pershings, complete with warheads, to an INF elimination facility where they would have been de-mated under the watchful eye of Soviet inspectors. Throughout the course of the INF negotiations, the United States refused to subject third country systems like the FRG Pershings to the INF Treaty, and insisted that the disposition of such systems was solely the concern of the sovereign countries concerned. This position was equally applied to French and British INF systems.

Most of the tension over the German missiles was released when Chancellor Kohl announced that his country's Pershings would be destroyed when all the Soviet and U.S. INF missile systems had been eliminated. As a consequence, the Soviets dropped their elaborate procedures for eliminating warheads and agreed (in paragraph 3 of Section II of the Elimination Protocol) that warheads could be removed prior to the missiles' arriving at elimination facilities. The sides further agreed (in paragraph 9 of that section) that they would complete the elimination of all their INF systems fifteen days prior to the end of the three-year elimination period, and that the U.S.-controlled reentry vehicles for the German Pershings would be removed from the FRG and moved to U.S. territory within that fifteen day period.

The Elimination Protocol was the first of the primary INF Treaty documents to be completed and agreed by the sides. It appeared to the U.S. negotiators that one of the reasons their Soviet counterparts were able to come to closure on this Protocol promptly was that the Soviet side of the Elimination Protocol Working Group was chaired by Sergei Kryuchkov, an official with high personal stature on the Soviet delegation, who seemed to be empowered by Moscow with considerable authority. Kryuchkov's father was a prominent KGB official at the time, and was later appointed KGB director.

Kryuchkov was officially serving on the INF delegation as a representative of the Soviet Foreign Ministry, but one episode during the final days of the talks indicated additional, overriding affiliations. Kryuchkov, who also acted as his delegation's legal counsel, was leaving the U.S. mission after a particularly difficult late-night negotiating session. The chief Soviet negotiator, who was talking with the U.S. ambassador, hailed Kryuchkov and told him he should stay behind at the U.S. Mission to work out with his U.S. counterpart some technical details of the portion of the agreement just reached.

Two aspects of the exchange caught the attention of the U.S. delegation. First, the Soviet ambassador, when hailing Kryuchkov, addressed him as "Colonel" (possibly a reference to KGB rank). Secondly, Kryuchkov's response to his ambassador's direction to stay behind to work with his U.S. legal counterpart was to reply, "No, I will not stay—I have my instructions," and to depart immediately.

As was the case with much of the rest of the INF Treaty, most of what is contained in the Elimination Protocol was unprecedented, going far beyond anything contained in previous arms control agreements. Given the fact that the elimination procedures were fabricated from whole cloth in the process of the INF negotiations, the two sides can take considerable satisfaction from the smooth implementation of these procedures, with all INF systems eliminated without diplomatic incident.

Vignette: The Long Flight Home

It was the morning of 7 December. It was the anniversary of Pearl Harbor, 46 years removed, although few ventured it a thought. The INF delegation was packed and moved from hotel rooms and apartments. Some had been ready for hours; others for days.

The organized energy of the U.S. Mission was reduced to silence. Safes formerly carefully locked and secure, now gaped open and empty with their contents either packed for return to Washington or consigned to the ubiquitous paper shredders. The long humming WANG word processors were finally silent with their library of documents archived onto computer disks. The corridors of the Mission were virtually filled with bags of confetti-sized shredding and the rubble of carry out, "fast food" that had sustained the delegation over the final week. All-American products were in the piles: Pizza Hut; Burger King; Kentucky Fried Chicken. This is the way the U.S. negotiates. But the long contemplated confetti snowstorm from the Mission windows was never held. Last minute second thoughts (or fatigue) saved the local maintenance crew a massive cleanup.

With the last details checked and the Treaty completed in English and Russian on the official treaty paper of both countries, the delegation loaded onto buses for the trip to the airport. Awaiting the delegation was a camouflaged C-141 Air Force cargo transport specially detailed to bring the delegation back together along with personal effects and scores of boxes of classified documents.

And accompanying the U.S. delegation were the Soviets. The final Treaty details, the checking and rechecking of the text, had absorbed so much time that the Soviets were unable to secure commercial transportation that would get them and the Soviet copy of the Treaty to Washington before Gorbachev and the rest of the Soviet official delegation. Always hospitable, the United States offered the Soviets a ride. So Ambassadors Obukhov and Medvedev (the latter an army general) and a shy, petite secretary who reportedly had typed every word of the Soviet draft Treaty thru its multiple revisions were perhaps the first Soviets ever to fly on a C-141.

The C-141, bigger than a box car roaring through the skies, was not your Pan Am 747! To the ear-plugged passenger it sounded as if you were flying inside a demented vacuum cleaner. Most of the delegation, however, was past caring. Draped over the temporary seats the bulk of the delegation initially slept the sleep of the exhausted. Some slept all the way to Washington.

Slowly, however, others became aware of still more history in the making. The Data MOU and the Inspection Protocol were being initialed—making INF the first treaty initialed in the air. Tables were set up on both sides of the aisle and the process of initialing began. A few of the delegation came forward with pens that they requested be used. The U.S. negotiators directly involved with the MOU and the Inspection Protocol took special pride. Again an occasional camera flashed. And then it was done with a smile, a handshake, and a few words of mutual congratulation.

Slowly the hours passed. There was a desultory bridge game. Noise quickly aborted the efforts of a delegation guitar player. The hungry sampled packaged meals, and if very hungry had the same meal again several hours later. A preteen style pillow fight enlivened the final hour. And the U.S. aircraft maneuvered through the air traffic controller over Andrews AF Base to bring the delegation C-141 down before the Aeroflot craft carrying Gorbachev, which arrived virtually simultaneously.

The plane was on the ground. The delegation was greeted by family, friends and Washington INF colleagues. The Treaty was now ready for history—and the Senate.

The Senate and INF Ratification

David T. Jones

Following is a detailed review of the Senate process for ratifying the INF Treaty. The author was a member of the State Department's Treaty ratification team. It was originally published as a monograph, Senate Ratification and the INF Treaty, *by the Army War College, in 1992.*

On 25 January 1988, when Secretary Shultz addressed the Foreign Relations Committee, the United States Senate began its review of the INF Treaty. On 27 May, the full Senate gave its approval in a vote of 93 to 5. Between the walls of these dates, the Senate conducted the most intensive and protracted scrutiny of an arms control treaty ever held. Legally, there is no question what the Senate was about. The Constitution of the United States in Article II, Section 2 requires the Senate to provide its "advice and consent," i.e., review and approval, to treaties and requires a two-thirds favorable vote for their acceptance. As treaties become the highest law of the land, the framers of the Constitution considered that this stringent approval process was appropriate.

But in the current era, perhaps least of all is treaty making a legal process. To be sure, there are intricate and fascinating legal issues, as any modern treaty is rich with lawyerly language and the proponents and opponents of any treaty often will couch their objections in such phraseology. The fundamental elements of the INF Treaty ratification process, however, were political and having far less to do with the technical merits of the Treaty than with demonstrating political power and "sending messages." What then were the parameters of this review? What were the problems and how were they resolved? What should the process tell the United States Government and the American people?

A Larger Context: The Politics of the INF Treaty

Although the Senate was about to begin its first ratification review of an arms control treaty in over a decade, the virtues and liabilities of the INF Treaty were hardly the only, and perhaps not the most important, aspects in play for the Senate. Of special note were political concerns (both domestic and international) and underlying these were an Executive- Congressional power battle over the making and interpretation of treaties.

The Politics of INF

First and foremost there were political considerations, both domestic and international. The INF Treaty was wildly popular. Every poll illustrated this popularity with endorsements ranging from the Veterans of Foreign Wars to Women's Strike for Peace: a coalition unusual in U.S. politics. Every domestic and international poll demonstrated similar, if not greater popularity. Endorsements came from every significant European political party in or out of power. Likewise, positive supporting comments from around the world deluged the INF Treaty, giving it a golden aura, akin to the development of canned beer and sliced bread. The Treaty, in and of itself, was a "Good Thing." Support was so high (and credible opposition so negligible) that the Reagan administration quickly concluded that "the Treaty sells itself" and deliberately determined not to create and dispatch a legion of official spokesmen to address domestic audiences, equivalent to the "SALT sellers" during SALT II ratification. Attempting to generate further support was deemed counterproductive; not only was it unnecessary to expend public affairs funds and energies on a topic so universally popular, but the administration feared individual senators would consider that they were being unfairly pressured/hustled if such a campaign were to be mounted.

Thus, following initial availability of a wide range of documentary information and official spokesmen in the days immediately following the Treaty signature to explain its content and ramifications to media and particularly to editorial writers, the administration took a low key public relations approach. Its officials mentioned the Treaty in the course of speeches on general topics, but, with the exception of a Saturday radio address by President Reagan, did not concentrate uniquely on INF.

The Treaty was popular for good substantive reasons: total elimination of a Soviet weapon system threatening NATO, asymmetrical reductions favoring the United States, and an unprecedented verification regime opening Soviet territory to inspection. But even more importantly in the 1988 election year, it appeared to signify a payoff for the "peace through strength" motif that had dominated debate over U.S. defense spending and strategy for dealing with the Soviets throughout the Reagan presidency. Moreover, it was clear that the Republican Party intended to use the INF Treaty as a keystone in its election strategy.

The Republicans had spent seven years and hundreds of billions of defense dollars to rebuild effective military strength *inter alia* on the grounds that only such strength would bring the Soviet Union to terms at the bargaining table. The INF Treaty, when ratified, would also demonstrate that President Reagan and the Republican Party had also effectively pursued "peace." Moreover, the INF Treaty would be a particularly effective counter to those domestic critics who had claimed that U.S. INF deployments would ensure that there would never be INF reductions. That these critics were Democrats would provide a "rub their nose in it" additional pleasure. Admittedly, some candidates for the Republican nomination, notably Senator Dole, were initially reluctant to endorse the INF Treaty, perhaps because then Vice President Bush gave it vigorous support. Senator Dole explained his reticence on the grounds that he had to "read" the Treaty. One wonders whether he ever actually read the hundreds of pages of Treaty-related material or settled for a precise and a close reading of the polls.

Nevertheless, even the most public-spirited Democratic senator had to recognize that the Republican Party had created the potential for major political benefit at a critical point in the election process. Every political party wants to run on the 1956 Eisenhower political slogan of "Peace, Prosperity, and Progress." With the INF Treaty, the Republicans in 1988 would have a lock on at least two of the three criteria for election. Thus for Democrats to admit that the Treaty was good, let alone excellent, was an indirect endorsement of President Reagan and Republican politics. To oppose the

Treaty, however, would run against the personal and political inclinations of most Democrats, as well as providing the Republicans
with the election issue that the "Democrats were against peace."
Coincidentally, opposing the Treaty would play into the hands of
the Republican conservatives for whom a number of Democrats
combined animosity with contempt.

Nor could the Senate, and the Democrats, be indifferent to
the international ramifications of the Treaty. Although bilateral in
form, dealing as it does with only U.S. and Soviet weapons, the INF
Treaty deeply involved NATO (and Warsaw Pact) territory and political concerns, and was also distinctly of interest to Asian friends
and allies. Ultimately the Senate could be cavalier about the SALT
II Treaty, as it applied only to U.S. and Soviet strategic systems having no direct effect on allies. INF, however, was the epitome of an
Alliance cooperative venture. From recognition of the problem of
Soviet SS-20s, through U.S. Pershing II and cruise missile deployments, and intensive consultation during the Geneva negotiations,
NATO had been intimately involved in the INF Treaty. NATO "basing countries" with U.S. INF missile bases had to accord parliamentary approval to provisions of the agreement permitting Soviet
inspectors on Allied territory. Removing Soviet INF missiles would
be a direct benefit for NATO and other allies. And they made no
bones about their desire for early Senate ratification of the Treaty,
to the occasional irritation of individual senators. Indeed, the judgment even by some skeptical of the Treaty, such as former Secretary
of State Kissinger, was that the Treaty should be approved if only
because the consequences of rejection would be more damaging to
U.S.-NATO relations than the consequences of the Treaty.

The Constitutional Question

A far deeper underlying issue was the constitutional concern of
making and interpreting treaties, as illustrated by the protracted
fight over the ABM Treaty. Epitomized in the arguments of the State
Department Legal Adviser, Judge Abraham Sofaer, the Reagan
administration contended that it was free to reinterpret the ABM
Treaty based on elements of the negotiating record that had not
been presented to the Senate during the course of the ratification

debate, even if the interpretation reversed what government witnesses had told the Senate. Unsurprisingly, the Senate vigorously dissented from this "Sofaer Doctrine" analysis. Consequently, the Senate was looking for an opportunity to assert its position, and the INF Treaty provided the perfect battleground to contest points such as providing the negotiating record to the Senate, determining when administration spokesmen were speaking "authoritatively" for the record, and pinning down what leeway, if any, the Executive branch had to interpret a Treaty beyond the confines of material that had been presented to the Senate. Thus, if the administration held the strategic advantage of the popular appeal of the Treaty to force its approval, the Senate held the tactical advantage of being able to arrange the conditions under which they would ratify it.

The Senate and INF: The Run-up to Ratification

The period of official review by the U.S. Senate was but one facet of the "advice and consent" process. The divisions between Executive and Legislative branches that have characterized U.S. domestic politics during most of the past generation have also put a strong imprint on U.S. foreign policy. Bluntly it is impossible simply to negotiate a treaty, let alone an arms control treaty, and send it to the Senate assuming sanguine legislative acceptance. The executive branch, whether controlled by Republicans or Democrats, does not command a partisan two-thirds Senate majority and has not done so since Christ was a corporal. Likewise, the era of "Executive Agreements," that is, foreign affairs agreements that are *de facto* treaty equivalents but ostensibly reached between ranking executive officials (and hence requiring only a congressional majority), has largely ended. The Senate has made it clear to the Executive branch that, particularly on arms control topics, it views an executive agreement as a subterfuge to avoid the Constitutional "advice and consent" process and has a plethora of mechanisms, particularly fiscal, to prevent such agreements from coming into effect even if they could be passed. (Ironically, elements of the House of Representatives will from time to time push for returning to "executive agreements," not from any desire to make it easier for the executive branch to conclude agreements, but to deal itself into the action.)

By 1985 the Executive Branch and the Senate had established the Senate Observers Group. With a small staff drawn from the Senate Foreign Relations Committee, this organization was designed as a bipartisan mechanism to receive information on arms control (and consequently develop senatorial expertise on the topic) and simultaneously to serve as a sounding board for Senatorial opinion for any emerging arms control agreement. Such a "stroking" operation was pursued both in Washington and Geneva. On a regular basis, senior administration arms control experts such as Ambassadors Nitze and Kampelman, or the Geneva negotiators, as available, would brief members of the Observer Group and selected Senate staff. Such briefings covered START and Defense & Space negotiations, as well as INF. Likewise, the group would travel to Geneva an average of once a negotiating "round" to discuss issues directly with U.S. and Soviet negotiators. This direct consultative process was a remnant of the SALT I negotiations, when senators held *ex officio* right to participate directly in the negotiations, a status still nostalgically recalled by some senators.

If the concept behind the Senate Observer Group was brilliant, the execution was less so. The concept would have created a core cadre of well informed senators who, on the basis of years of knowledge and familiarity with the emerging agreement, would have led the subsequent ratification debate. Thus Observer Group membership was always rather small and stable to foster greater technical expertise and Legislative-Executive branch trust. The unfortunate reality, however, was that during the years of negotiations, little "homework" was done. Proffered briefings were politely turned down or poorly attended, and then primarily by staff.

Visits to Geneva during work-a-day sessions often attracted a sparse senatorial turnout which, when combined to visits elsewhere in Europe, could be criticized as merely junketeering, a charge which made some senators further leery about participating. And, until close to the very end of the negotiations, it was not obvious that agreement was imminent. In short, INF arms control negotiations fell victim to the "Hill syndrome" that if a subject isn't being voted on tomorrow, or the subject of attention of a constituent pressure group providing significant financial support, it is not going to get regular attention. Arms control has to fight for the limited hours and minutes in a senator's attention span that is also clamored for by abortion supporters, prayer in school advocates, reelection campaigns, veterans rights, welfare reform, individual DOD weapons programs, local dam/river projects, and all the hundreds, indeed thousands, of topics that surge across the U.S. political scene lodging in one way or another in the Senate.

Analysts in the Executive branch recognized and regretted this phenomenon, but moved ahead. Ultimately, with the exception of Senators Nunn and Stevens, the Senate Observer Group did not play a significant leadership role in Treaty ratification. Nevertheless, the limited feedback available from staff and senators, helped familiarize the INF negotiators with some politically sensitive points, such as the disposition of nuclear warheads. Past experience with the Senate analysis of SALT II assured that the INF Treaty did not have the obvious "treaty killer" loopholes that particularly incensed senators during that review, e.g., potential interference with National Technical Means, encoding telemetry, and inadequate inspection. The INF negotiators flagged the prospect of ultimately having to obtain Senate approval for the Treaty to the Soviets in negotiating sessions on specific points, particularly for inspection/verification concerns. Indeed, occasionally the Soviets attempted to counter-pressure, asserting that the Supreme Soviet would have to give its approval. Although the Soviets doubtless believed that we overdid the specter of Senate ratification and were openly dubious, we were more credible than they.

A Bureaucratic Structure: The Administration Organizes to Ratify

No one at senior levels in the Reagan administration had ever managed the ratification of an arms control agreement. The most recent precedent, the SALT II Treaty, had been a catastrophe, and the willingness to duplicate its bureaucratic structures was commensurately lacking. Ultimately, the officially designed structure for coordinating the Executive Branch ratification effort was centralized and cumbersome. The structure placed White House Chief of Staff Senator Howard Baker in overall command of ratification, with top level White House political and substantive officials coordinating USG policy on specific aspects, e.g., legal matters under White

House Counsel Culvahouse. The State Department Counselor, Ambassador Max Kampelman, for example, was one of the representatives on this high level policy committee. The White House also took direct responsibility for the "treaty interpretation" issue as it was a political/constitutional question rather than a substantive INF concern. Subordinate levels within the NSC coordinated working level action. Great emphasis was placed on "singing from the same sheet of music," with the concurrent requirement for full interagency coordination of all official statements and responses to Senatorial questions. Each agency involved in the substantive issues (State, DOD, JCS, ACDA, and CIA) set up its own internal organization to manage ratification-connected issues, e.g., official testimony, responses to Senatorial inquiries.

The State Department, which had the lead agency responsibility, had a relatively elaborate two tiered structure. In overall control, Ambassador Kampelman chaired an INF Policy Group which included Assistant Secretaries of the major bureaus dealing with INF (European Affairs, Politico-Military affairs), long-term arms control experts such as Ambassadors Nitze and Rowny, Chief INF Negotiator Ambassador Glitman, and high-ranking technical experts from Legal and Congressional Affairs as well as from ACDA. This group set policy and addressed major problems, reporting to Secretary Shultz.

Backstopping this Policy Group was an "INF Ratification Task Force," directed by a senior Foreign Service officer, which included several State INF experts empowered to draw widely on Department resources to handle questions and problems. INF negotiator Ambassador Glitman was maintained and supported separately as a spokesman for the administration as a whole, and testified more frequently and extensively on the Treaty than any other administration witness on the negotiating history and interpretation of the Treaty.

The complex theoretical structure broke down over time. High level attention to the ratification process waned as the committee hearings and testimony ground forward over the months, and ranking officials at the White House and State met less frequently. The NSC continued to insist on centralized control over "authorized" responses, but mid level officials operated with substantial autonomy.

Providing Paper for the Senate

Recognizing the prospective role of the Senate, the Executive began a full court press with the arrival of the Treaty in Washington for signature. The Summit signing ceremony between the President and General Secretary Gorbachev was attended by a selection of ranking senators, with an eye toward co-opting possible doubters and flattering presumed supporters. Copies of the requisite Treaty documents had been rushed to the Hill on the day of signature, to assure that the public relations aspects of the impending ratification were not neglected. Simultaneously, the Executive branch worked to complete an official transmittal letter from Secretary Shultz to the Senate. This letter of transmittal, officially delivered when Shultz provided opening testimony before the Senate Foreign Relations Committee on 26 January, also provided an article-by-article explanation of the Treaty, ostensibly in layman's language, but carefully reviewed by Department of State and other government lawyers to assure full conformity between the legal and "informal" text.

The Negotiating Record

One of the elements on which the administration quickly yielded was providing the "record" of the negotiations to the Senate. The elements of this record were extensive, but not exhaustive. They consisted of formal decisions issued by the President on INF, official statements by U.S. and Soviet negotiators, formally presented ("tabled") documents such as draft treaties, summary and detailed reporting on the individual negotiating sessions, and official reporting on meetings between ranking U.S. and Soviet officials, (e.g., meetings between Secretary Shultz and Foreign Minister Shevardnadze). This material covered the entire period of the INF negotiations from their inception in 1981 (interrupted by the Soviet walkout in 1983) to their conclusion in December 1987. Protected from Senate review, however, were the policy recommendations from the U.S. delegation to Washington, personal reports and evaluations by negotiating team members to their respective agencies (so called "backchannels"), and the internal agency memoranda upon which agency positions were based. The requirement to produce all the official reporting, however, generated a frenzy of effort within the vestigial elements of the disbanded U.S. Geneva negotiating team.

Although each Geneva negotiating meeting had been carefully covered by specifically assigned reporting officers and a detailed summary message transmitted to Washington, reporting had lagged on the very detailed, semi-verbatim follow-up telegrams. Eventually all material was tracked down, although a couple of pieces were located and added only after the "record" (thirty-two volumes and five feet of material) was officially transmitted to the Senate on 25 January. In fact, the record was not really available for Senate review, following staff logging and indexing, until 22 February. In accordance with the agreement governing handling of the record, the Senate rigorously limited access to the material in quarters designed to secure classified documents and did not permit its duplication or removal. Ultimately the record played little part in the ratification debate. The "smoking guns" suggesting negotiating error or shortcomings which some had hoped (or feared) would be discovered did not exist. The sheer bulk of the material presumably deterred some prospective critics. Others may have recognized that a negotiator must have room for hyperbole. Thus while a negotiator, addressing his counterpart across the table, may rhetorically "fall on his sword," saying "I absolutely must have this point" on a specific topic and thereby have his demand "on the record," it does not always necessarily mean "absolutely, positively."

Briefings and More Briefings

At the same time that the paper record was being prepared, the interagency teams designed intensive briefings. Some were one-on-one discussions between senior negotiators and senior senators, or any senator who wanted such a review. Other briefings were carefully tailored for the rank of the audience. Weeks were spent drafting and coordinating interagency briefings on political, military, and intelligence aspects of the Treaty, with hierarchies of ranking agency representatives designated to brief increasingly senior Senate staff and senators. There were, of course, glitches. An early effort to brief Senate Majority Leader Byrd was hindered by a slew of questions he had to a long-superseded early draft of the Treaty.

Byrd's staff apparently had not provided him the final version of the Treaty. Likewise, the carefully crafted hierarchy of briefings proved overly elaborate. Few were requested, and few attended those briefings that were presented. Instead, Senate staffers worked through the committees designated to hold hearings on the Treaty (Foreign Relations, Armed Services, and Intelligence) or spoke directly to knowledgeable individuals when seeking information.

Senate Consideration: The Committee Process

Upon presenting the INF Treaty to the Senate, the Reagan administration largely lost control of ratification. Under Constitutional procedures, this would be the norm for any treaty as the responsibility of the Executive for a treaty ends (other than responding to Senatorial questions) when the Senate begins its ratification review. Any attempt to "hustle" the Senate in its deliberation is counterproductive. Such a normal phenomena, however, was doubly true when combined with a Reagan White House, and a Senate restored to Democratic control only a year earlier with a presidential election campaign in the offing. As a consequence, the Executive branch had virtually no influence over when and how Senate committees would take up their review or when the Senate leadership would schedule debate. In retrospect it is instructive to note that administration insiders predicted the Senate would conclude its Treaty review by the Easter recess at the end of March. Of course, "prediction" is just another word for "guess," and the "end of March" was a very bad guess indeed.

It is also instructive to recall that the Senate was going about INF ratification with minimal recent experience. It had been seventeen years since the Senate last successfully ratified an arms control treaty (ABM Treaty in 1971). Only eighteen of the senators then present were still active for the INF debate, and none of them had played a major role in the ABM Treaty ratification. Three Senate committees (Foreign Affairs, Armed Services, and Intelligence) had authority to hold hearings on the INF Treaty. Close to fifty senators were represented on one or another of the committees. All senators were not equally engaged in debate, and each had different perspectives and personalities. Although official responsibility for treaty ratification rested with the Senate Foreign Relations Committee (SFRC) chaired by Senator Pell, the chairman of the Armed Services Committee (Senator Nunn) was widely regarded as the most powerful individual personality in the Senate Treaty review. This perception created a degree of tension between the SFRC and the Senate Armed Services Committee (SASC). The SFRC with the exception of conservative Republican senators, Helms and Pressler, was the most committed to timely completion of ratification, while the SASC repeatedly found points in the Treaty with which Senator Nunn in particular disagreed and consequently was determined to "fix." The Senate Select Committee on Intelligence (SSCI), whose interest in the INF Treaty was primarily concerned with its monitoring and verification, had a more limited initial role.

Committee reviews can be divided into two parts. The first set of formal reviews began on 25 January and were concluded by the end of March. The second, stimulated by verification questions and the issue of the role of future technology for INF range missile systems, was played out in May, particularly by the Intelligence Committee, and led into Senatorial involvement in negotiating agreed interpretations of the Treaty.

Round I: The Intelligence Committee (SSCI)

Chaired by Senators Boren (D-Oklahoma) and Cohen (R-Maine), the SSCI was dominated by long term, expert staff highly knowledgeable in the techniques and lore of intelligence. A substantial number of their sessions on the INF Treaty were "closed," focusing on classified material and systems which would be employed to verify the INF Treaty (and any subsequent arms control treaty). The result of initial hearings was a cool-eyed review of INF monitoring possibilities, starting from the premise that "no verification and monitoring regime can be absolutely perfect." The essential conclusion was that while there were areas of potential weakness in the Treaty (the unresolved dispute over numbers of SS-20s and the potential for developing a covert GLCM force), "the Soviets have little or no incentive to cheat" primarily because their nuclear inventory remained large enough, even after INF reductions, to cover desired targets "and still have several thousand warheads in reserve."

Although the SSCI report was approved unanimously on 21 March with no recommendations for alternations in the Treaty, the calm technocrats of the SSCI had their own ax to grind in the report. The SSCI analysis of the INF Treaty, while providing the required review of INF Treaty provisions, was primarily a launching pad for a judgment on any prospective START agreement. A START treaty, requiring fifty percent reductions and consequent monitoring of a complexly structured residual force, would be significantly more difficult to verify than the global elimination INF Treaty. The SSCI report strongly recommended "investing more" in modernized intelligence systems to verify a prospective START Treaty. Indeed, it was rumored that SSCI senators considered conditioning their agreement to an INF Treaty on expanded funding for satellite systems which the Executive branch deemed currently unnecessary, and ultimately extricated a commitment for two billion dollars for increased NTM capability.

The Foreign Relations Committee (SFRC)

Chaired by Senator Pell, the SFRC had primary jurisdiction over the Treaty review and other committees reported to it. Consequently, while the SSCI and SASC worked in the shadows and often in closed sessions, the high visibility testimony by Executive Branch witnesses and Treaty critics was played out before the SFRC. Weeks of hearings saw the Secretaries of State (twice) and Defense, the Chairman of the Joint Chiefs of Staff and the individual service chiefs, the director of the Arms Control and Disarmament Agency, and a wide variety of second level critics and supporters. Testimony filled five volumes with a sixth volume devoted to the SFRC report including Minority positions and observations.

During the SRFC review, the Treaty faced a number of criticisms (primarily from Senator Helms), the most prominent of which were:

Non-destruction of Nuclear Material

Much to the surprise of administration witnesses, who anticipated attacks on issues such as Treaty verifiability, Senator Helms chose to focus on an obscure point, the exclusion of nuclear material from the INF Treaty, during the period of maximum public and media attention in the opening days of testimony. He charged that INF warheads could be "bolted on" to other Soviet missiles and that excluding nuclear material from elimination gave the Soviets an advantage. Senatorial reaction was that the issue was not just a red herring but a "crimson whale" as the utility of the nuclear material without the missile to deliver it was nil. In fact it had been the United States which insisted on excluding nuclear material from the Treaty, *inter alia* to preserve the confidentiality of nuclear weapon design information which otherwise might be compromised during its destruction and to avoid the potential environmental problems associated with destruction of nuclear material.

A "Covert" SS-20 Force

Senator Helms argued that, in the absence of the right to search the territory of the Soviet Union "anywhere, anytime," the Soviets could hide and maintain an SS-20 force. He noted differences in U.S. intelligence estimates to justify his contention that the Soviets had not declared as many SS-20s as they had produced. The question of a "covert" force was legitimate, particularly given past Soviet history of compliance with agreements, and deserved serious examination. It was an issue which the negotiators wrestled with repeatedly, and sought to guard against through specific Treaty provisions.

Intelligence "estimates" lie at the bottom of the argument over a covert SS-20 force. There are many ways in which an intelligence judgment over an enemy force is reached. Absent a spy who can provide day-to-day order of battle figures and production statistics, any intelligence judgment is a construct based *inter alia* on previous Soviet practice for its missile force, observed systems, patterns of deployment, estimates of factory production, etc. Thus different intelligence analysts working from the same information, but making different judgments (e.g., will a factory produce 24 hours a day/365 days per year or at some lesser rate), can come to different conclusions, each of which are logically "valid." Something of this nature occurred in estimates of the Soviet SS-20 missile force, and consequently agency conclusions differed. The DIA estimate subsequently cited by Senator Helms and other Treaty critics was at the high end of the interagency spectrum of estimates. This does not mean that it was illogical, simply that it was wrong. Nevertheless, *proving* it wrong was an attempt to prove a negative, i.e., that there is no covert missile force.

The INF negotiator, Ambassador Glitman, noted that an INF "covert force" was akin to the Loch Ness Monster in that he could not *prove* that it did not exist. U.S. negotiators considered it illogical for the Soviets to attempt to maintain a covert SS-20 force, as the numbers would be militarily trivial and the financial costs of maintaining such a force significant (even discounting negative international reaction if the missiles were discovered).

Additionally, by eliminating all SS-20 training missiles, prohibiting test flights in INF ranges, and monitoring the SS-20 final assembly facility, intelligence specialists judged that the military reliability of any hidden missiles would quickly degrade.

Don't Prohibit the Conventionally Armed Cruise Missile

Some critics, particularly former Assistant Secretary of Defense Perle, argued that not all INF range GLCM should be banned. He proposed revising the Treaty to permit cruise missiles armed with high explosives while banning only cruise missiles armed with nuclear weapons. Such officials projected a significant future for such conventionally armed cruise missiles, which they hypothesized could become a major element in NATO arsenals, by being able to strike distant targets at low cost and extreme precision. Military authorities, however, disagreed, stating that there was no military requirement for such systems.

Nevertheless, the most significant reason to ban all INF range GLCM was that it was impossible to distinguish between nuclear and conventionally armed GLCM. Bluntly, a conventional cruise missile could not be verified. Despite extensive study, there was no method to guarantee that a conventional GLCM could not quickly be converted into a nuclear GLCM. An exception for a "conventional GLCM" would have been a major loophole providing the Soviets with a virtually irresistible incentive to cheat. Indeed, the military judgment was that it would have to regard all "conventional" Soviet GLCMs as nuclear armed.

The Armed Services Committee (SASC)

Headed by Senator Nunn, with Senator Warner the ranking minority member, the SASC took a more skeptical approach to the Treaty. Throughout February, the SASC mixed testimony on the INF Treaty with the status of the conventional forces balance in Europe, reflecting Senator Nunn's earlier expressed concern that an INF agreement should be linked to reductions in conventional forces. Toward the end of February, however, the SASC began two days of testimony by the INF negotiator, Ambassador Glitman, based on 135 questions prepared by the SASC staff on points of interpretation and clarification in the Treaty. As the Committee began to "walk through" the Treaty article-by-article, many of the formal questions were answered on the spot along with those occurring to senators during the course of discussion. The official responses to questions unanswered during two days of testimony were not completed and returned to the SASC until 14 March, whereupon Ambassador Glitman returned for further testimony on 18 March, and still further supplementary questions.

On 22 March, Nunn was due to present the SASC report to the Foreign Relations Committee; however, the additional testimony from Glitman, detailed review of the negotiating record, and internal Committee discussion delayed the report. Consequently, on 22 March, Nunn spoke to the SFRC "in his personal capacity" pending his Committee presentation. Nunn was remarkably unenthusiastic about the Treaty, freighting his remarks with concerns over the European conventional force balance and NATO's military shortcomings while urging follow up action in both conventional arms control and force modernization. Nunn coldly observed that NATO was "within its rights" to celebrate the Treaty but without a START agreement, "its military significance is, at best, marginal." He grudgingly concluded that the Treaty could "make a modest but useful contribution to NATO security" and, on balance, "the positive features of the Treaty outweigh the weaknesses." However, as well as the festering issue of a treaty interpretation amendment, he, and subsequently Senator Warner, signaled difficulties *inter alia* over what INF-related activities (research, technical assistance programs) would be permitted with NATO members, whether to permit conventionally armed cruise missiles, whether a "double negative" in Article VI would permit the Soviets a loophole to produce a second stage of the SS-20, and how "future systems" would be regulated.

Unsurprisingly, when the formal SASC report emerged on 29 March, the observations and conclusions closely reflected Nunn's initial "personal" comments. Of particular concern were "futuristics" (explored in detail below) and the "double negative."

Grammarians to the Fore: The Double Negative

The most difficult issue in the INF negotiations was unveiled close to their end. In the course of protracted discussion over verifying that all "stages" (sections) of INF missiles were eliminated, the United States discovered that one SS-25 stage was "outwardly similar but not interchangeable" with an SS-20 stage. In short, the Soviets were using the first stage of the SS-20 as the first stage of their ICBM, the SS-25. Obviously they were not going to give us a "two for one" deal by agreeing to eliminate the SS-25 in the course of eliminating the SS-20. Equally clearly, we were not going to permit an obvious Treaty circumvention by permitting the Soviets to continue to build an unregulated stage of the SS-20. After much high pressure negotiation, the sides agreed that each would have the right to build a ballistic missile incorporating a stage in effect identical to an INF missile stage. Thus the Soviets could build the SS-25 (incorporating a virtual duplicate of an SS-20 stage) and the United States could build a short range missile or an ICBM that used one stage of the Pershing II. This agreement was embodied in the Treaty as follows:

> *Notwithstanding paragraph1 of this Article [which* inter alia *bans production of INF missile stages] , each Party shall have the right to produce a type of GLBM not limited by this Treaty which uses a stage which is outwardly similar to, but not interchangeable with, a stage of an existing type of intermediate-range GLBM having more than one stage, providing that that Party does not produce any other stage which is outwardly similar to, but not interchangeable with, any other stage of an existing type of intermediate-range GLBM.*

The SASC and particularly Senator Nunn argued that this language created a "double negative" the effect of which would be to permit the Soviets to produce not only a missile with a stage which was "outwardly similar to, but not interchangeable with" an SS-20 stage but also another missile stage that was outwardly similar and interchangeable with an SS-20 stage. Administration witnesses and particularly Ambassador Glitman vigorously disagreed, noting in particular that a stage that was outwardly similar *and* interchangeable with an SS-20 stage would *be* an SS-20 stage and thus banned. Although admitting that the record demonstrated that there was a "meeting of the minds," the SASC concluded the paragraph was "technically flawed and should be clarified" perhaps by an exchange of diplomatic letters. In contrast, the SFRC examination of the issue concluded that while the provision was "awkwardly phrased," there was no risk it would be misunderstood and thus no need for further clarification with the Soviets. The point, however, was to arise again during formal Senate debate.

Questions Questions Questions

A remarkable sidelight of the INF ratification process was the blizzard of questions posed by Congress to the Executive Branch. In the normal course of testimony, official witnesses will "take" questions on which they do not have instant expertise, or senators will provide "follow up" questions either based on testimony or covering areas not addressed by official statements. Such questions, while not exceptional, are usually relatively few and precise in scope. For the INF Treaty, however, the volume and extent of the questions became a complicating factor for ratification. Although there were official legislative questions prior to the opening of ratification debate, the beginning of formal testimony unleashed a torrent of questions from individual senators and committees. Recognizing that the Reagan administration was on the hot-seat to respond to senatorial inquiry, questions ranged considerably afield from purely Treaty-related issues: U.S.-Soviet relations; military force planning; U.S.-NATO relations; future of arms control. Most questions sought to clarify Treaty points or elicit detail, but others were of the purely "have you stopped beating your wife" variety.

These "packages" eventually mounted to approximately 1,300 questions, each of which had to be answered in "authoritative" detail and approved through the dauntingly tedious interagency process. Of particular note was a long study of the Treaty by Senator Helms, containing approximately 250 questions and an analysis by the American Enterprise Institute (AEI) on a variety of technical points. Officials responsible for answering and managing responses to the questions slowly sank beneath the waves. Policy prevented submitting responses to the "packages" of Senatorial questions until all the questions in a specific "package" were answered. Invariably there was at least one question per "package" that generated problems in creating a response, frequently on an arcane substantive point over which the administration was divided. Creating an artful response or resolving the specific substantive issue took considerable time. The heavier the question load, the slower the response time. The slower the administration responded, the greater the senatorial irritation.

Unfortunately, the mass of answered questions had limited utility: they were rarely circulated beyond the individual senators or committees that had posed them and many were not available to the Senate as a whole until after ratification was complete, when they were printed in the volumes of the hearings. Thus they served more to put the Reagan administration "authoritatively" on record for the history books than to inform the Senate on individual points for the ratification debate.

SFRC "Markup"

Having finished hearings and received reports from the SASC and SSCI, the SFRC turned to the "markup" of the Treaty: in effect, a final review by the Committee to determine whether conditions or amendments should be added to the Treaty. The Reagan administration and the INF negotiators had viewed this process with some concern fearing that Senator Helms would engage in a protracted marathon of discussion, punctuated by proposals for detailed amendments which would be "treaty killers." Such action, the committee equivalent of a filibuster, could have been facilitated by traditional SFRC reluctance to limit comment by individual senators even if the result was considerable delay. Indeed, Senators Helms and Pressler appeared rehearsed for such a performance as copies of more than fifty theoretical amendments were unofficially circulated on the Hill. To counter this anticipated assault, the administration quietly drafted ripostes to each of the hypothetical amendments and circulated them to selected Committee members. As amendments could be included by majority vote, there were fears that ostensibly noncontroversial, "motherhood" amendments such as support for human rights or general requirement for compliance with previous agreements might be attached to the Treaty during Committee action, if only to provide minority critics with a "bone" of consolation for their overall defeat (but nevertheless a "bone" which could require renegotiation or at least delay Treaty implementation).

However, despite the heavily foreshadowed medley of amendments and anticipated delaying tactics, "markup" was completed in six days, with the SFRC voting out the Treaty (seventeen to two) on 30 March. Senator Helms engaged in only one bit of gamesmanship when he noted on the first day that a Committee quorum was not present without him, and forced the end of the session by his departure. Of the mass of amendments prepared for them by their staff, Helms and Pressler formally presented only a scattered selection (seven) for a vote, *inter alia*, a requirement that the President certify the Soviet SS-20 numbers were accurate; an amendment to permit conventionally armed cruise missiles; and a requirement for the President to certify that the Soviets were in full compliance with the Helsinki Final Act. All were defeated by massive margins with the two Republican conservatives attracting virtually no support from even party colleagues.

Still more satisfying to the administration, the SFRC rejected the proposals for modification and amendment proposed by the SASC (outlined above). Doubtless inter-committee rivalries played a part in this tactic, but each of the points raised in the SASC report and emphasized by Senator Nunn was effectively dismissed or downplayed by the SFRC. The most important of these, a possible clarification of "weapons delivery vehicle" as an element of the "futuristics" debate, was judged "desirable [but] not absolutely necessary." The administration, at Senator Pell's request, had provided comment, i.e., rebuttal, to the SASC report on each of the five areas highlighted by Nunn. Thus the Treaty was "clean": free from substantive amendments.

A Single Condition (But Not a Small One)

That said, the SFRC report included a "fly" in the administration's ratification ointment the size of a California condor. The Committee report and draft instrument of ratification incorporated a "condition" on treaty interpretation stimulated by the ABM Treaty reinterpretation debate. In ostensibly innocuous language, the "condition" required the "United States" (i.e., the Executive Branch) to interpret the INF Treaty in accordance with the "common understanding" between the Executive Branch and the Senate at the time of ratification and not to "adopt an interpretation different from that common understanding" without Senate approval. The "common understanding" was to be based on Treaty text and "authoritative representations" (the bureaucratic equivalent of speaking *ex cathedra*) by Executive branch officials. Adopted by a twelve to seven vote (with Republican senators Helms and Murkowski joining the Democrats), the condition represented a significant defeat for the administration's attempts to avoid a condition which it perceived (regardless of the detailed legal rationales of its proponents) as a mechanism by liberal Democrats to thwart any reinterpretation of the ABM Treaty that would permit development of the Strategic Defense Initiative ("Star Wars").

At various points in the ratification process, the administration had advanced remedies for Senatorial concerns which it hoped would defuse the issue. On 9 February, for example, Secretary Shultz responded to a letter from Senator Nunn by offering assurances that Executive Branch witnesses and supplied material on the INF Treaty could be regarded as "authoritative," and "the Reagan administration will in no way depart from the INF Treaty as we are presenting it to the Senate." Clearly waiting on this response before opening detailed examination of the Treaty, on 22 February, Nunn quoted the letter in detail at the opening of an SASC session concluding that, "What these assurances mean is that the committee can now proceed with detailed testimony on the treaty, confident that the treaty the Senate is being asked to approve is in fact the treaty that will be respected by the executive branch now and in the future."

Although it is problematic whether the artfully crafted Shultz letter ultimately would have satisfied the political requirements of Democratic senators for a "treaty interpretation" amendment, any such hope was blasted by a letter from White House legal counsel Culvahouse on 17 March, responding to a request by Senator Lugar to analyze a proposed "treaty interpretation" amendment. Aggressive in tone (and uncleared by Executive Branch agencies), the letter suggested that the Executive Branch was bound only to interpretations "...authoritatively shared with, and clearly intended, generally understood and relied upon by the Senate..." during ratification. SFRC lawyers concluded that this formulation although it "may appear straightforward" was designed to create criteria that "would be so difficult to meet that the Executive would almost never be bound by its own presentation to the Senate." Recognizing too late that he had kicked a dozing dog, Culvahouse attempted to recoup with a follow-up letter on 22 March aligning himself with the Shultz interpretation, but Senate Democrats were now less willing than ever to be lenient. Brushing aside various backstage alternative formulations floated, for example, by Senator Lugar during the SFRC hearings and "markup," Committee Democrats determined that it would be done their way or not at all.

"Futuristics": Ratification Surprise

The issue of "futuristic" INF systems was completely unanticipated by the administration negotiating/ratification team. It grew, however, from the proverbial "cloud the size of a man's hand" to a point where it threw ratification itself into doubt and required *de facto* renegotiation of a portion of the Treaty. The "futuristics" issue consisted of two parts: The first of these dealt with the "hypersonic boost glide vehicle" and whether it could be used for INF weapons. "The what?" was the first reaction by the INF negotiating team. None had ever heard of the system until it was identified in the American Enterprise Institute study. After substantial probing, the system was identified and isolated as essentially a theoretical concept still on the drawing board. A hybrid system designed for strategic ranges, it would have one portion of its flight path a ballistic launch and the remainder a non-ballistic, unpowered "glide" to target. Was this system covered by the INF Treaty? The administration chose to duck, avoiding a "yes" or "no" and providing a response that said a system would be covered if it met the four Treaty criteria of range (500-5,500 km), weapons delivery, ground-launched, and cruise or ballistic missile. Although grumbling, the SASC ultimately set this point aside.

"Futuristic" INF Technology

The second "futuristics" concern proved far more complex. The issue as eventually posed was clear: Could some future technology, e.g., high powered laser, microwave, *Star Trek*-style "phaser," etc. be deployed on INF range missiles and used as a weapon? The instinctive response by INF negotiators was "no" but proving first that this was the U.S. position and then that the Soviets also agreed that such technology was banned was significantly more difficult.

The origin of the problem was rooted in the development process for U.S. weaponry. To simplify greatly, a selected number of "black" programs examining and developing potential weapons on the cutting edge of technology are maintained in great secrecy, with information about them highly restricted and released only on a "need to know" basis. Clearly under normal circumstances, no negotiator would "need to know." Nevertheless, in July 1987, when the INF negotiations moved from a proposal which would have permitted a residual force of INF missiles to the "zero" proposal which would eliminate all such systems, the United States began an internal review over what U.S. programs would be affected by such a proposal. The consequence of the review was a recommendation to seek two "exceptions" to the treaty: (a) for "booster stages" (Article VII, para 12) which permitted stages that had not been used in INF systems but technically had INF range to be used for space tests; and (b) for ABM and ASAT systems (Article VII, para 3) which had been used only against targets in air or space but which technically would be banned as they have a "slant range" greater than 500 km. These were the only exceptions the INF delegation was instructed to seek and, after considerable discussion and education, the Soviets recognized that the provisions would be mutually beneficial.

SASC Testimony

The question of "future systems" began to emerge during Ambassador Glitman's testimony before the SASC on 22 February. At that point, Senator Quayle pressed for information to differentiate between remotely piloted vehicles (RPV) and systems banned by the INF Treaty. Glitman emphasized that systems which met the four Treaty criteria (range; weapon-delivery; ground-launched; and cruise or ballistic missile) were prohibited. "Weapon-delivery," however, was not one of the terms separately defined in the Treaty: the negotiators having believed it to be self evident. Nevertheless, at that juncture, Senator Quayle began a more intensive effort to define "weapon delivery" in a manner which would apply only to currently deployed weapons technology such as nuclear or conventional explosive warheads. He was aided in his argument by the wording of the "article by article" analysis, supplied to the Senate by the Executive Branch on 26 January (see above) which noted that the Treaty applied to GLCMs "tested or deployed for weapon-delivery, i.e., flight-tested or deployed with any type of warhead device or simulation thereof." The senator may have hoped through this effort to leave open the potential for future development of INF range missiles armed with high powered lasers or other exotic technology. Other senators, however, quickly spotted this issue as a potential treaty interpretation/compliance issue akin to ABM Treaty interpretation problems and demanded clarification. Administration officials recognized this as a potential treaty stopper, since there was no chance that the Soviets would agree to alter the fundamental meaning of a "zero" INF Treaty by cutting a giant Treaty loophole which would permit INF missiles carrying "futuristic" weaponry.

Proving the Administration's Case: Easier Said Than Done

After an internal caucus, the administration determined that it did intend to ban all futuristic weapon technology for INF Treaty limited systems. Then it began what proved to be an uphill fight to prove that both the Soviets and the United States had agreed that such "futuristic" systems were indeed banned. The administration was hindered, moreover, by the absence of explicit Treaty provisions defining "weapon-delivery" and future technology. Consequently, they had to prove their case by logic, implicit Treaty circumstances, and circumstantial evidence drawn from the Treaty negotiating record.

Nevertheless, the issue was not publicly debated, with the SFRC essentially willing to accept the administration's arguments and the administration again attempting to explain its case in closed hearings with the SASC on 18 and 24 March. When Senator Nunn's testimony and the Armed Services report were delivered at the end of March, however, the "futuristics" moved into higher gear. The SASC comment on the "futuristics" issue termed it "critical" and recommended an "authoritative" administration definition of "weapon-delivery" and assurance whether this definition "was clearly agreed to" by the Soviets. If the Senate was unsatisfied with Executive explanation, the report warned, an "appropriate understanding" with the Soviets would be necessary to determine the scope of "weapon-delivery." Consequently, during the SFRC "markup" hearings, Senator Pell requested a response to the SASC report and Senator Helms asked for specific negotiating record citations to substantiate Executive branch conclusions on Soviet positions.

A vigorous search of the largely un-indexed official negotiating record quickly unveiled a number of indicative references demonstrating that the Soviets sought to ban all ground-launched weapon-delivery systems in INF ranges. These citations were sent to Senator Pell in early April. Particularly definitive in the INF negotiators' view was a plenary statement by Soviet Ambassador Obukhov which emphasized their desire to ban all types of INF range ground-launched systems "regardless of how they are armed" (which clearly covered "futuristic" as well as existing armament). To further substantiate its position, the administration, after detailed interagency review of other points of criticism by Nunn, also sent Pell a response (known internally as the "five issues" letter) emphasizing the accuracy of its interpretation. In it, the

Executive Branch averred that the United States and Soviets jointly understood "weapon-delivery vehicle" to mean "any mechanism or device which when directed against a target is designed to damage or destroy it" and sanguinely suggested it was not necessary to confirm this understanding with Moscow. Additionally it concluded that all ground-launched, INF range "weapon-delivery vehicles" (GLCM and GLBM) both "present and future" were banned.

Attempting to Satisfy Senator Nunn

Despite this brave front, the administration was aware prior to its official transmission of the letter to Senator Pell that these assertions would not satisfy Senator Nunn's continued concerns. Staffers made it clear that while the administration had a reasonable case, the legacy of the ABM Treaty reinterpretation battle had too poisoned the atmosphere to allow the Executive Branch any benefit of the doubt.

In what appeared at the time a fortuitous development, however, Secretary Shultz was already scheduled to meet Soviet Foreign Minister Shevardnadze in Geneva on 14 April to discuss preparations for the Moscow Summit. A short session with Shevardnadze could be used to pinpoint the Soviet position on "weapon-delivery vehicle" and "futuristic" INF systems. Approaching the Soviets was hardly the USG's first choice. The negotiators believed their technical position both in the Treaty and throughout the negotiating record was definitive; therefore, to approach the Soviets as demandeur would suggest we were unsure of our ground. Additionally, there were concerns that the Soviets would extract a price by reopening other points, or perhaps seeking to expand the definition of "futuristic" technology to include selected effects such as electronic jamming. Nevertheless, the administration, supported by some members of the Senate, determined to make the approach.

Getting wind of the Executive Branch plan to approach the Soviets, however, Senators Quayle and Dole attempted to short-circuit any diplomatic demarche. In a letter to the Secretary, Senator Dole urged Shultz not to take the issue up in "premature discussion" with Shevardnadze and to let the Senate play out its review and analysis of how decisions on "futuristics" in INF might affect other arms control negotiations. A portion of this debate was played out in a closed hearing of the Armed Services Committee on 14 April. Here Senator Quayle released a letter he had sent to former Secretary of Defense Weinberger and former ACDA Director Adelman on 12 April. In his letter, Quayle asked each if he knew that the INF Treaty would ban "futuristic INF weapons carrying payloads unrelated to nuclear, chemical or high explosive munitions." In presumably prearranged responses, each dated 13 April, Weinberger and Adelman stated that they did not recall any discussion of "futuristic" systems in an INF context. Weinberger further obliged Quayle by stating that if he had known such "futuristic" systems would be banned, he "would have opposed it in the strongest possible terms." Senator Quayle's letters were a bit disingenuous as, in the context of the debate over banning conventionally armed cruise missiles, he had warned then NSC advisor Carlucci in a 10 September 1987 letter that such a ban "could eliminate our option to deploy new technology weapons...and that it would be politically imprudent to so jeopardize our future option on these military technologies." Courtesy copies were sent to Weinberger and Adelman.

During the course of the hearing, administration witnesses went through the "what did he know and when did he know it" Watergate-style drill. Knowledgeable military witnesses testified that the issue of applicability of "futuristic" technology to INF systems had been discussed in sufficient scope and detail to inform ranking Defense Department officials. In effect they had determined that "futuristic" technology could be accommodated on other delivery systems, such as ALCM.

A Letter from Shevardnadze

Earlier, however, members of the administration had concluded that Quayle (and Dole) were attempting to keep open the potential for "futuristics" in INF range weapons: a move that the now alerted Soviets would never accept. Consequently, Shultz broached the topic with Shevardnadze on 14 April (the day of the SASC hearing) and, in a remarkably rapid response, on 15 April Shevardnadze provided a letter agreeing with the U.S. position and stating that the Treaty covers INF systems "however armed" and that they would be banned "irrespective of their armament, nuclear or any kind of non-nuclear." The administration considered the response definitive and authoritative and rushed it to the Hill.

Rather than closing off the topic, however, the Shevardnadze letter turned into a mini catastrophe. Although the letter appeared quite satisfactory to the administration, to the jaundiced eyes on the SASC it was seriously lacking. Not only did it fail to repeat precisely the formulation that the United States had been using to define "weapon delivery vehicle" (Shevardnadze had attempted to short-hand agreement by simply stating that Moscow agreed with the United States) but it used "warhead" (now a buzzword for confusion) in the text. Additionally, a flawed (informal) translation provided by the Soviet Embassy was initially circulated on the Hill creating further linguistic confusion before the U.S. formal translation was available. Again, Senator Nunn concluded that greater precision was required. A formal clarification would be necessary and in a 22 April floor statement Nunn spelled out this requirement, while critically dissecting and dismissing the administration's arguments that such clarification was not necessary.

An Exchange of Notes

Therein followed a protracted—and virtually unique—drafting exercise between the Executive and Legislative branches. For days, texts were exchanged on a set of official messages that the United States would exchange with the Soviets. To satisfy our concerns (and assure the perfect response), the United States drafted both the statement outlining the U.S. position on the definition of "weapon delivery vehicle" and the concomitant ban on "futuristic" INF systems and the Soviet response (little more than "*da*"). Drafting was tedious with the NSC, State, and staff from several senators involved in the process. The result was one element of the final return to Geneva on 12 May.

Blindsided by the Soviets: The Technical Talks

However, still another problem was lurking in the wings—a series of issues raised during technical discussions of the Treaty.

Although the Treaty was scheduled to go into effect one month following the formal exchange of documents (ultimately performed on 1 June 1988 at the Moscow Summit), both sides realized that there was more than a month of preparation necessary to assure that Treaty implementation proceeded without any of the embarrassing "glitches" that would play into the hands of Treaty critics. Thus, although the Treaty was unprecedented in its detail, it was still only a structure upon which a good deal of procedural implementing detail was necessary. These details were addressed in a series of "technical talks" in Geneva (March) and Washington (April) and, more or less predictably, stimulated problems of their own. The most important of these was a Soviet challenge concerning whether the U.S. inspectors could look for an item the size of a missile stage or were restricted to inspection for an item the size of a complete missile. Nevertheless, administration observers did not consider the problems serious and, indeed, the technical discussions had been accorded less substantive attention than the ratification debate: after all, if ratification failed there would be no implementation.

These interpretation problems, however, quickly moved from technical to political levels with publication of a *New York Times* article by Michael Gordon on 28 April identifying several of the issues in play and stating that the United States was preparing to press the Soviets to resolve them. And indeed the State Department Counselor, Ambassador Kampelman, called in Soviet Ambassador Dubinin late on Friday, 29 April to present the U.S. requirement that nine inspection/verification-related issues be resolved prior to the Senate debate. Delayed by the weekend and their Monday celebration of May Day, the Soviets did not respond until late on Sunday, 8 May. Unfortunately the Soviets had failed to take the problem sufficiently seriously, and their answers, although positive in tone, were incomplete; they left unresolved the vital issue of inspections at Votkinsk and raised an unacceptable demand for accounting and elimination of FRG missiles stored in the United States.

Consequently, the SSCI was unimpressed in a 9 May hearing to examine the Soviet responses. Focusing on the inadequate Soviet responses, following the hearing, SSCI Cochairmen Senators Boren and Cohen announced that ratification debate must be delayed pending resolution of the issues. The INF Team then prepared to return to Geneva "one last time."

The final session was memorable in its own right. Arriving late from Washington on 11 May, the U.S. team, led by Ambassador Glitman, began meeting immediately with the Soviets. By 12 May, all issues were resolved. The formal diplomatic note on "futuristics" was signed by Ambassadors Kampelman and Karpov. Agreement was reached on the nine verification issues in a "minute" signed by Glitman and Colonel General Chervov, although not until 10 hours after Secretary Shultz announced at a press conference that everything had been completed. One of those "loose ends" required an all night negotiating session to tie down. But with it all, the Treaty was finally ready for Senate floor debate.

Senate Ratification Debate

The two weeks of Senate floor debate was a self contained drama. It was political theater with the requirements for formal "speechifying." It was a litmus test of ideology against which supporters and opponents will be labeled for all time. It was a last chance to make a statement by modifying the Treaty text, and to lay down "markers" for other arms control negotiations, particularly START. It was a political science text book of parliamentary maneuver with various candidates for most clever senator. It had the internal dynamic juxtaposing the much desired Memorial Day week long recess against the political requirement to approve the Treaty for the approaching Moscow Summit. A daily question was "will the Treaty be done in time?"

Perhaps least of all, however, was it a "debate" in which the fate of the Treaty was in doubt. Throughout the long Senate review, the administration and Treaty supporters knew they "had the votes" and that the Senate would give its consent. Thus, the problem for INF ratification was not persuading doubting senators, but getting the Treaty to the floor for debate where approval would be just a matter of time whether formal discussion took one week or ten.

Administration preparations for floor debate were painstaking. Indeed, probably they were overdone. Detailed "books" on the Treaty were prepared for each senator and key staff. Very detailed master books were prepared for floor leaders and major senatorial spokesmen. Speeches were drafted for "friendly" senators on general Treaty topics and specific topical problem issues, e.g., "futuristics," to be deployed as necessary. Counters for possible hostile amendments were game-planned. The State Department, which unlike several other Executive Branch departments, does not have permanent offices on the Hill, opened a temporary office in the Capitol Building near the Senate Gallery. This operation, headed by INF Treaty negotiator Glitman, was designed to permit administration officials to respond quickly to fast-breaking developments during the floor debate.

The First Week

Nevertheless, the first "week" (opening Tuesday, 17 May and ending Friday) of floor debate was desultory. Debate started late in the morning and concluded in normal business hours. Set piece speeches were read into the record: speeches which reflected good staff drafting and the pounds of material in the public record explaining the Treaty.

During the first week, the sides maneuvered, with the Democratic majority attempting to create a list of amendments/modifications to the Treaty so these could be scheduled for debate and vote. Treaty opponents avoided any such listing and instead angled for devices to delay action. In a definitively indicative voting test, however, on Thursday, 19 May, Senator Helms again attempted to resurrect his claim that the INF Treaty was improper because Gorbachev was not a legal representative of the Soviet state but a political party official. That claim had been extensively rebutted in Foreign Relations Committee hearings (essentially international law permits anyone to sign a treaty if it is clear that their state authorizes them to do so.) It was hard to claim with a straight face that Gorbachev did not have the authority to commit the Soviet state. Consequently Helms point of order was tabled ninety-one to six, suggesting the limits of die-hard opposition to the Treaty.

Also during the later part of the first week of debate, the Senate examined several other amendments to the Treaty. These were offered one by one, presumably after coordination by Senate opponents, to keep the debate going without giving any indication of an outer limit for the length of formal debate. The first amendment, proposed by Senator Symms (R-ID), called for Presidential certification that the Soviets were in compliance with all past arms control agreements prior to entry into force of the INF Treaty. Clearly designed to appeal to traditional conservatives, Symms outlined an extended list of Soviet treaty violations as identified in annual Presidential arms control compliance reports associated with the ABM, LTBT, SALT I, BW, and SALT II agreements which the Soviets would have to rectify before the United States would implement the INF Treaty. Without engaging Symms on his own grounds of the validity of the violations or previous Soviet non-compliance with agreements, the five individual elements of the proposal were voted down by margins ranging from 82-15 to 89-8. Essentially, the Senate had concluded that the INF Treaty "stands on its own" and, by providing the opportunity for a fresh start in U.S.-Soviet relations, should not be linked to past failures.

In a similar vein, Senator Humphrey (R-NH) offered an ostensibly "motherhood" amendment requiring Presidential certification that there was a fifteen-day stockpile of munitions and fuel for NATO conventional forces prior to the Treaty's entry into force. By drawing attention to shortcomings in Europe's conventional defenses, the Humphrey amendment was designed to be attractive not only to standard conservative Republicans but to "defense Democrats," such as Senator Nunn, who had deeply held reservations over the need to improve conventional defenses. Not at all discomfited over the prospect of ostensibly ignoring the need for conventional force improvements, Democrats agreed with Humphrey's premise that such conventional stocks were needed ("motherhood" is good) but simply indicated by defeating the amendment seventy-three to eight that the INF Treaty was not the vehicle to redress conventional force problems.

Thus, by the end of the first week of debate, Majority Leader Byrd had begun to evidence a touch of irked frustration. Clearly, in his view, the Republicans had had their fun and it was time to settle down to work. Byrd had continued to attempt (to no avail) to elicit a definitive account of the amendments that would be offered. Minority Leader Dole was unable to supply any such listing, as conservative Republicans simply indicated there would be in unspecified numbers, an unidentified "more." Byrd turned the heat up by stating that the Democrats would propose no individual amendments, thus making it clear to the media that any delay in completing Senate debate would lie with the Republicans. Procedurally, Byrd threatened to invoke the complicated "cloture" rule, which if passed by three-fifths of those present and voting would limit debate to thirty hours and reduce the ability to introduce further amendments. In ordinary circumstances, the Senate is loath to invoke cloture, valuing the comity produced by letting a minority have its say, even at extended length, if there is a "gentleman's agreement" that the minority will not attempt to take advantage of this permissiveness.

Simultaneously, on 16 May, there was still another set of questions directed by Senators Helms and Humphrey primarily at elements of the Glitman-Chervov 12 May "Agreed Minute." The questions reflected essential misreadings of the content of the Minute, which expanded and clarified U.S. rights rather than surrendering them as charged in the questions. But while the questions were substantively thin, the threat by Senators Helms and Humphrey to filibuster until answers were produced was taken seriously. Consequently, there was a full court press within the administration and intelligence community to produce answers, which were completed in record time for the Q&A process: seven days.

The Second Week

With the opening of the second week, the earlier dilatory pace began to change. During this final week, debate was dominated by a number of amendments which in one form or another eventually found their way into the ratification document, and the increasing pressure to complete the advice and consent process, as the President had already left Washington for the Moscow Summit. By Tuesday afternoon, Byrd and Dole had filed a petition for "cloture" which could not be officially acted upon by the Senate for 48 hours, but if voted upon at that point would sharply limit further debate. Byrd adroitly used the threat of a cloture vote on Thursday and Friday to push for accelerated progress on the thicket of amendments.

Ultimately, through a series of "unanimous consent" agreements, Byrd avoided a cloture vote and worked out a timeline permitting individual senators to "have their say" and introduce specialized amendments. And as the week heated up, such amendments came thick and fast, frequently with no warning over their introduction, little or no coordination, frantic redrafting, compromises, and occasionally acceptance, virtually "on faith" by voice vote.

Technical Corrections and 12 May Agreements

No agreement is perfect, and the INF Treaty proves that maxim. Following the 8 December 1987 Treaty signature, a number of typographical errors were noted in the Treaty and the diagrams of sites to be inspected. These errors were identified and rectified in standard diplomatic exchanges of notes. Likewise, the "futuristics" issue and the series of verification and implementation issues were resolved on 12 May, also by legally binding exchanges of notes. Senators, however, questioned whether this process was satisfactory and Senator Helms, in particular, sought specific individual amendments to reflect the technical corrections. Helms played footsie with his amendments, advancing them for debate and then withdrawing them, but ultimately combined his proposals with Senators Nunn, Warner, Boren, and Cohen in an amendment to require the President to secure final confirmation of Soviet agreement to the 12 May exchange of diplomatic notes. This omnibus (and superfluous) amendment was approved 96-0.

Double Negative

Both the Armed Services and Foreign Relations Committees had examined in detail the Treaty language prohibiting the sides from making more than one stage of a non-Treaty-limited missile that is "outwardly similar to but not interchangeable with" a stage of a banned missile. The battle of grammarians had appeared on the surface to be a draw, but reappeared in an amendment on 23 May by Senator Wallop to clarify "ambiguous and tortured language." The administration opposed the amendment which was eventually tabled (68-26). Nevertheless, it had attracted a greater range of Republican and Democratic support than any previous proposal and clearly weighed on the minds of Senate leadership. Consequently, early on 27 May, Senator Dole (without discussion with the administration) reintroduced language to clarify that only one such "outwardly similar" stage could be produced and quickly secured voice vote approval.

The "Biden" (Treaty Interpretation) Amendment

Source of most of the political tension during the ratification process, the amendment as originally offered by the SFRC was modified by Senator Byrd to be optically more attractive to the administration. Nevertheless, in running debate throughout 26 May, it was vigorously and inventively attacked by Republicans, arguing *inter alia* that it would bind the United States to standards more stringent than those accepted by the Soviets. The point was made obliquely by Senator Wilson (R-CA), who offered a further, ostensibly bland amendment late in the evening to the effect that the United States would not be bound to any interpretation of the Treaty not shared by the Soviets. Fearful that their point of binding the Executive Branch to its stated interpretation of the INF Treaty was about to escape, Byrd threatened an immediate cloture vote (which would presumably have delayed completion of the Treaty past the Moscow Summit) if the Wilson proposal was not defeated. Although tabled by a virtual party line 53-45, it was hardly satisfying to Byrd who labeled Republican tactics "Mickey Mouse" and abruptly concluded the session for the night.

"Human Rights"

A multiple-sponsored "declaration" (which did not have to be communicated to the Soviets) stated that the United States should inform the Soviets of our strong commitment to human rights and emphasize that they should comply with the Helsinki Final Act. As a hortatory, "motherhood" proposal, it was approved by voice vote.

START Cautionary Notes

Strategic issues were much on the minds of senators during debate.

Among other messages being delivered to the administration, the Senate clearly wanted to lay down "markers" on START: essentially do not rush to judgment and preserve the conventional cruise missile. These declaratory markers were contained in two separate proposals, the first initiated by Senator Helms and intensively debated and modified during the course of the week, and the second introduced late on 26 May by Senators Murkowski and Quayle and adopted without significant discussion.

The latter emphasized *inter alia* that "it should be the position of the United States that no restrictions should be established on current or future nonnuclear air- or sea-launched cruise missiles..." in any START agreement. The Senate could not send a stronger message that its acceptance of the INF cruise missile ban had been a hard pill to swallow (a final effort by Senator Hollings to amend the Treaty to permit conventionally armed GLCMs had been defeated 69-28), and they did not want to see a "logical" extension of the GLCM ban appearing in a START agreement.

Senator Helms, however, had sought more detailed Senatorial control over the START negotiations. Rather than simply defeating the amendment, the administration elected to do extensive "face saving" modification. As ultimately modified and cosponsored by Dole and Byrd, the amendment declared that START negotiations will be conducted with "close and detailed consideration of the advice of the United States Senate" and that any "framework" START agreement would only guide further negotiations and "not constrain any military programs..." Appropriately sanitized, the amendment passed 94-4. Nevertheless, as the Senate had repeatedly telegraphed its fears over a "rush to judgment" for a START Treaty (one proposal being a START "framework" agreement), the amendment made it clear it did not desire further START action in an election year.

As a side note, the paired START provisions were at least somewhat contradictory on a secondary point: future approaches to verification. The Murkowski-Quayle declaration noted that "the United States should rely primarily on its own national technical means of verification rather than any cooperative verification scheme, such as the on-site inspection procedures agreed to in the INF Treaty" while the Helms, *et al* amendment stated that "the negotiations...shall also seek to secure regimes of effective verification and mechanisms for full compliance *which build upon the verification regime and compliance mechanisms of the present Treaty,* strengthening them appropriately for any subsequent treaty..."

Clearly the first requires greater reliance on NTMs, while the second contemplates an enhanced on-site inspection regime. The explanation for the inconsistency is relatively simple: inadvertent oversight. Murkowski-Quayle was available only in a scratched up, largely handwritten form on the night of 25 May and advertised as a cautionary note on the conventionally armed cruise missile. Passed by voice vote, it was not seen nor reviewed by the administration prior to passage. The "Helms Amendment," however, was thoroughly reviewed and redrafted to adjust its text into acceptable form. The consequences of this internal disconnect were not considered major, but simply as points to be worked out during renewed START negotiations. It is illustrative, however, in microcosm of the results, of high-pressure negotiation.

A Final Note

In mid afternoon on 27 May, the Senate, in careful attention to ritual, provided its consent to the INF Treaty. Following the 93-5 (Helms, Hollings, Humphrey, Symms, and Wallop) approval, the packed Senate gallery burst into rare spontaneous applause. The President would have his Treaty at the Moscow Summit. The Memorial Day holiday had been preserved. Particularly appreciative of the results, the administration flew Senators Byrd and Dole to Moscow for the official exchange of ratified treaties. Ambassador Glitman, the INF negotiator, however, was not invited.

Conclusions

With the experiences of the INF Treaty ratification completed, what lessons can the observer draw from the experience, particularly for a START Treaty?

Learn to Love Ministerial Government

The divided nature of U.S. government has been the essential political factor in domestic politics for almost 40 years. It appears likely to continue. The INF Treaty demonstrated the political impetus for the Senate to be seen as "equal partners" with the Executive Branch in the treaty-making process. As arms control agreements appear more rather than less likely in coming years, the Senate will be regularly involved in the process. To a degree, this phenomenon is simply an extension of the steady expansion of Congressional authority into the conduct of foreign affairs: a circumstance familiar to parliamentary systems where ministers of foreign affairs and defense are drawn directly from elected parliamentarians, but largely foreign to previous U.S. experience.

Unfortunately for the Executive Branch, the Senate comes to a Treaty, not, apparently with the expectation of reviewing a good job well done, but of anticipation that there are mistakes in need of correction. Presumably this reflects their personal experience with drafting legislation. It also, however, reflects the basically adversarial attitude between Executive and Congress; the "checks and balances," which are often played as a "zero sum game," in which the successes of one branch of government are viewed as losses by the other. This innate tension is now complicated by intense suspicion rooted in what the Congress sees as the covert Executive approach to the Hill of "put one over on them/slip it by them" embodied in the Reagan administration effort to reinterpret the ABM Treaty and the management of Iran-Contra issues, but leading back as far as conflicts over the management of the war in Vietnam. Thus, if the Executive branch really wants something, the first Congressional response tends to be "what's the matter with it" or, at best, "how can we benefit too"? It does not apparently matter to the Senate that the Executive-Congressional partnership implicit in Constitutional review of treaties is not a requirement to engage in the detailed task of Treaty drafting.

In addition, there are many intelligent, highly motivated Senators and staff on the Hill. This concentration of talent means that any complicated compromise or infelicitous wording will be seized upon quickly, and potential ambiguities examined. If the staff does not notice a problem area during its own review, internal administration critics will point it out to them. It appears to be a truism that the outcome of any complicated compromise has its "winners" and "losers." While the "winners" are willing to smile quietly, the losers are "sore losers" and anxious to reargue the issue on the Hill. There seems little tolerance for ambiguity at this juncture in history: either from the right (citing SALT I and II) or the left (citing the ABM Treaty interpretation fight). However, words are not tooled steel, and "precision" in Treaty language less easy to obtain than in tool and die manufacture. Indeed the two substantive problem areas in the INF Treaty were at worst mildly ambiguous: "Futuristics" and the "double negative," but that saved neither from painful reworking.

The question of the role of future technology under an INF Treaty became a ratification issue primarily because Senator Nunn was dissatisfied with the administration's explanation of the subject, and Senator Quayle did not want the INF Treaty to serve as a precedent for helping the Soviets to block the use of "futuristic" technology in the SDI program. The administration, and particularly the negotiators, clearly believed that the Treaty text and negotiating record supported a ban on "futuristic" INF range missiles. Senators Nunn and Quayle, however, contended the record was not clear. Nunn argued that the administration's position on the reinterpretation of the ABM Treaty demanded further clarification of "futuristics." Quayle sought to limit "weapon delivery" to existing weapon systems but, ironically for his cause, by forcing the issue he stimulated those who might have missed the point to insist on resolving it three times over.

Certainly following the 15 April letter from Soviet Foreign Minister Shevardnadze, the Reagan administration believed (despite initial translation difficulties) that there was no further ambiguity. Senator Nunn still did not agree. The consequence of Senator Nunn's dissatisfaction was an unparalleled joint administration-Senate drafting of an agreed exchange of notes with the Soviets. Thus, an exchange which should have been a technical exercise conducted by a mid-level career diplomat escalated to the status of a major Hill-Executive Branch negotiation with legal language dictated by Senate staffers which diplomats dared at their peril to vary. Even this capitulation by the Executive to Senatorial authority proved insufficient, as the Senate ultimately insisted that the Exchange of Notes be incorporated as a "Category III" amendment to the instrument of ratification, requiring still another affirmation of Soviet acquiescence before the Treaty could enter into force. It is difficult to argue at that point that the Senate was being appropriately cautious, and not simply demonstrating its muscle.

Having developed a taste for such drama, it is easy to predict that the Senate will continue along similar lines. The INF ratification experience will be cited as precedent and justification. The lesson the Senate will draw from the "futuristics" debate will be that the United States needs simply tell Moscow to "change it," and they will. Since administration concerns that the Soviets would use U.S. desire to clarify the "futuristics" issue to reopen major issues of their own proved largely groundless in INF, Senatorial proponents of renegotiating other points will argue that it can be done quickly, painlessly and at low cost. It will be easy to forget that banning future technology on INF range missile systems was to Soviet advantage.

Don't Lose the 1986 Election (or, Alternatively, Win the 1990 Election)

There is no question that the Reagan administration paid a substantial price for being the minority party in the Senate. Losing control of the Senate in the 1986 election left the management of the INF Treaty in the hands of the Democratic majority: a majority which, having regained control of the Senate after being out of power for six years, had interests and priorities often not amenable to White House suggestion. The Senate treaty ratification process and the "checks and balances" process in general are deliberately constructed to protect the rights of the minority. But the rights of the minority are designed to prevent action. It is a different story indeed when the minority wants action. Had the Reagan administration retained its previous Senate majority, INF ratification may well have been considerably easier as:

- The pace of testimony and committee markup could have been stimulated; Senate floor debate could have been scheduled for immediately after Easter instead of being shunted aside for over a month while the Senate addressed the Omnibus Trade Bill; and

- It would have been far more difficult to have forced the "Biden Amendment" on Treaty interpretation into the Treaty. Without control of the SFRC, the Democrats could not have attached "Biden" to the SFRC Committee report and would have had to present it on the floor of the Senate, where including it in the final document would have been more difficult. Moreover, a Republican-directed SFRC might have been able to secure acceptance of one or another of the compromises on Treaty interpretation floated by the White House.

This assessment is not to imply that Senators Pell, Boren, and Nunn as Committee chairmen were Treaty opponents, or that the prospect of steering the Treaty through an SFRC chaired by Senator Helms would have been painless ratification. Nevertheless, Senator Byrd as Majority Leader made a game of deliberate prickliness in response to any implication from the White House that Senate action was in order. The Reagan administration was forced to play by Byrd's rules and come to him, hat in hand. As a consequence of persistent delay by Byrd on scheduling Treaty debate, further review expanded to fill available time and a non-issue such as "futuristics" absorbed a month of Congressional and Executive Branch effort.

Don't Ratify an Arms Control Agreement in an Election Year

INF as a political football? Absolutely. For one party it was a "historic" agreement. For the other, a "modest first step." While the Treaty was vigorously opposed by conservative Republicans and supported by liberal Democrats, nevertheless, the Treaty posed more of a political problem for the Democrats than the Republicans. The core of the Republican Party, centered in the Executive Branch supported the INF Treaty and intended to make it a major plank in the election campaign, disowning conservative treaty opponents as necessary. Democrats, critical for years about lack of Reagan commitment to arms control, were faced with a diplomatic success (which they supported) that was also of considerable political value to the Republicans. Consequently, Senate Democratic leadership frequently had two competing agendas: (a) Get the Senate to finish its advice and consent process approving the Treaty; and (b) Make sure that the Republicans could not claim the millennium from a ratified Treaty.

Additionally, there was a shared feeling that the Senate was able to deal with only one arms control agreement in 1988, and that was going to be INF. Senator Byrd (echoed by others) made it clear as early as February, following the Verkunde Conference in Germany, that there should be no rush to judgment on START. Nevertheless, if the INF Treaty were to have been approved at the end of March (the original estimate), it would have provided START with considerably greater impetus to move to completion: impetus difficult to gauge in retrospect, but certainly not desired either by Democrats or conservative Republicans. The consequence was a tacit alliance to prevent early action on the Treaty, wrapped in professed concern that the Treaty be "right" and "accurate."

The conclusion was predictable. Following extended public spats over issues such as an SS-20 "covert force" and prohibition of any "futuristic" technology on INF range missiles, the INF Treaty emerged from the Senate just in time for the Memorial Day recess and inclusion of several prominent senators in President Reagan's official party at the Moscow Summit. Although public support for the Treaty held up well, the impression that it was better than "Classic Coke" had dissipated, and the Senate emphasized in the media that it was an equal partner that had "fixed" the Treaty.

Resolve the Treaty Interpretation Problem and the "Sofaer Doctrine"

Beyond any question, the Senate Democrats expended more ire over their interpretation of the "Sofaer Doctrine" than any other aspect of the INF Treaty. The Reagan administration was well forewarned that problems of "treaty interpretation" created by its re-interpretative review of the ABM Treaty would be fought out in the INF Treaty: Forewarned, yes. Forearmed, yes. But still unable to dodge the bullet. With the INF Treaty as hostage, both sides engaged in extended pressure tactics, attempting to make the other back down. Ultimately, the Democrats had a firmer grip on the political realities, to wit, President Reagan had to "eat" what the Senate Democrats gave him on treaty interpretation, as the Executive could not face the consequences of refusing to ratify its own Treaty.

Despite the bruising nature of the battle, treaty interpretation is not dead. The Executive Branch can still back away from the "Sofaer Doctrine" and claim to be the sole interpreter of treaties. Alternatively, it can take the INF Treaty's ratification document interpretation amendment at face value as applying only to the INF Treaty, and continue to argue its case for START (or any other Treaty). The latter course assures a battle over this issue with each presentation of a treaty to the Senate.

Remember the Limits of the European Card

One highly valuable prop for the INF Treaty was strong, persistent international support of which NATO backing was only the most obvious component. In contrast to SALT II, the INF Treaty was an agreement affecting far more than U.S.-Soviet relations. We could not lightly consider rejecting an agreement that reflected a decade of U.S.-European consultation and negotiation. Ultimately most Treaty critics, such as former SACEUR General Rogers and former Secretary of State Kissinger, justified their grudging support for the Treaty on the grounds that rejecting the Treaty would be worse than ratifying it, so far as our relations with Europe and even European defense were concerned.

Some prospective arms control agreements, such as accords on Conventional Armed Forces in Europe (CFE) and Chemical Weapons (CW), will also have broad international ramifications if they ever face Senate ratification. Nevertheless, a START Treaty would not have such a natural advantage. Although we can assume that there will be consultations with European and other friends and Allies, they will be informative rather than deliberative. While Europeans and Asians may inform Senators that, for example, a reduction of strategic arms by fifty percent will also affect them and note their support for such an outcome, Allied opinions will hardly have the weight they had on INF. Any START agreement will be weighed in the balance of U.S.-Soviet bilateral relations rather than multilateral views. The precedent for START will be SALT II, not INF.

Nor Will Domestic Support Be Automatic

The INF Treaty benefited from massive domestic and international support. It was perceived as the right treaty at the right time. Historic "firsts" such as asymmetric Soviet reductions and on-site inspections reinforced the impression that it was a "good deal" for the West. The atmosphere for a START agreement will be very different. While INF systems were important, they were ultimately a threat to Europe and Asia, not the U.S. and constituted only three to five percent of nuclear arsenals. Strategic systems, however, are the ultimate guarantee of U.S. independence. The numbers of nuclear systems involved in reductions (even fifty percent reductions) will be massive. The restrictions on remaining forces and the manner in which they are to be constituted will stimulate intensive strategic debate and, at the same time, imply budget commitments for the next twenty years. Thus, we can anticipate that even with continued Soviet political evolution and a smiling General Secretary Gorbachev, START will be opposed by reputable groups. It cannot count on the grand coalition of support, ranging from VFW to Women's Strike for Peace that rallied behind the INF Treaty. Instinctive opponents of arms control agreements, who ultimately voted for the INF Treaty because they lacked a legitimate constituency to justify a "no" vote, will be able to find reputable support for opposing START.

A Delayed and Revised Treaty

A corollary of intensive legitimate domestic opposition will be extreme care in Senatorial review. Every Senator will view his START vote as an election issue. Even those who support a START treaty will be compelled to be "picky, picky, picky" to alleviate constituent concerns. Committee hearings, particularly Intelligence Committee review of the START verification regime, will be painstaking. Thus, if the INF Treaty took over six months from signature to ratification, a START Treaty could easily take twice that long. Nor will it emerge unscathed. The substantive and political atmosphere surrounding any START Treaty would mean that even if it had been carved on tablets of gold with a finger of fire, the Senate would declare itself agnostic.

Whatever the substantive quality of the Treaty, it will be revised, amended, and elaborated upon through "understandings." Some Senators will seek to walk back U.S. "concessions" through amendments. Others will insist on putting their mark on the Treaty through amendments whether these be substantively irrelevant "vanity amendments" or deeply felt substantive differences of opinion. There will not be a "clean treaty" (no amendments), and those presenting a START Treaty would be ill advised to press for one. Rather, the effort should be to strike bargains quickly with serious critics who have an honest concern, even if of questionable substantive validity, and co-opt such critics into opposing others with "treaty killer" reservations. This approach may require renegotiation of some issues (always diplomatic anathema) with the associated danger of Moscow reopening other issues. The alternative to accommodating the Senate on such points, however, will be a failure to ratify.

Learn to Love the Media

INF benefited from positive media treatment. At the same time, key journalists writing on the issue were exceptionally well informed and substantially knowledgeable. The INF Treaty "sold itself." START will not, however, and will need all the help it can get. Deliberate effort to mobilize media support is a two-edged sword, and primary media interest remains a "good story." If supporting START is that story, it will be easier to gain ratification support. But if START has even pinholes, let alone "loopholes," writing a negative story—if it is a scoop—will be equally attractive.

Vignette: The Altar of Tack

American culture is frequently scored as tawdry, crass, commercialized or just plain "tacky." But is the U.S. alone guilty of questionable taste? Upon viewing elements of European culture, the U.S. INF delegation came to a corporate judgment that, lo-and-behold, some aspects were questionable and determined to preserve selected samples, if not for posterity, at least for the moment. Qualification criteria were flexible: essentially to be small, cheap, and distinctive. In short, something a traveler might encounter during normal shopping. Thus the Pompidou Center in Paris did not qualify. Pure obscenity was frowned upon, but the clever excursion skirting ill taste became a delegation delight. A book case in the office of a popular delegation member slowly became the repository of such mementos and thus "The Altar of Tack" was born, incorporating inter alia:

- a battery powered, blinking light bow tie;
- a box featuring a Swiss alpine scene and a cow which when inverted made a noise roughly equivalent to "Moo";
- a Soviet teapot of remarkable dimensions and striking orange and black design;
- an all-day-sucker carrying the features of Pope John Paul II;
- the traditional Belgian statue "Manaken Pis" of a naked little boy with a corkscrew substituted for the prominent organ; and
- assorted toy dolls, swizzle sticks; post cards; invertible snow scenes and light up gadgets.

Over the weeks, the "altar" generated much comment and delight from visiting dignitaries as well as delegation members.

Recent additions were commented upon and judgments passed on whether this material was up (down?) to existing standards. The romantic inclinations of various toy dolls were discussed. Slowly the conclusion was reached that the collection should be made permanent. Rumor had that it was offered to the Department of State for permanent exposition. Pending such decision, the still-expanding "altar" remained housed in a State Department office. Ultimately, transferred to a private residence, it was destroyed in a hurricane and now resides in a Northern Virginia landfill.

NATO and the Treaty

The following three articles—the first two by David Jones, the third by John Woodworth—address elements of the negotiating process within the North Atlantic Alliance and subsequent specific issues, such as the prospective status for NATO's basic protocol for defense strategy and the Alliance's next steps for addressing tactical nuclear weapons.

The INF Treaty: Lessons Learned for Dealing with NATO

David T. Jones

Originally published as *"What Has NATO Learned from INF?" in the* Foreign Service Journal, *December 1989.*

Drawing "lessons" from any event is akin to the fable of the blind men describing the elephant. The first grabbed the tail and said it was a rope; the second, the trunk and announced it a serpent; the third, wrapped his arms around a leg and declared it a tree. Indeed, the consequences of the INF Treaty are also a matter of perspective. Supporters count the pluses; critics accentuate the negatives. The negotiating team member is "blind" to certain nongovernment viewpoints; the outside observer lacks the first hand experience of the negotiator.

It is traditional in discussing "lessons learned" to focus on what is learned about adversaries. This is both exciting and amusing, and usually adversaries do not leap into print to refute published comment. At least as important, however, is what is learned about dealing with friends and allies. The following analysis of the INF negotiations and negotiating process examines some lessons that can be extracted concerning our NATO Allies.

Lessons Learned for the NATO Alliance

INF was the principal armament and arms control preoccupation for the NATO Alliance for a decade. The fact that the INF negotiations ended with a resounding success for the Alliance will be closely examined for years; the whys and wherefores analyzed to determine the potential for equally successful duplication. Although there will be as many conclusions and nuances as there are observers (and all will be second-guessed by the ultimate graduate student), the principal lessons learned about the Alliance during the INF process appear to be the following:

- Allied cohesion held;
- The customized mechanisms for Alliance consultation worked;
- NATO achieved all its negotiating goals;
- There has been a price, particularly in terms of NATO's future nuclear options; and
- On balance the costs to the Alliance of concluding the Treaty were far less than the costs of rejecting it.

Principal Implications from the Treaty

- The United States can use the INF experience to convince NATO that strengthened conventional forces are a prerequesite to successful conventional force reductions negotiations;
- Given limited defense budgets on both sides of the Atlantic, the United States should use still existing concern over Soviet conventional superiority to stimulate more efficient use of defense resources within NATO;
- The United States should focus on the concept that INF has demonstrated the need to deal with the Soviets from a position of military strength and political cohesion; and
- A clear sense of direction and astute Alliance management will continue to be needed to ensure that the INF Treaty leaves the Alliance stronger, not weaker

---

Alliance Cohesion Held

NATO is frequently considered the "worst dressed" Alliance: always in disarray. But during the ten years in which INF seized the Alliance (two years for decision making and eight of deployments and negotiations), NATO was never more unified on the essentials of an issue. We are fortunate that this unity persisted inasmuch as the Alliance itself was at stake. Failure to deploy U.S. INF systems in

1983 would have been interpreted as a failure of NATO. Perhaps in retrospect, INF will be regarded as NATO's "mid-life crisis," which galvanized an aging Alliance to face and master a new challenge. Memories of that INF experience should stand NATO in good stead as it enters its fifth decade, after celebrating its fortieth anniversary in April 1989.

Nevertheless, we should not forget that INF deployments were a "near run thing." Even after we began deployments, the Soviets had a reasonable hope that one or another basing country would lose a critical election, or lose its nerve. Moscow tried very hard to win the INF negotiations through the domestic politics of our Allies. Indeed, each basing country fought and won an election in which political opponents criticized U.S. INF deployments. A single loss could have unraveled the entire fabric of agreement, and we were not out of the woods until the 1986 Dutch decision confirming they would also deploy INF missiles if necessary.

The point is not one of self congratulation, but a useful reminder that those characterizing various allies as "weak links" can be stupidly wrong. The NATO Alliance can absorb astonishing pressure if its members accept the objectives.

Consultations Worked

No issue in Alliance history was more comprehensively consulted upon than INF, and the Allies can recall that they were key decision makers on many points throughout the INF decade. NATO Allies were instrumental on topics such as the requirement for parallel deployment and negotiating tracks, the decision for a "double zero," and the firm exclusion of third country systems (UK and French nuclear weapons) from negotiations. Consequently, we were positioned to reap a harvest of comprehensive Allied support for the Treaty, and received endorsements from virtually every Alliance leader in and out of government. Opinion polls showed that the INF Treaty was universally popular throughout Europe, and has remained so.

The mixed blessing from this success is that now we are obligated to follow the INF consultation model as our NATO management tool on Alliance arms control issues, even if we might prefer a looser arrangement, or believe the issue does not warrant a comparable commitment in U.S. bureaucratic time and energy. Success can be a straitjacket.

We Got What We Wanted, and More

It is a rare negotiation that at the end of the trail can honestly conclude that we got what we originally asked. Alliance cohesion and consultation clearly paid off as measured against NATO's guidelines for the INF negotiations. We achieved what NATO wanted, and more. Without belaboring the parameters of technical negotiating success, the INF Treaty set precedents for future negotiations in obtaining Soviet agreement to principles such as asymmetrical reductions to equal global limits, exclusion of third country systems from bilateral negotiations, and comprehensive on-site inspections.

The most dramatic element of the negotiations is the inspection and verification regime. In this regard, our negotiators got more than we anticipated, or perhaps even dreamed possible. The entire concept of practical arms control verification has been redefined by the depth and detail of the interlocking net of INF verification measures: on-site inspection of system elimination, inspection of operating bases, semi-permanent monitoring of a key production facility, and cooperative measures for satellite inspection of selected missile operating bases.

The conclusion from this experience is that clear conceptual knowledge of objectives, as epitomized by thoroughly worked out guidelines, will serve the Alliance in good stead. We are better off as an Alliance to be confident of our first principles and how we want to go about them—no matter how long it takes—than to permit our substantive moves to be dictated by artificial deadlines, e.g., a ministerial, the conclusion of a CSCE Review Conference, or a Heads of State Summit. It is hard indeed to ignore such pressures, but the United States and the Alliance are stuck indefinitely with its basic proposals whether made at leisure or under pressure.

But There Was a Price

Not to put too fine a point on it, INF has weakened the defense consensus in Europe. Previously it did not really matter for U.S.

policy if conservatives or socialists held power in the European basing countries. Both equally supported NATO defense policy. Now, however, it matters a great deal, as the socialists in all basing countries, (except Italy) publicly espouse a substantially weaker defense policy than the United States now supports. Although it will help basing country incumbents to run on the INF success story, the vibrancy of the success weakens over time, and normal democratic turnover will doubtless bring the "outs" to power in one or more basing countries over the next decade. While we can hope that the responsibility of power will prevail over ideological preference, we could be in for some unpleasant surprises.

The INF experience has also limited NATO's military flexibility, particularly in nuclear modernization. No NATO government, not even a conservative one, wants to repeat the domestic political upheavals of 1983-84 by deploying new nuclear weapons systems, or even modernizing old ones. Consequently, although it would be permitted under the terms of the INF Treaty, the chances of ever deploying a new missile called a "Pershing IC" (using one stage of the PII as the SS-25 uses one stage of the SS-20) are virtually zero. Indeed the increasingly uphill struggle within the Alliance over a modernized "follow-on" Lance missile of less than 500 kilometers range is the most obvious consequence of the INF Treaty. Popular aversion to nuclear modernization, epitomized in the infelicitous phrase "the shorter the range the deader the German" has grown beyond Bonn, although the INF Treaty leaves Soviet SNF, including SCUDS and FROGS, unconstrained. Despite previous ministerial commitment to selective nuclear modernization, the NATO heads of state summit in May 1989 recognized the depth of German concern by deferring a nuclear modernization decision until 1991, and implicitly linking it with a conventional forces agreement.

Although the logic of Lance modernization and the political weight of major supporters (United States and UK) may ultimately result in a positive deployment decision, it is an increasingly long shot, especially when balanced against professed Soviet willingness to eliminate all SNF. At best there will be badly bruised feelings and extensive deployment and arms control compromises incorporated into what, without an INF Treaty, would have been a ho-hum modernization program.

Indeed, the Alliance is in danger of learning the wrong lesson from INF: that nothing is better than anything. "Zero" may look like the magic answer to deadlock: zero short range missiles, zero nuclear artillery, zero dual capable aircraft, zero nuclear weapons in Europe. Trends toward denuclearization may be hard to stave off, and we can anticipate that public receptivity toward nuclear free zones in various parts of Europe will grow. Europeans appear to be intellectually convinced that "arms control works" while forgetting the corollary that military strength makes it work. The continued positive operation of the INF Treaty will make public opinion more vulnerable to Moscow's promises about a new doctrine of "reasonable sufficiency," "weapons reductions"—conventional, nuclear, and chemical, etc. This public mood appears to be emerging irrespective of whether the Soviets take concrete actions to fulfill those promises or whether residual Soviet strength is still disproportionate to Moscow's defensive needs.

The successful INF Treaty and the evolving Vienna CFE negotiations may also create difficulties for NATO conventional improvements. Opponents of these improvements may try to use the INF Treaty to prove that arms control is a proven, inexpensive alternative and to suggest that the allies place their bets on a conventional force reductions agreement.

Balance Sheet

The surest and best thing to be said about the Alliance in this affair is that it identified a specific set of INF objectives and fulfilled them with patience and determination. When the Soviets essentially bought NATO's terms, there was no turning back. Whatever one's misgivings about eliminating U.S. PIIs and GLCMs, they pale in comparison with the upheaval that would have ensued if the United States had rejected Gorbachev's double global zero proposal and the INF negotiations consequently collapsed.

Nonetheless, we must continue to recognize that the INF Treaty had a shock effect on the Alliance. Many conservative Europeans were visibly discomfited by the reality that the Treaty spelled the end of the painfully deployed U.S. INF systems by mid-1991. Consequently, as epitomized by the intense and fractious debate over Lance modernization, they remain "twice shy" about commitment to new nuclear systems.

Still, if carefully managed, European concerns in general and their perception of the INF experience in particular can be guided to serve Alliance long term interests.

Conventional Strength Is the Key to Negotiating Success

The United States can draw upon the successful INF "double-track" experience to continue to encourage the Allies to negotiate effectively in CFE by strengthening their conventional force capabilities. This is a valid thesis regardless of Gorbachev's December 1988 commitment to unilateral Soviet force reductions, and subsequent Soviet and NATO proposals that suggest convergence on the terms for a CFE agreement.

Glasnost Is Not Enough

Pending any CFE agreement, the United States should link continued European concerns over Soviet conventional preponderance, even following any *glasnost*-stimulated unilateral reductions to a renewed effort to revive NATO's longstanding effort to enhance effectiveness through standardization, coproduction, and interoperability, and use of advanced technologies.

A Wider Allied Role

The United States, facing the prospect for a declining defense budget, should make it even clearer that it does not consider its interests threatened by a stronger Allied national security role in NATO. Likewise, we should press to further strengthen the recently revived WEU and enhance Franco-German cooperation all leading to greater European defense cooperation. Whether or not there is a CFE agreement, such European politico-military cooperation is long overdue.

To turn Alliance concerns over the consequences of the INF Treaty to U.S. and Allied advantage, however, the United States must make every effort to hammer home to European opinion one elemental INF lesson: namely, that NATO can bargain successfully with Moscow only from a position of strength. NATO's strength, both military and political, will not guarantee agreement, but weakness and disunity are a guaranteed formula for failure.

Decisive U.S. leadership and sensitive Alliance management will be required to ensure that the Treaty's after-effects strengthen and not weaken the Alliance. The aftermath of the INF Treaty continues to offer a unique opportunity to revivify and improve the Alliance. Although military improvements in nuclear weapon systems may prove very difficult, improvements in the conventional area and the possibilities for enlarged intra-Alliance cooperation, both within NATO and among individual Allies, may be increasing. The post-INF world promises a full measure of challenge for both West and East.

The INF Treaty: NATO Nuclear Strategy and Arms Control

DAVID T. JONES

This article was drafted in 1990 as a possible "stand-alone" piece. It has not been previously published.

"Emcee Fourteen Slash Three. MC 14/3."[4] These are the labels that identify NATO's defense and deterrence strategy, shorthanded as "flexible response." To identify the doctrine is to ask the questions: how has the 1987 INF Treaty affected Alliance nuclear deterrence strategy? In the light of the INF Treaty, where is the Alliance headed on arms control (both for conventional and nuclear forces) and nuclear force modernization? What does "flexible response" mean today, and should it be replaced by an "MC 14/4"?

So what is MC 14/3? Sooner or later, weapons generate policy to handle them. One can imagine a Cro-Magnon oral tradition on missile employment (arrow range from lighter or heavier bows; superiority of flint versus bone arrow heads). And the more powerful the weapon, the more complex and sophisticated the procedural and political rationale underpinning its employment. The most powerful weapons in the NATO defense inventory are nuclear; the Alliance's most fought over and thought over defense questions have been its nuclear deterrent strategy. This issue has been quiescent as an element of public debate for more than twenty years following the creation of MC 14/3 in 1967, but each Alliance question of nuclear modernization, deployment or possible use has been linked to the basic NATO position on deterrence.

Ostensibly, MC 14/3 and the strategy epitomized by the shorthand term "flexible response" is simple. The NATO Alliance declares that any Warsaw Pact aggression will be met as NATO believes appropriate. NATO is not constrained to meet an attack by conventional weapons with only conventional weapons. It does not shy away from being the first to use nuclear weapons and rejects a "no first use" policy. Nor does it promise that its first use of nuclear weapons will be "tactical" or restricted to the immediate battlefield. NATO strategy does not rule out immediate strategic strikes against an aggressor's homeland. Thus, NATO is unpredictably free to respond to any level of Warsaw Pact aggression with any level of response.

Earlier NATO nuclear policy (MC 14/2) reflected the U.S. Dulles-Eisenhower era strategy of "massive retaliation." That is, Warsaw Pact aggression would be met by direct, immediate, large scale attacks on the Soviet homeland. As the Soviets developed their own survivable, second strike strategic forces in ever greater numbers, reaching rough strategic equivalence with the United States toward the mid-1960s, the credibility of "massive retaliation" declined. Europeans deemed it less likely that a U.S. leader would order the equivalent of national suicide in response to what might be a relatively low level Warsaw Pact military challenge in Europe.

"Flexible response" sought to resolve this perception. Deterrence of any Warsaw Pact attack was not to be based on a single system or a single type of response. Deterrence was to be a seamless web based on the full spectrum of NATO's military capabilities, from front line rifleman to silo-based Minuteman. The Warsaw Pact (WP) would be deterred from aggression based on this full range of NATO forces, both conventional and nuclear. Should deterrence fail, NATO would choose how it would respond to aggression, both to restore deterrence and the *status quo ante.*

Such a strategic concept, however, requires that deterrence be "credible," that is, that Moscow must regard all the elements of the military spectrum as technically effective, and NATO's political will to employ them as enduringly firm. Consequently, each of these points, e.g., military components of the spectrum of deterrence, demonstration of political will, etc., has stimulated endless, virtually theological debate over its credibility and how to maintain it. For example, while a single rifleman or a single infantry platoon would not be regarded by anyone as a credible conventional force, Europeans have had no compelling desire to build conventional forces that would match Warsaw Pact forces. While the United

States has traditionally urged stronger conventional forces to "raise the nuclear threshold," and despite a superior population and resource base that would have permitted NATO to equal WP military forces, Europeans have been reluctant to build matching military forces. Ever practical, Europeans have noted that nuclear weapons would negate even the largest and best equipped conventional force, and such forces are very expensive. In addition, large conventional forces would imply a willingness to fight a conventional war, and NATO Europeans, with the extensive historical experience of destruction from two world wars, had no desire to make Europe "safe for conventional war."

Reasonably enough, Europeans seek to deter any war, not just nuclear war. The tension, however, between allies over the role conventional forces should play in deterring war has been a major strain in NATO relations, most frequently ventilated in debates over "burden-sharing."

Likewise, there is a basic requirement to assure that the nuclear component of the deterrent is credible. NATO cannot simply declare a theoretical commitment to use nuclear weapons in its own defense and assume that the verbalization is regarded seriously by Moscow. Consequently, NATO has concluded that a wide range of these weapons, varying in yield and type, able to be delivered by land, air, and sea forces, and employing the delivery systems of as many NATO allies as possible, is necessary to convince Moscow that all NATO members are committed to this policy and that NATO military and political planners have a wide variety of options with which "flexibility" can be demonstrated. Thus, NATO "political will" to employ nuclear weapons would be illustrated by a combination of the numbers of nuclear weapons deployed, the wide selection of weapons, their systems and ranges, the systematic modernization of these weapons, and the semi public manner in which training and exercises for the possible use of nuclear weapons is conducted.

Nevertheless, there is an obvious and persistent tension between defense and deterrence when nuclear weapons are involved. In its crudest terms, Europeans fear the United States wants to confine any war, conventional or nuclear, to Europe, leaving a "black spot between two green spots." Conversely, Americans believe

Europeans want any instance of aggression to be met by intercontinental strikes, the outcome of which would leave "a green spot between two black spots." While these may be the underlying, never-publicly-voiced ultimate concerns, the more mundane issues are those of nuclear weapon numbers, the timing and focus of nuclear force modernization, and scenarios for NATO exercises.

Over the years (although this judgment can be overstated), the United States has tended to emphasize the ability to implement nuclear strikes. Our planners have sought to ensure that NATO forces have the technical capability to carry out military war plans (Can SACEUR execute his SIOP?)[5]. Consequently, the requirement for specific types and numbers of nuclear weapons and modernization of individual nuclear capable systems has been regarded first as a military/technical issue, and only second as a political concern.

In contrast, the Europeans have emphasized the deterrent aspects of nuclear weapons. Of particular concern to Europeans over the decades has been maintaining the capability to strike Soviet homeland targets with European based systems. Such systems were viewed as demonstrating to Moscow that Soviet cities and installations would be at risk from any combat in Europe, and that Europe could not be isolated ("delinked") from U.S. based strategic systems. For the European nuclear cognoscenti, there is a sophisticated understanding of the need for nuclear weapons as the ultimate sanction against any war: the final politico-military illustration that use of conventional military force will not yield political advantage. They agree that there must be substantial numbers of weapons with nuclear delivery systems deployed as widely as possible among NATO members, both to avoid any one state being "singularized" as a host for U.S. nuclear weapons, as well as to emphasize the "shared risk" of nuclear deterrence. The conclusion of such reasoning, explicit in MC 14/3 and again advanced in NATO's recently completed, "comprehensive concept"[6], is that U.S. nuclear weapons deployment in Europe will remain necessary, regardless of conventional force levels.

Nevertheless, this is fairly sophisticated reasoning which is rarely advanced in any public dialogue. It requires several minutes to elaborate, and is not amenable to a 30 second sound bite, while "no nukes" is a catchier slogan. There is, after all, no rational manner in which European politicians can discuss a nuclear war in Europe with their constituents. As a consequence, over the past 20 years, the public rationale for the stationing and modernization of nuclear weapons has been simplistic: compensate for Soviet conventional force advantages or match the Soviet SS-20 threat. And, as we shall see, current and projected developments have undermined these facile mechanisms for mobilizing and maintaining public support.

Challenges to Flexible Response

As noted above, the viability of the "flexible response" strategy is contingent upon maintaining a substantial array of nuclear weapons, modernizing these weapons and their delivery systems as necessary, and demonstrating *inter alia* through planning and military exercises that the Alliance has the will to employ these weapons. In the mid-1970s, it was widely known that there were approximately 7,600 U.S. nuclear weapons in Europe. These consisted of bombs, missiles, artillery shells, air defense missiles, anti submarine weapons, and land mines. Military planners reportedly had targets for every weapon, and wanted still higher deployments: presumably to augment deterrence further.

Currently, however, through systematic reductions and modernization (sometimes with new technology permitting a conventional weapon to substitute for a nuclear system), the U.S. nuclear inventory in Europe has been reduced to approximately 4,000 weapons. Nuclear mines, antiaircraft missiles, and anti submarine systems have been totally eliminated, while stocks of other nuclear systems (bombs, artillery shells) presumably reduced or retired, e.g., land-based missiles such as Sergeant, Honest John, and Pershing I. Of the systems introduced during the last decade, the practical military utility of the 8" nuclear artillery shell is in question and the INF range systems (GLCM, Pershing II) are being eliminated. SACEUR has additionally suggested that under certain circumstances, e.g., SNF modernization, further reductions can be made, particularly in nuclear artillery rounds.

Deterrence itself has proved to be at least numerically flexible, with requirements for nuclear weapons in the mid-1980s barely half those of a decade earlier without suggestion that deterrence is weaker. At the same time, there is a political impetus against modernization of nuclear systems, which previously was approved routinely by military technical experts. Moreover, publics are impatient with cautious bureaucracies unwilling to move instantly to tune their arms control proposals to the siren songs emanating from Moscow. As a consequence, there is a steady pressure to reduce the number and mix of nuclear weapons, and the questions must be posed, "Is there a lower level for deployed nuclear weapons beyond which NATO must not reduce if deterrence is to be credible?" And the corollary concern, "Are arms control negotiations driving Europe toward 'denuclearization'?"

The INF Treaty: Wonder Boy and Whipping Boy

The INF Treaty stands in the center of this controversy. Completed in December 1987, ratified by the U.S. Senate in May 1988 and in full operation since July 1988, the INF Treaty normally is assessed as the politico-military success story of the decade. A uniquely unified NATO Alliance met the challenge of Soviet SS-20 deployments by agreeing to deploy U.S. INF systems. After years of intense negotiations with the Soviets, U.S. diplomats in close consultation with NATO Allies secured Moscow's agreement to Alliance conditions, such as asymmetrical worldwide reductions, extensive inspections, and exclusion of dual capable systems and British and French nuclear forces. Soviet INF reductions will be far greater than U.S. reductions. The INF negotiating logic will be directly applicable to NATO's benefit in other arms control fora. The "bottom line" is that, for the first time in history, an entire category of weapons will be eliminated.

Such a judgment has very wide, but not universal acceptance in Europe. To the degree that the European equivalent of "Joe Lunchpail" thinks about it at all, the INF Treaty is a "good thing," but mostly it has faded from the public consciousness. For politicians from the center on leftward, it provides a useful rhetorical touchstone when expounding upon prospects for peace and improved East-West relations. Foreign affairs and defense bureaucrats and intellectuals reflect the equally predictable "shades of grey" views. The most conservative and militarily oriented of these officials profess more or less grudging acceptance, but if permitted their "druthers," they would either have retained some LRINF (1,000-5,500 km range) or at least some SRINF (500-1,000 km range) systems, or even initiated nuclear force negotiations with the Soviets with some other systems, e.g., nuclear capable artillery or short range nuclear forces (SNF) of less than 500 km range.

The second of these observations can be dismissed rather quickly. Diplomats and politicians deal with the issues as presented them in the context of the day. In the mid-1970s, NATO was akin to an individual with several long-term ailments (conventional force imbalances, nuclear force modernization) who suddenly suffers an attack of appendicitis (SS-20 deployments). Addressing and resolving the issue of Soviet INF deployments became the most important politico-military challenge of the era. If it had not been successfully resolved, the NATO patient may not have survived.

Those who argue that some undefined amount of LRINF and SRINF should have been retained in the NATO force structure contend, in effect, that elimination of those systems and the concomitant capability to strike targets in the Soviet Union with missiles based in Europe weakens the "linkage" between U.S. based strategic systems and the defense of Europe. Illustrating the abstractly theoretical nature of these arguments, Treaty proponents argue conversely that elimination of these systems, particularly LRINF, strengthens linkage by removing Soviet systems that could strike most European targets, but not the United States. Both the United States and Europe are equally threatened by Soviet strategic forces.

Elimination of SRINF, even proponents admit, does reduce NATO (and Soviet) flexibility, but strict constraints on SRINF were going to be necessary in any event to prevent the Soviets circumventing INF Treaty provisions by large increases in SRINF. But (again the counter argument) if the Europeans are that concerned over elimination of SRINF, they should support modernizing current short range nuclear forces (SNF) and extending their range to close to the INF Treaty floor of 500 km.

Whatever the arguments and counterarguments over linkage/ delinkage, one point is irrefutable: the INF Treaty reduced the numbers of U.S. nuclear systems. The iron bar around which NATO arms control policy swings is the objective of increased security (read deterrence) at a lower level of armament. The lower level of armament stemming from the Treaty is self evident; the question of increased security/deterrence from the INF Treaty, and consequently from other prospective arms control treaties, is as always an abstraction and consequently open to indefinite debate.

Arms Control and Nuclear Modernization: Background to the SNF Debate

Continuing their arguments with some verve, the INF Treaty critics have blamed the INF Treaty for the now temporarily resolved NATO debate over how to manage SNF modernization and/or negotiations over these systems with the Soviets. In their eyes, the INF "double zero," eliminating both SRINF and LRINF missiles, has stimulated anti-nuclear sentiments, and greased the skids toward a denuclearized Europe. Although it is akin to crying over spilt milk, the critics deserve a response. To an extent they are right.

If there had been no INF Treaty (presumably because NATO rejected Gorbachev's acceptance of its own proposal for zero LRINF), there would be political debate over NATO's inability to "take yes for an answer." Do the critics of the INF Treaty seriously believe that NATO and basing country cohesion would have held under these circumstances? Likewise, in the NATO discussion of Gorbachev's proposal to eliminate, rather than limit SRINF, the United States made it clear that it was willing to reject the Soviet proposal, but that such a rejection would be simultaneously a NATO decision to deploy a U.S. SRINF force (a system in that range, the "PIb," had been tested but never deployed). NATO members instinctively shied from a decision to deploy new nuclear weapons in a category where the Alliance had none, and where the Soviets proposed to destroy hundreds of their own systems.

Indeed, if NATO is concerned about the challenge posed by Gorbachev's arms reductions, consider the difficulties the Alliance would have faced in sustaining a "no/non/nein" position on "zero-zero" in a modern democracy, when juxtaposed with a smiling Gorbachev appealing to European populations to be reasonable. Political suicide is not a viable electoral platform.

In another regard, the critics are also right in suggesting that the

INF Treaty led to SNF problems, albeit not for the reasons they postulate. Almost by definition, if there had not been an INF Treaty, it is unlikely that negotiations on CFE would be moving so smoothly, or that there would have been any significant discussion of SNF negotiations. Bureaucracies are surprisingly limited concerning the number of topics they can seriously address at any given time. Diplomats, although intelligent, are not omniscient; while energetic, they are not omnipotent. NATO and Soviet bureaucracies, already engaged with negotiations at one stage or another on INF, strategic systems, chemical weapons, confidence building measures, and conventional forces, were not likely to open another worm can (and indeed at the Reykjavik Ministerial in 1987 NATO, carefully avoided decanting SNF).

Thus, virtually by definition, if INF negotiations were still in process there would be no SNF debate. But in truth, the critics have it backwards. The INF Treaty is not driving NATO toward political accommodation with Moscow, but instead was the consequence of political change in Moscow, identified by the West as *glasnost* and *perestroika* in a halting attempt to put a label to what retrospectively looked ultimately like a second Russian revolution. In the INF negotiations, the Soviets came to us, met our requirements, and "bought" our demands. They are doing so again in CFE, and repeatedly expressing willingness to meet the traditional United States and NATO concern for greater security at a lower level of forces, in whatever fora the West professes interest. This is hardly to suggest that the Soviets are now born again altruists, offering the diplomatic equivalent of milk and honey instead of vinegar and bile. They operate as always according to Moscow's perception of Soviet national interest.

NATO's arms control specialists have spent a generation struggling through the desert, and are deeply concerned that the prospect before them will prove to be a mirage, and that the choice fruits apparently in their hands will turn to sand. Consequently, the debate over SNF modernization/negotiations is but the veneer on a basic problem. That deeper concern is how to determine what force levels and structure are necessary to maintain the credibility of NATO's nuclear deterrent. Nuclear artillery (8" shells) was modernized without popular attention. SNF is the first of what will probably be a long series of debates over how much defense is necessary in an era of warming détente, instead of the previous wrangle over how much defense is necessary to maintain a cold peace. With the INF Treaty, NATO has proved that it can conclude a modernization program that terminates in an arms control reductions agreement. Nevertheless, if the nuclear element of deterrence is to be sustained over the long term, NATO must demonstrate that it can sustain a nuclear modernization program not directed at arms control. Our very success in negotiations, however, is becoming our opponent in force modernization.

SNF: The Issue

"SNF" or short range nuclear forces are those forces able to strike targets only up to 500 km, the INF Treaty range "floor." The key elements of these forces are nuclear capable artillery and ground launched missiles, specifically the Lance missile, with a 90-100 km range, initially deployed in 1973. As there has been relatively recent modernization of 8" nuclear artillery rounds, attention has focused on potentially modernizing the eighty-eight Lance launchers which military sources judge will be obsolete in the mid-1990s. NATO military commanders have concluded that modernization is necessary, and have argued that a new "extended range" follow on to Lance (FOTL) should have a range close to the INF range floor of 500 km.

This military judgment has directly collided with German political realities: an overwhelming majority of the FRG public (whether seventy percent, eighty percent, or some higher figure depends on the date of the poll) does not wish such systems deployed. They have apparently become convinced of the accuracy of the infelicitous phrase "The shorter the range, the deader the German." Instead, the clear FRG public preference is for arms control negotiations addressing these systems, concluding in their elimination. While, if operating in a vacuum, the conservative CDU/CSU political leadership in Bonn would probably support SNF modernization, the FRG is far from such a vacuum and, consequently, Bonn has increasingly pressed to open SNF negotiations, as much to dampen the political heat as actually to find a solution. Nevertheless, the FRG clearly believes that it is unjust to delay indefinitely any discussion of systems of special interest and concern to Germans. Moscow has played to these sentiments, announcing unilateral reductions in its SNF forces, and clearly suggesting that it would be willing to zero out its more than 1,500 SNF systems in the course of a negotiation.

Fearing that any such negotiations would be the fatal banana peel on the already slippery slope to a denuclearized Europe, the United States and UK in particular, and other NATO members more quietly (Italy, France, Netherlands) have opposed SNF negotiations. At the Reykjavik Foreign Ministers Ministerial in June 1987, the official communiqué was artfully vague in suggesting to some that SNF negotiations would be possible only after successful conclusion of conventional force and chemical weapons agreements, and authorized preparing a "comprehensive concept" to define Alliance views on defense and arms control. Consequently, it was not immediately necessary to make a decision on SNF modernization.

This device bought the Alliance some time, along with the hope that SNF might be finessed in some undefined manner. Bonn, however, read the communiqué language to accept its premise that SNF issues could be negotiated concurrently with other arms control topics and continued to press this view. German irritation was exacerbated by UK comment that a "firebreak" needed to be constructed to prevent swift movement toward a denuclearized Europe. Bonn saw in the comment a suggestion that there was an area in which the "fire" could burn freely: presumably Europe from the Urals to the English Channel. Governed by such thinking, SDP opposition and Foreign Minister Genscher's Free Democrats within the FRG governing coalition regularly reemphasized the need for SNF negotiations.

SNF: The Bargain

By the beginning of 1989, time was running short. The "comprehensive concept" was grinding forward in NATO bureaucracy, but not toward agreement on the basic juxtaposition of SNF modernization and/or negotiations. Clearly hoping again to kick the issue down the road, the United States announced in February that it was not necessary to decide immediately on modernization, presumably permitting the FRG to hold its 1990 election without having made an SNF modernization decision. Instead of accepting this way out of the controversy, Genscher struck for more when, during a subsequent Washington visit in March, he emphasized the need to begin SNF negotiations quickly.

Thus, the stage was set for crisis at the May [1989] NATO Ministerial Summit, and required a mighty effort to prevent an open split. Whether such conciliatory efforts are "condemned to success" remains to be seen, but the consequence compromise was a complex interlock of the CFE negotiations and SNF. The Alliance will attempt to complete the CFE negotiations in six to twelve months, following which, during implementation of the CFE agreement, SNF negotiations could begin. A modernization decision on SNF would not be necessary until 1992 "in the light of overall security developments." The tight timetable for completing CFE and beginning SNF permitted Bonn to back off its demand for immediate SNF negotiations. The FRG commitment to a specific decision date for SNF modernization, and the NATO "comprehensive concept" emphasis that any SNF negotiations would encompass only "partial" reductions were important concessions for the United States.

SNF: The Prospects

The die has now been cast. With it, however, the likelihood of SNF modernization and deployment of a FOTL diminishes even further. In its CFE negotiations, the Alliance has put substantial pressure on itself to complete what will be an enormously complex negotiation on conventional forces involving twenty-three nations and a wide variety of systems (tanks, artillery, armored troop carriers, aircraft, and helicopters) as well as personnel levels.

Data Must Be Exchanged

Provisions will be necessary to determine how systems will be destroyed. A complex framework of inspections will be necessary to verify any such agreement, especially as there will be residual force levels for all systems. Each of these vast subjects encompass thousands of individual details, any one of which can become (even when all concerned are cooperating to make maximum progress) the object of protracted discussion. When NATO committed itself to this hypothetical time table, there was not a single word of tabled CFE treaty text to begin to address these points.

To put the task before the CFE negotiators in perspective, in comparison, it took almost nine months from the time a draft bilateral INF Treaty was presented until its agreement. Moreover, many of the elements and issues of the INF Treaty had been discussed for years, and INF negotiations addressed only one type of weapon with a relatively simple inspection concept (how to verify that all INF is eliminated.) As a consequence, arms control professionals privately deem a six to twelve month CFE negotiating schedule impossible, conceivable only if heads of state and government did virtually nothing except negotiate a CFE agreement. Indeed, the firm-jawed, publicly positive attitude toward completing the negotiations is reminiscent of the condemned man who undertook to teach the king's horse to sing.

Although it is virtually impossible to complete CFE in the near term, this does not mean that the injunction against an SNF negotiation will be equally stringent. As NATO must take seriously the six to twelve month projection to complete CFE, it must also begin work on an Alliance mandate and negotiating position for SNF. Not to do so would suggest bad faith with Bonn (and after all the CFE "horse" might learn to sing in twelve months). This SNF mandate promises itself to be complex. A solid argument can be made that drafting a negotiating mandate for SNF prior to a modernization decision on these systems is logically backwards. What SNF systems, after all, will the Alliance wish to retain: current Lance at reduced levels? A modernized Lance of the same range? An extended range FOTL? Without a modernization decision, these points cannot be resolved. Numbers are at least to some degree dependent upon weapon capabilities. What numbers are envisioned by the Alliance, and where should they be deployed?

Logical as it may be to make the modernization decision first, however, NATO has already decided, as announced during its May 1990 Summit, that the decision need not be made until 1992. Consequently, we may presume that NATO will reach agreement on an SNF mandate following detailed internal examination of desired numbers of SNF (a number less than eighty-eight but more than zero is foreordained, but may not initially be specified) and extensive debate over how to verify limits on such small, mobile systems. Although the Alliance may deliberately delay coming to closure on such a mandate, it is clear that it will be easier to complete than a CFE Treaty, if only because it can be vague while the Treaty must be very specific.

The concern is not so much that the Alliance will rush the completion of the CFE agreement to meet an artificial self imposed deadline, but that a completed SNF negotiating mandate "all dressed up with no place to go" will precipitate negotiations, whether the United States wants them or not. If there is negotiating progress in CFE, whether a treaty is completed in twelve or twenty-four months is not of great moment to Western publics. It will, however, be much harder to delay opening an SNF negotiation if a NATO negotiating mandate is *de facto* complete, and Moscow continuing to present a smiling mien. One can imagine the following scenario:

Projected Timeline of Arms Control Agreements	
CFE Negotiations	Projected completion between January-June 1990
SNF Mandate:	Completed by June 1990
CFE Negotiations	Actually completed June 1991
SNF Negotiations	Begun January 1991

In suggesting that an SNF modernization decision will be taken in 1992, NATO's "comprehensive concept" does not specify whether this decision will be on 1 January, or 31 December, or some date in between. Indeed, once an SNF negotiation begins, there will be massive domestic and international pressures to conclude a simple straightforward agreement at "zero." It is disingenuous to suggest, as do some officials, that NATO can avoid being driven to an SNF zero agreement simply by making its decision on "partial" reductions and sticking to it. That is as simplistic as insisting that the slogan "just say no" will end the drug problem. Unfortunately for the desires of NATO's military commanders and U.S/UK strategists, there is no public constituency for SNF modernization.

In this regard, a comparison with INF deployments is salutary. There was a European pull for INF deployments. The Soviets were deploying massive numbers of SS-20s. They refused to negotiate. Europeans felt threatened. Europeans had to convince a reluctant United States that deployments were necessary. So when the political opposition mounted, European leaders had to tough it out. They may not have enjoyed the heat, but they had provided the cook with the recipe and had to stay in the kitchen.

In contrast, for SNF, there is only a U.S. push. The Soviets are reducing, not deploying SNF. They are eager, not reluctant to negotiate. They are eager to eliminate, not retain such systems. The Europeans feel less threatened: indeed, they are less threatened. Under such circumstances, where is the European incentive to expend scarce defense resources, to endure domestic turmoil over new nuclear deployments, or to do what "U.S. militarists" rather than local voters want? And all this discomfort and expenditure for a system that, if ever used, would primarily be killing German citizens on German territory. Selling SNF is harder than selling iceboxes to Eskimos; it is more akin to making the damned ask for more brimstone when the opposition is offering asbestos underwear.

Nevertheless, the question of nuclear modernization will not go away. If not SNF, what systems, when, and where? If not nuclear modernization in the short term, whither flexible response in the long term?

Military Exercises: Increasingly Controversial

The third key element in nuclear deterrence has been planning and exercises. For more than twenty years, NATO has conducted "war game" exercises. On an annual basis, the NATO committees in Brussels, military commands throughout Europe, and selected officials in national capitals have participated either in a "high level exercise" (HILEX) or a "winter military and civilian exercise" (WINTEX-CIMEX). These exercises are conceptually different. HILEX is designed without a strict, formal scenario but is partly "free play" and responsive to direction by players. WINTEX-CIMEX, however, has a closely scheduled scenario, designed to examine the full range of NATO emergency and crisis reaction procedures, to test them against hypothetical, but predictable circumstances and re-familiarize the bureaucracy with the frequently complex intricacies of formalized crisis management. Consequently, WINTEX-CIMEX has addressed nuclear release procedures by NATO's BLUE forces against the euphemistically designated aggressor, ORANGE.

Such procedures have always been handled gingerly with NATO members, recognizing the requirement to reinforce deterrence by demonstrating the political will to request, release, and employ nuclear weapons. Even if performed during an "exercise," NATO presumes that Moscow receives the appropriate signal. Nevertheless, the signal had two tones/frequencies, and there was an equally strong desire within NATO not to alarm domestic populations with apparently blithe employment of nuclear weapons, even if performed during an "exercise." In 1989, however, the consensus for handling WINTEX-CIMEX apparently broke down over nuclear release policy. Although the circumstances are confused, the exercise scenario apparently called for use of nuclear weapons against ORANGE military forces about to overwhelm NATO troops, one in a specific location in the FRG, and the other elsewhere in NATO Europe.

Although this is not an illogical scenario, apparently it was one of the few times, if not the only time, that such a hypothetical circumstance was examined, and the military scenario hit the political fan. Bonn reportedly protested the development in a very early morning demarche by its acting NATO ambassador to the U.S. NATO mission in Brussels. Then, the FRG discovered previously unavailable "reserves" to reinforce the threatened sector, and the projected employment of nuclear weapons on FRG territory was cancelled (the other nuclear strike against ORANGE forces on NATO territory went forward as scheduled). The resulting political controversy in Bonn and elsewhere in the Alliance was submerged in the ongoing debate over SNF modernization/negotiation, but clearly the Alliance had sent a message of its own to Moscow: even hypothetical discussion of the use of nuclear weapons under tactical, battlefield circumstances is strictly proscribed. The net effect on the flexibility of "flexible response" and Moscow's perception of NATO's political fortitude can only be imagined.

Does Flexible Response Have a Future?

The foregoing suggests profound limitations and restrictions in NATO's flexible response Model '89 vs Model '79 or Model '69. Previous force modernizations and recent arms control agreements have substantially reduced nuclear weapons and nuclear capable systems deployed in Europe. Questions over SNF modernization imply limits on future modernization. Debate over hypothetical training exercises suggests NATO is communicating a negative image of its unity and political will regarding nuclear weapons use. Nor is this the end of questioning. Should a CFE agreement be completed, it will stimulate basic questions concerning the nature of conventional defense. The NATO conventional strategy of "forward defense" is barely sustainable at current force levels. Continued at significantly lower force levels, it would be a guarantee for quick defeat.

There are in Europe a variety of critics quietly professing that "flexible response" is dead. This attitude is particularly evident in Bonn where FRG President Von Weisaker is a skeptic. The FRG's SPD opposition proposes a "no first use" commitment for nuclear weapons—a refutation of an essential element of NATO's strategic doctrine. That element of the FRG population always dubious about nuclear weapons (reportedly about 40 percent of the public) has had its position strengthened by Soviet transigence/flexibility over the past two years. Indeed, there are those who believe that the "third zero" is not zero SNF, but zero nuclear weapons in Europe.

Nevertheless, although the storm is rising, the boat has not swamped. NATO government officials repeatedly stress that NATO must retain U.S. nuclear weapons stationed in Europe as a key element of deterrence. They take one of two lines of comment:

(a) "Flexible response" remains unaltered. It was valid before U.S. INF was deployed. It will be equally valid when INF is eliminated. As long as nuclear weapons are deployed and there is a concept for their employment, deterrence will hold. Sufficient weapons and systems exist to strike required military targets. War is probably less likely than at any time since NATO was constituted. If the strategy had failed, deterrence would have failed, i.e., war. No war, hence no strategy failure and no need to change.

(b) "Flexible response" may be dead, but the odor is not yet noticeable. It would be more dangerous and publicly disruptive to attempt to create an "MC 14/4" than it is to keep "flexible response" on the politico-military equivalent of a life support system and await developments. After all, development of "flexible response" followed, rather than led strategic evolution in the mid-1960s. In two or three years, by the early 1990s, the consequences of current arms control negotiations will be clearer, and Gorbachev's ultimate prospects easier to discern. Given time, a new NATO strategic doctrine may write itself.

These relatively sanguine analyses are essentially accurate. Determining a course of action on "flexible response" is not so much concluding that "if it's not broke, don't fix it," as it is recognizing that it is unknowable whether it is broken or not, but attempting to fix it now will most assuredly break it. There are, however, actions that can be taken that will strengthen either "flexible response" or whatever new NATO strategic defense doctrine may emerge from the interlock of arms control negotiations and Soviet political evolution.

Prudent Modernization

SNF modernization has been directed at the wrong system at the wrong time. Although doubtlessly useful in its specific military context, modernized SNF has no political constituency. While not publicly retreating from the technical commitment for SNF, and continuing with development to retain negotiating leverage, we should recognize that absent a total reversal of current trends, there is no public willingness to accept SNF deployments. We could even "win" at the negotiating table with the Soviets agreeing to accept, for example, equal levels at fifty SNF launchers, and be unable to find an ally willing to accept deployment of modernized SNF, while the Soviets regularly remind Europeans of their willingness to accept zero. We should be willing to "trade" zero SNF with the

Soviets for tight inspection measures to assist in effective SNF verification, and simultaneously strike an ironclad bargain with NATO
Allies to secure a public commitment to modernize other nuclear
systems.

Modernize What Systems?

The critical question will be "what systems." The only viable conclusion appears to be the tactical air-to-surface missile (TASM),
which is no more than an airborne cruise missile. It has the advantage of being able to strike targets at longer or shorter ranges, i.e.,
it is not limited to 500 km range and its range and mobility is enhanced by air delivery. This extended range has value in European
eyes in particular as such systems could strike targets in the Soviet
Union and, to European observers, provide greater linkage to U.S.
strategic systems. Moreover, potential launchers (aircraft that can
carry TASM) are widely spread throughout NATO inventories, so
deployment will not "singularize" one or two allies. Additionally,
the potential domestic opposition to TASM does not appear as
wide spread or emotional as SNF opposition, for two main reasons:
TASM would not be a new system, only an addition to already existing aircraft, and its range would eliminate the spurious criticism
that SNF will kill only Germans.

Obviously, there are negative elements to any nuclear modernization, and some axiomatic critics of any NATO policy are poised
to charge that TASM will circumvent the INF Treaty in spirit, if not
in letter. Such critics simply do not know either the content or the
negotiating history of the Treaty, which was carefully restricted to
ground-launched missiles. More serious potential criticisms are the
anticipated CFE limitations on nuclear capable aircraft, and the vulnerability of any airbase assumed to be housing nuclear weapons
to preemptive Soviet attack. In this regard, increasing capabilities
involving stealth technology should make it more likely that TASM
will arrive on target, and increased base hardening and dispersal
will be necessary to assure survival of NATO aircraft, whether or
not nuclear capable.

Greater Cooperation with French and British Nuclear Forces

Steadily and effectively, but without attracting much public notice, UK and French nuclear forces have grown considerably. By the mid-1990s, UK Trident submarines and French SSBNs will carry significant numbers of warheads. Additionally, the French continue to produce Hades INF-range missiles in still to be determined numbers.

These forces are now well beyond the rather primitive "tear off an arm" nuclear deterrent strategy, which characterized previous French and British views of their nuclear forces. Consequently, the potential clearly exists for NATO nuclear force planning, including French as well as UK nuclear forces, either informally or officially. We do not have to belabor the potential for such a development at this point or construct hypothetical bureaucratic structures to contain it, but simply to note its logic.

Conclusion

Nothing lasts forever. We have had a very good run with a military strategy that was conceived in a substantially different era. If "flexible response" has been no more than a tent under which all manner of NATO opinion on deterrent strategy could shelter, nevertheless it has kept the rain off Alliance members for more than twenty years. Nevertheless, "flexible response," by pleasing (at least minimally) so many, has been badly understood, and public rationales for the presence of U.S. nuclear weapons in Europe have been advanced at the lowest common denominator of understanding. Weapons and modernization have been presented as necessary, either to match Soviet actions or to counter WP conventional force superiorities. The "comprehensive concept" has made a start in emphasizing that nuclear weapons by themselves are a fundamental component of NATO's political and military security, not a compensation for or a response to Soviet action. More action along these lines will be necessary to build a sophisticated European understanding of the role of nuclear weapons.

What Should Be Done about Tactical Nuclear Weapons

John Woodworth

Ambassador Woodworth was the deputy and DOD representative on the INF Delegation. The text of this article was originally published March 1999 as an Atlantic Council Occasional Paper

Arms control negotiations on U.S. and Soviet strategic and nonstrategic nuclear weapons during the Cold War were driven by goals of sustaining deterrence and enhancing stability. Ten years into the post-Cold War era, however, the problems of nuclear arms control with Russia have evolved. Earlier goals remain important, but new concerns have emerged. Particularly with respect to tactical nuclear weapons (TNW), these concerns include proliferation dangers, reinforcing the viability of prospectively low START ceilings, confidence-building, and strengthening cooperative security in Europe. These concerns, and the changing strategic environment, create circumstances where traditional approaches to nuclear arms control, at least with respect to TNWs, are not likely to offer optimal approaches for meeting the most important challenges ahead.

The TNW problem, simply put, centers around the prevailing situation of Russia holding on to an untenably large number of TNW as a legacy of the Cold War. In contrast, the United States and its Allies have abandoned the bulk of their TNW capabilities. The resulting imbalance, combined with new goals and strategic opportunities, make notions of traditional bargaining over each sides' TNWs not only of dubious efficacy but also potentially dysfunctional.

To get at the heart the TNW problem (getting rid of the large number of Russian TNWs while at the same time overcoming adversarial legacies of the Cold War) there could be distinct advantages to pressing for solutions that directly reinforce the broad strategic goal of bringing Russia into a security partnership with the United States and the West. Getting to this goal will involve construction of expanding networks of cooperation that reflect and contribute to growing common interests. TNWs could be made a deliberate part of this process.

Goals and Interests

The U.S goal of greatly reducing, or even eliminating, the excessive numbers of Russian TNW has nothing to do with gaining strategic advantage, nor even of reinforcing some nuclear *modus vivendi* in Europe. Rather, specific key objectives have to do with clearing away some dangerous and counterproductive "underbrush" from the Cold War.

Reducing Warheads

U.S. and Russian policymakers have recognized in the 1997 Helsinki Statement that even in the context of strategic arms, warheads must now be addressed. This is all the more true with TNW, where delivery systems are essentially all dual-capable and serve conventional needs. This makes controlling warheads the only meaningful way to get at the TNW problem. Moreover, Russian retention of large numbers of TNW warheads that can be used "strategically" as well as "tactically" will undercut agreements significantly lowering U.S. and Russian strategic arms.

Controlling Proliferation Risks

The United States and other countries are rightfully concerned about the proliferation dangers posed by the large number of Russian TNWs. These concerns are heightened in direct proportion to doubts about the effectiveness of Russian control and security, not only of warheads, but also of nuclear materials and components from weapons it is dismantling. Unfortunately, Russian good intentions on these problems are not reassuring, because of dangers of disorder and criminal behavior.

Removing Destabilizing Threats

Russia's current excess of TNW will remain an existential threat to its neighbors, especially in Europe. Even with the decline of the saliency of nuclear weapons in East-West relations, and the absence of public controversy today compared to earlier periods, Russian TNW can only chill possibilities of fully integrating Russia into a cooperative security partnership. Russia must be brought to realize this.

As for Russia's possible objectives and interests concerning TNW, the apparent growing attachment to nuclear weapons accompanying the sharp decline of its conventional military capabilities could dampen Russian willingness to eliminate a significant part of its TNW. Still, Russia will almost certainly draw down some of these nuclear weapons, if for no other reasons than costs and obsolescence. At the same time, it would seem reasonable to assume that Russia would share concerns about proliferation dangers in general, and would be interested in cooperation to lessen them. Whatever its motivations, Russia will predictably try to bargain hard for any TNW reductions. They will seek to maximize U.S. financial help for nuclear safety and security measures. Beyond this, U.S. nuclear SLCM and NATO dual-capable aircraft will almost certainly prove irresistible objects of Russian negotiating ploys. But since these systems have now been reduced to bare minimums, it will be hard to paint them credibly as dire threats, which is not to say they should be excluded from future solutions. More generally, in the wrong context, Russia could be tempted to play the TNW issue to leverage various political goals, the most obvious being its current objection to NATO enlargement.

Ultimately, how and whether these different interests and objectives can be reconciled will depend more than anything else on the direction of internal change in Russia, and the players who exercise dominant influence there. Nonetheless, success in dealing with TNW and with achieving broader objectives could be influenced importantly by how the issue is approached.

Approaches

For a variety of reasons, approaching the TNW issue as a matter of defense and security cooperation, rather than through traditional arms control negotiations, could afford important advantages for advancing broader U.S. and NATO policy goals toward Russia. This approach could be strongly in Russia's interest as well.

We may need to turn ultimately to traditional nuclear arms control negotiations, out of necessity if not choice, for dealing with TNW. Such negotiations could take various forms, e.g., separate U.S.-Russian negotiations on TNW, folding TNW into negotiations on strategic arms, or multilateral negotiating venues. These alternatives are far from being equal in their implications, but what they share from Cold War experience is their use as tools in helping to manage adversarial relations between nuclear rivals.

Today, however, it is precisely because we are working to move away from the adversarial relations of the past that relying on traditional arms control negotiations for TNW could be out of step with our main goals. The very dynamics of negotiations in this form reinforce the adversarial nature of the proceedings. Trust is not presumed, nor is it necessarily sought. Once underway, opportunities for capitalizing on more productive forms of cooperation could be lessened. The temptation to indulge in political grandstanding, reminiscent of INF, could be present. Moreover, such negotiations will play to Russian proclivities to bargain relentlessly and sometimes obsessively. Results could be prolonged or delayed indefinitely. While traditional arms control negotiations should certainly not be foreclosed, there would be distinct advantages to an approach that could represent progress toward a qualitatively new stage in working with Russia.

What, then, are the features of an approach that seeks to emphasize activities of defense and security cooperation, rather than negotiations? The most useful models are the kind of planning processes found in NATO. Under this approach, the practical outcomes that would be sought with TNW would remain much the same, and hard bargaining could be part of the process, just as in NATO planning. However, such activity would be conducted in a framework of cooperative, rather than adversarial rules-of-the-road. Emphasis would be on reconciling and reinforcing mutual security goals. Results would be sought in practical forms of cooperation. Transparency would be a constant feature.

A variety of measures and activities could be pursued under this approach, building on past efforts while also breaking new ground. Some could be undertaken in a NATO or NATO-related framework (e.g., the Russian-NATO Permanent Joint Council), others through supporting bilateral or other discussion channels. Such measures and activities could include:

- A sustained discussion of doctrine, force structure, and planning;
- Data exchanges, moving emphasis to warhead numbers, types, and locations;
- Consolidation and inspection of storage sites, at minimum initially for warheads withdrawn from operational inventories;
- Joint measures for accounting for warhead dismantlement; and
- Joint measures for storage and control of nuclear materials.

This approach would build on steps that have already been made, such as the Bush-Gorbachev unilateral reductions of 1991-92, the U.S.-Russian Joint Working Group experience during 1994-95, and the first airings of the TNW issue in the Joint Permanent Council (PJC) in 1997. These undertakings have fallen far short of expectations, e.g., Russia's lack of accounting for its unilateral TNW reduction, absences from the JWG, and lack of openness in the PJC. But it would seem premature at this stage to write off more productive possibilities in the future.

The suggested approach does not operate on the premise of the rigidities of equal arms control ceilings. It acknowledges that the United States, NATO, and Russia may have different nuclear roles, requirements, and priorities that are not linked to each other's forces. However, it does imply the necessity of transparency and accountability as an intrinsic part of an evolving security relationship, and it does aim toward the major reduction and perhaps virtual elimination of TNW. The prospects for this are not necessarily dim. As noted, Russian officials and commentators have variously cited the need for Russia to reduce its nuclear forces greatly due to costs and obsolescence. There are no plausible threats that would justify Russian retention of large TNW nuclear forces; one of the goals of the approach suggested here is to convince them of this. Moreover, TNW reductions could significantly benefit Russian interests by facilitating the cooperation it needs with the West.

The relationship of TNW to U.S. and Russian strategic arms will be important. As indicated, strategic arms reductions on the order of those envisioned in START III will heighten the significance of TNW, and make their reduction of greater importance. Since warheads are expected to become a subject of discussion under START III, there are real questions about how or even whether TNW and strategic warheads can or even should be dealt with separately. However, there is no reason to presume that the suggested approach for TNW could not interface, nor indeed even integrate with measures relating to control and accountability of warheads under a future strategic arms agreement.

Ultimately, the object of this approach would be not only to secure desired outcomes on TNW but also to use the issue as an integral part of a strategy of engaging Russia in an expanding partnership. There could be many ancillary benefits, not least being help in overcoming Russia's misplaced concerns vis-à-vis NATO.

Caveats and Objections

It would be fatuous to suggest that the approach sketched above would be easy, practicable, or certain of outcome. Cold War habits of mind die hard, and suspicions of U.S. and NATO motives run deep with many Russians. Ultimately, adverse developments in Russia could thwart any hope of progress. But these uncertainties ought not to be allowed to stunt ambitious efforts to move to a qualitatively different stage in relations with Russia. Optimum policy should focus on creating the openings and generating the inducements for cooperation. This holds true on the TNW issue as in other areas.

One could fairly question the prospects of mounting a "security cooperation" approach to TNW, given the less-than-encouraging role that Russia has played on many nuclear issues in recent years. The lack of assurances concerns implementation of its 1991 commitments to unilateral TNW reductions, uneven cooperation in nuclear safety and security talks, and disappointing response to date to efforts to vet the TNW issue in the PCJ framework. Other developments, like the stalemate on START II and continuing development and production of new nuclear weapons, add to concerns. While the picture is clearly mixed, it nonetheless remains possible to see strong incentives for Russia to favor cooperation. Regression to old patterns of hostility offers Russia nothing for breaking out of its deeply serious current troubles.

Could a "security cooperation" approach, which seeks to foster transparency, fail to provide the precision, obligations, and account-ability that an arms control verification regime might otherwise provide? Are legally binding agreements essential? The question, along with the underlying skepticism, is reasonable. Getting verifi-cation on warheads, in all the dimensions this would involve, poses daunting challenges no matter how the problem is approached. A network of transparency measures might need a formal and com-prehensive character. The problem could well be tackled on several fronts that reinforce each other. The overlap or even integration of approaches to the control and accountability of strategic and TNW warheads together (with or without combined ceilings) warrants detailed consideration.

Vignette: Shall We Give Thanks?

Thanksgiving is the most "family-oriented" of American holidays. The thoughts of turkey, cranberry sauce and "all the trimmings" evokes Norman Rockwell images of a shared heritage that even high tech eve-of-the-twenty-first century America accepts as its norm. But in November 1987, the INF delegation was far from home and none would consider proposing a holiday, as for weeks each side had been vigorously working through each other's holidays, not to mention Saturdays and Sundays. And the implicit early December deadline for the Washington Summit was moving ever closer.

Nevertheless, Ambassador Glitman and his wife had looked beyond the workaday grind. Sensing the delegation mood, they planned a dinner at their home on the Sunday before Thanksgiving. Although planning to leave for Vermont to organize Thanksgiving for their five children, Mrs. Glitman first assembled a "traditional" dinner for the INF delegation. It was a short, ten-hour working day and little by little the delegation assembled at the Glitman's home for a rare social occasion.

So as we gathered, with the cocktail hour slowly merging into the sit-down at four large tables. Soup to nuts, bracketing the turkey and serving as the backdrop to conversation both transitory and profound. There was a touch of the awkward, a portion of the grateful, a recognition of sacrifice, and, above all, an abiding hope that the efforts of all would not go for naught.

As the evening drew to a close, the delegation gathered to the fireplace and, as guitars appeared, sang a wide selection of classic American folksongs. Unanticipated talent appeared. Mike Glitman, showing surprising skill on the guitar, punctuated the moment with a song for his wife alone that we also were privileged to hear.

On Thanksgiving proper the delegation worked until 8 p.m. and the ambassador ate a very late dinner with his chauffer.

How to Negotiate with Gorbachev's Team

David T. Jones

This article was published in the Summer 1989 issue of ORBIS *and edited slightly to make it more current.*

To what extent did the United States confront a new diplomatic posture when negotiating with the Soviet Union of Mikhail Gorbachev? Without belaboring the issue of change versus continuity in Russian negotiating style, it is possible to draw a few conclusions from the experience provided by the 1988 Intermediate-range Nuclear Forces (INF) Treaty, the first major U.S.-Soviet diplomatic engagement of the Gorbachev era.

Owing to personal interest, and the vagaries of Foreign Service assignments, I was in the rare position of having been involved with the INF issue at its beginning and at its climax. I was at NATO during the December 1979 decision that simultaneously launched INF deployments and began the parallel negotiations to curb those weapons. Then I was in Geneva during the fall of 1987 for the final INF Treaty negotiations. Based on this experience, I offer the following observations as a few of the lessons that current and future U.S. negotiators might draw from the INF experience.

Negotiating behavior under Gorbachev unquestionably illustrated new features, including much sharper public diplomacy and definite effects from *glasnost*. But these changes were not extensive enough to warrant abandoning some time honored and basic guidelines for American diplomats negotiating with the Soviets. The old maxims remained valid:

- Negotiate from a position of strength
- Remember that Moscow watches U.S. election returns

- Establish clear guidelines and hold to them
- Make agreements stick in writing
- Exploit Russian weakness at the delegation level
- Expect Russian bureaucrats to drag their feet

Background

The INF Treaty had its roots in the mid-1970s, when most European states of the North Atlantic Treaty Organization (NATO) began to worry about the Alliance's ability to deter Soviet aggression against Western Europe.

Specifically, Europeans were worried that Soviet weapons programs were tipping the nuclear balance in the USSR's favor. Because the Soviets already possessed huge conventional military advantages, it was NATO policy to use nuclear weapons first if necessary, and the threat of doing so was assumed to deter a conventional attack. But such a threat was a credible deterrent only if NATO was perceived to have both the military tools and political will to escalate to nuclear weapons. Soviet nuclear weapons building programs during the 1970s made a successful escalation doubtful.

Throughout the early and mid-1970s, European anxiety levels rose. With the Soviets' deployment of modern mobile SS-20s in 1977, the Europeans began to insist on a NATO response. To deter the new Soviet threat, NATO decided in December 1979 to station in Europe several hundred U.S. long-range INF missiles, Pershing II ballistic missile systems and Ground Launched Cruise Missiles (GLCMs). With deployment scheduled to begin in late 1983, these would be the first Europe-based missiles capable of reaching the Soviet homeland.

Consequently, the Soviets could no longer threaten Europeans with the implication that a nuclear war could be restricted to Europe without significant danger to the Soviet territory. The presence of U.S. INF forces in Europe targeted against the Soviet Union would clearly commit the United States to a superpower war, with all the deterrent effect on Soviet action that commitment implied. They would "couple" American strategic arms and the defense of Europe.

A corollary of such a coupling, however, would be the potential for Western defeat at the strategic level if America's central strategic forces were inferior to those of the Soviet Union. Consequently, a few analysts argued that it would be better to create a "Eurostrategic balance" in which U.S. nuclear forces in Western Europe could be viewed as matching comparable Soviet forces. In this view, nuclear deterrence would be more certain if the Soviets were aware that American resort to nuclear weapons did not quickly engage strategic systems. Such an approach appeared, however, to most Europeans to be a prescription for "war fighting" rather than deterrence which, in their view, should be a seamless web from riflemen to Minutemen with no distinct breaks. Ambiguity of strategic response might serve U.S. interests, but Europeans argued that predictability was a more likely deterrent. Thus, a weapons system such as the Pershing II, which would escalate the conflict in both violence and geography, added credibility to deterrence.

In the very communiqué that announced the Alliance's deployment decision, however, NATO also declared, "Arms control efforts to achieve a more stable overall nuclear balance at lower levels of nuclear weapons on both sides should...now include certain U.S. and Soviet long-range theater nuclear weapons." In short, the Alliance said it was "pursuing two parallel and complementary approaches of TNF [Theater Nuclear Forces] modernization and arms control." This became known as the "dual track" decision.

Initially, NATO agreed that arms control should not entirely preclude NATO deployments in the belief that such deployments re-coupled America's strategic deterrent to European defense, and were not designed merely to offset Soviet deployments of SS-20s. After the Reagan administration took office in January 1981, however, a new debate ensued within the American bureaucracy over the proper U.S. negotiating stance. The State Department sought negotiating flexibility with a formula proposing equal INF ceilings at the lowest possible levels, including zero.

The Defense Department, represented by Secretary of Defense Caspar Weinberger and Richard Perle, Assistant Secretary of Defense for International Security Policy, favored the dramatic clarity of a zero option, based on the minority assessment outlined above. For political reasons, the zero option had by now also become popular in West Germany. In the end, President Reagan supported the zero option, and serious negotiations on limiting INF missiles began in Geneva in November 1981.

The negotiations made little progress, as the Soviet Union hoped that European publics would negate the deployment decision by ousting the governments that had agreed to them. This did not happen, and in November 1983, after the United States started to deploy its INF missiles as planned, the Soviets walked out of the negotiations.

In March 1985, Mikhail Gorbachev became general secretary of the Communist Party of the Soviet Union, and that same month the negotiations resumed. While the power of personality can no doubt be overdrawn, it is difficult to conceive of Brezhnev, Andropov, or Chernenko pressing as hard as did Gorbachev for an INF agreement acceptable to the United States. In the end, the United States got the zero option, and more besides. The Soviets' shorter-range missiles (SS-12 and SS-23), which if left unconstrained could have threatened most of the same targets vulnerable to SS-20s, were eliminated also. By agreeing to zero weapons on both sides, Soviet concessions had the effect of eliminating worries about the transfer of SS-20s from the Far East, and of reducing problems with the verification regime designed to implement the Treaty.

Of course, the Soviet Union remained capable of waging nuclear war in Europe, as did the United States. The INF Treaty did not eliminate the strategic nuclear and general military balance in Europe but rather reshaped it. More important, the INF Treaty created a special cache of political problems for the Alliance, centered on the future role of West Germany. Some opponents of the Treaty remained concerned over its military aspects, believing still that it decoupled the United States from the security of Western Europe; Others were concerned over its political aspects, believing that it singularized West Germany and undermined the political unity that is the *sine qua non* of NATO's effectiveness in any crisis.

These were not trivial concerns. What is important in this context, however, is not whether the United States got in the INF Treaty something that will stand the test of time, but more simply that, for the first time in the history of U.S.-Soviet arms control negotiations, the United States got precisely what it wanted in a long, complex, and protracted negotiation. Looking at the full arms control agenda before us, we need to review just how we did it. Maybe we can do it again. The key is to understand how much of the success was reasonably attributable to our skill, to Gorbachev's decisions, or to some combination of the two.

Even as Gorbachev's tenure brought change within the Soviet Union, so it brought some nuances to Soviet negotiating behavior.

Improved Public Relations

In his memorable summer 1985 interview with *Time,* Gorbachev denied the old saw that the Soviet Union wanted to drive a wedge into NATO, splitting the United States from its Allies. Nothing could be further from the truth, he claimed. But his claim was disinformation. If anything, the Soviets accentuated their NATO-splitting tactics during the INF negotiations, and raised their public diplomacy efforts in Europe to new levels of sophistication.

Early in the resumed Geneva negotiations, the Soviets dispatched many ambassadors, led by their chief negotiators, Ambassadors Viktor Karpov and Aleksei Obukhov, to NATO capitals to hammer at U.S. arms control positions. It had been standard U.S. practice to provide comprehensive explanations to allies and adversaries alike, but this practice was new for the Soviets, who performed with greater sophistication than anticipated. Following each major meeting with the United States, Soviet "spin controllers" quickly circulated to ensure that the most convincing case for their positions was understood. The Soviets increasingly used Moscow press conferences, featuring hitherto anonymous Soviet generals, to stake out positions. Most remarkable, the Soviets generally made themselves far more accessible to the press than previously. Compared to the grilling usually accorded to U.S. military representatives, the Soviet spokesmen were not pressed for specifics; the media appeared more interested in the new phenomenon of relative openness itself than in pursing the nuances of specific details in the Soviets' presentations.

The Soviet INF delegation members played a special role, making themselves available to visiting dignitaries; they were especially attentive to lawmakers and staff from the U.S. Senate Observer Group during the latter's periodic Geneva visits. Dogmatic and ideological during negotiating sessions, the Soviets demonstrated flexibility and reason to outsiders. The Soviet INF delegation in Geneva also issued press releases more frequently than its counterpart from the United States, including a remarkably nervy press release on 2 December 1987, accusing the United States of delaying data exchange; this after it had spent days refusing to execute an already agreed exchange (the maneuver was given the "chutzpah of the year" award by the U.S. delegation.)

The U.S. government is often puzzled as to why, with Madison Avenue in its territory, its side of the arms control story is so poorly conveyed—or at least why its listeners so often remain un-persuaded. Public opinion polls in Europe prior to the INF Treaty suggested that Gorbachev was perceived as more popular and believable than the U.S. leadership. The INF lesson, subsequently reinforced by Gorbachev's unilateral commitments to reduce Soviet conventional and nuclear forces, suggested that there would be more of the same. Gorbachev's smile doubtless hid iron teeth, but he said what European publics wanted to hear, there was a new dawn in Moscow, and the price of peace became cheaper. Despite the assistance of the security-minded governments in Europe, the United States would be hard-pressed to ensure that the post-World War II generation understood the underpinnings of the military realities in Europe. If the Soviets had proposed sweeping, attractive reductions at the scheduled Conventional Forces in Europe (CFE) negotiations, the painstaking negotiations on technical issues may well have taxed the patience of European populations, to the disadvantage of the West. Indeed, the ostensibly attractive Soviet opening moves in CFE stimulated positive public reaction, even before the details were examined.

At the same time, by entering the public relations sweepstakes, Gorbachev committed Moscow to playing under new rules. No longer could the Soviets make wildly implausible proposals or simply stonewall reasonable U.S.-NATO positions, because now there was an international price to pay. On the other hand, the West could no longer expect axiomatic Soviet intransigence to save it from tactical errors, such as "anywhere, anytime" on-site inspections.

Glasnost

The INF talks were a major proving ground for Gorbachev's policy of *glasnost* or openness. The Americans wondered whether *glasnost* would lead to a greater Soviet willingness to accept intrusive verification and to provide detailed information on Soviet forces.

Despite Gorbachev's statement in January 1986 that Moscow was prepared for all forms of verification, including on-site inspection, and Deputy Foreign Minister Vorontsov's subsequent boast that "we will demand even more verification than the U.S.," the Soviet team in Geneva refused to go beyond the old platitudes. *Glasnost* was slow in coming to INF.

However, after introducing their April 1987 draft of the INF Treaty, the Soviet delegation became somewhat more willing to discuss specific verification measures in depth. But the turning point came only in October 1987, on the sixth of that month, to be exact, when the Soviets in the INF Elimination Protocol Working Group displayed photos and line drawings of Soviet intermediate-range missiles: an unprecedented action reportedly authorized personally by Marshal Sergei F. Akhromeyev. With this step, the Soviets presented hard information never before seen in the West: albeit comparable to the information on U.S. armaments that Moscow could get in *Jane's Weapon Systems.*

This single act, more than any other, showed that the Soviets were seeking an early INF agreement. Thereafter, Soviet representatives were distinctly more responsive, especially in the technical working groups. Although high-level diplomatic efforts were still needed before the Soviets would present disaggregated data and site diagrams, the data they did provide were far more extensive than anything ever before made available. Although Soviet military leaders clearly resisted concessions every step of the way, eventually they resigned themselves to the highly intrusive verification regime advocated by the United States. Some Soviets appeared stunned by their own openness; one military representative commented, "If an enlisted man gave you this information, he would be shot."

Under the banner of *glasnost*, the West could anticipate greater Soviet flexibility on materials that were routinely unclassified here, but that Moscow considered state secrets for decades. For example, a detailed conventional-forces data exchange, with each side responsible for the accuracy of its data, could clarify points in the CFE negotiations that remained at issue throughout the Mutual and Balanced Force Reductions negotiations. Also, if the INF precedent held, individual Soviet delegates would be more willing to reveal inside information and to explore unresolved issues. Moreover, the precedent was set for extensive inspection of specific sites, continuous presence of inspectors at key production facilities, and "cooperative measures" to assist the effectiveness of national technical means of verification such as spy satellites.

In the past, Soviet negotiators were inflexible, assuming that the United States must make the moves to generate progress. Stimulated perhaps by *glasnost*, the INF negotiations suggested that the Soviets would be more creative. American negotiators should have insisted that they be.

The Soviets shifted ground many times during the course of the INF negotiations, particularly after Gorbachev entered the scene, but certain constants in their conduct reinforced old truths about negotiating with the Soviets.

The Soviets Remained Firm Devotees of Power Politics

Indeed, the entire INF affair, from the Soviets' deployment of SS-20s in 1977 to the Treaty banning them in 1987, serves as a vivid reminder of how Moscow used its nuclear arsenal to intimidate weaker states. The SS-20s were being deployed throughout much of the 1985-87 negotiations, and were probably good for another 10 to 20 years. Moreover, a modernized version of the SS-20 was also being tested, indicating that the Soviets were prepared to keep their SS-20 force indefinitely. Yet, in the end, the Soviets were willing to destroy the entire SS-20 force, suggesting that this force was originally deployed not for coherent military reasons, but as an instrument of political pressure and intimidation.

Likewise, negotiation of the INF Treaty demonstrated beyond doubt that the Soviets took you seriously only when you had "battalions" big enough to match their own. The proposal of the North Atlantic Treaty Organization not to deploy INF missiles if the Soviets destroyed their intermediate-range missiles was risible, an attempt to trade "a bucket of ashes for a bucket of coal," and the

Soviets treated it with contempt. Only when NATO had absorbed the political and financial costs of INF missiles, proving that it could deploy them, did the Soviets seriously weigh U.S. proposals and Alliance supporting statements.

It is hard to overstress this lesson and its implications. Effective negotiation with the Soviets was not possible without negotiating chips. They did not give you the time of day unless you were wearing a watch. This is not to suggest that U.S. INF deployments were sufficient for an INF agreement, but they certainly were necessary. Obviously American actions did not force the Soviets to accede to a specific agreement or, indeed, to any agreement at all. Even with U.S. INF deployed, the Soviets could have elected to maintain and modernize their INF missile force at maximum levels, or they could have accepted an agreement at equal levels above zero. Without U.S. deployments, however, the best possible agreement that the United States and NATO could have extracted would have been Soviet SS-20 reductions (perhaps to 1979 levels), but with the United States committed not to deploy any INF missiles. That, of course, would have meant conceding a Soviet monopoly in INF missiles.

This truth, that *a U.S. counter is necessary for any Soviet system*, had to be kept in mind in the START negotiations, where the United States sought objectives such as the elimination of Soviet mobile missiles, even though the comparable U.S. missile is little better than a drawing-board construct. This is not to say, however, that the negotiating chip must appear in exactly the same form as its Soviet counterpart. Both U.S. mobile missiles (MX and Midgetman) were unpopular in different domestic quarters and so were never deployed. But the media had been touting the B-2 "Stealth" bomber as a counter to Soviet mobile missiles. Because stealth technology enjoys a popular mystique, deployment of a stealth bomber was far more credible than deployment of a mobile missile, and this might have prepared the way for a trade-off between the B-2 and Soviet strategic mobile missiles.

Anticipate Soviet Electioneering

Certainly, the Soviets were no less dutiful about observing NATO's domestic electoral scene than the Alliance was about Kremlin-watching. This was clear following the Soviet walkout at the INF negotiations in November 1983 after U.S. INF deployments. The U.S. administration was facing a presidential election in which some candidates, such as Senator Alan Cranston (D-CA), opposed INF deployments by the United States. The alternative of a freeze in INF deployments by the United States was widely bruited, with the intimation that U.S. deployments would make an INF agreement impossible; and the Soviets had to ask themselves whether "President Mondale" might be more flexible. Indeed, Viktor Afanasiev, a member of the Soviet Central Committee and editor in chief of *Pravda*, has confirmed that "an unwillingness to help promote Reagan's reelection was one reason for the Soviets' negative stance on arms control in 1984."[7]

Domestic critics had also made deployment an election issue in those countries that hosted NATO INF bases, namely the United Kingdom, West Germany, Italy, Belgium, and the Netherlands. In every one of them, the government fought an election focused in part on its commitment to INF deployments. Thus, the negotiating walkout on 23 November 1983 was a low-cost strategy for the Soviets. If the Allies or the United States had broken ranks or altered deployment commitments, the Soviets would have reversed a major NATO security decision; and, if Western cohesion held, Moscow could always return to the negotiating table.

The latter proved, indeed, to be the case. Promptly after the 1984 presidential election in the United States, the Soviets renewed their interest in arms control negotiations. Other European elections were still to come, however; the United States obtained a fully reliable political endorsement of INF only in July 1986, when the Dutch government gave its final commitment to deploy missiles.

Again, the lesson verges on the obvious. The Soviets would not come to significant arms control agreements in the final year of a U.S. administration. In an election year, the U.S. administration grinds into immobility as campaigning absorbs the energies of decision makers. Lacking pertinent guidance, negotiators march in place. Incumbents do not want to give their opponents anything as concrete as a finished treaty to criticize and prefer to claim that "the process" is moving in a promising direction. "Better no agreement than a bad agreement" becomes the campaign slogan.

Further, the Soviets would not propose concessions that the

current administration might not have had time to act upon, and that the next administration could pocket as given. The temptation to see whether the next administration would be more flexible on neuralgic points was overwhelming. If the Soviet bureaucracy considered whether to press for a START agreement in 1988 or to see if "President Dukakis" would offer a better deal on "Star Wars," the proponents of delay clearly won.

The U.S. delegation at the INF negotiating table had well-defined objectives, and these were critical in eventually reaching an agreement. Since 1981, NATO guidelines had been clear: equality of rights and limits, globality (no transfer of the threat from Europe to other regions), no negotiation on or compensation for the systems of third countries (meaning those of the United Kingdom and France), no adverse effect on NATO's conventional capabilities (that is, exclude nuclear-capable aircraft), and effective verification. In addition, the Alliance later decided that an INF Treaty must include collateral constraints on shorter-range systems (a detail that may have been overlooked initially, owing to the U.S. negotiators' single-minded focus on the SS-20 missile system). Most of the INF negotiations were devoted to convincing the Soviets that the United States would continue to support these principles.

Sound positions were worth repeating to the Soviets, as many times as necessary. Repetition helped American messages get through to Moscow, even if the reporting by Soviet negotiators was spotty, distorted, and self-serving. Americans take some pride in approaching problems in a flexible and creative way ("if at first you don't success, try the outfield"); but in negotiations with the Soviets, flexibility was usually not a virtue. The Soviets were not very subtle in their presentations, preferring the sledgehammer to the rapier. They expected their interlocutors to hammer away at them in a similar fashion. They therefore tended to misinterpret a position as weakly held if it was not delivered repeatedly and vigorously.

For their part, the Soviets were less than clear about their own principles after having failed to prevent U.S. deployments. Although they accepted the initial position of total INF elimination in July 1987, it remains unclear whether, during the first year of resumed negotiations, they hoped to maintain Soviet INF preponderance, or planned to use INF as a bargaining chip for U.S. concessions in START. Recalling how long it takes a new U.S. administration to conduct substantive reviews of major issues, some of the fits and starts of Soviet negotiating policy might have reflected a similar shakedown during Gorbachev's first year in office. Until the Dutch reaffirmation in July 1986, the Soviets also no doubt harbored hopes that one or another host country would falter, and the entire deployment scheme would subsequently unravel.

It appears clear that Moscow's final decision to accept the zero option was prompted by recognition that a residual INF force based in the Asian portion of the Soviet Union would be militarily trivial. Such a force would accentuate verification problems, while indefinitely troubling relations with Asian states. Clearly, prospective removal of SS-20s aimed at East Asia removed an irritant with the Peoples Republic of China, helping pave the way for a potential rapprochement with Beijing.

In groping toward final acceptance of the basic U.S. zero proposal, however, the Soviets spun a series of maneuvers, playing shell games with their positions, sometimes demonstrating confusion within their own ranks. For example, they shifted their line innumerable times on the linkage between the INF negotiations on the one hand, and START/Defense and Space Negotiations on the other. At one point following the Reykjavik Summit in October 1986, Gorbachev and his chief negotiator, Ambassador Viktor Karpov, made contradictory statements on the issue of whether INF was part of the package or not.

The United States was well served by an initial negotiating position which was clearly articulated and comprehensively agreed within the Alliance. In retrospect, the protracted effort to reach agreement on such positions was worthwhile, if only to convince outside observers of the unlikelihood of significant changes in the U.S. position. Similar care would enhance the American position on START.

Get Written Agreements

American positions are fought out in interagency discussion, with decisions made at the highest level necessary to resolve debate. Working through the delaying mechanisms available to each powerful agency and personality until a decision or compromise is reached has frequently been a problem in this process, and advocates of policies not adopted often leak their positions to the media, giving the impression that the issue remains unsettled. Nevertheless, the results of these high-level discussions are usually treated as gospel in negotiations. U.S. negotiators can therefore speak with confidence that their positions will not be reversed.

In past negotiations, there was an impression that, while it was often extremely hard to bring the Soviets to agreement on an issue, once they agreed on a point, they would hold to it. This was not true during the INF negotiations. Whether the issues were major (such as the INF-START-SDI linkage) or minor (timing the elements of data exchanges), there was a repeated need to revisit issues that ostensibly had been solved. American delegates characterized the process of reaching specific agreements with the Soviets on INF as comparable to "nailing Jello to a wall."

Final Soviet decisions were only made at the very top. Soviets at the delegation level, presumably on instruction, reversed agreements reached at higher levels between ranking U.S. and Soviet officials and tried to sell the same horse twice, or as many times as they thought they could find a purchaser. For example, some of the technical commitments made by ranking members of the Soviet political-foreign affairs establishment following Summit discussions in Geneva with U.S. representatives in November 1987 simply did not hold up in subsequent negotiations. Consequently, we learned that when we needed a definite agreement, we had to ensure that the highest levels of the Soviet military were clearly involved: otherwise, it was prudent to hold onto our positions.

The United States, then, needed to pin down agreements in unambiguous writing. Meetings that do not result in written agreements, even those at the highest level, can create serious difficulties. Soviet-American meetings were always held under great logistical and political pressures, and there was more to talk about than time permitted; but the emphasis had to be to secure solid written confirmation of what was agreed (and clear identification of what was still unresolved). Even written language can be ambiguous and hence held hostage to bad faith, but a solid treaty text is the best protection negotiators can secure, both for establishing a clear national understanding of the rights and obligations enjoined by the treaty, and for maintaining the support of friends and allies in instances of disagreement between parties.

Exploiting Soviet Weakness

In the course of the INF negotiations, thousands of substantive points were addressed—from large issues such as the exclusion of British and French nuclear systems to the minutest details, such as the question of whether verification inspectors should be allowed to carry tape measures. This process of negotiation was normally adversarial; at best, it was tedious and businesslike. In any case, it proved that Soviets at the negotiating table were not ten feet tall, even under Gorbachev. American negotiators had more flexible instructions, were less hamstrung by compartmentalization, and had greater in-depth expertise. During the weeks immediately after the September 1987 Shultz-Shevardnadze meeting in Washington, the Soviets in Geneva, although apparently under instructions to expedite the process, lacked the specific guidance to complete the Treaty rapidly. The result was *de facto* filibustering by Soviet negotiators (privately labeled "numb-alogues" by the U.S. delegation) designed to fill time. At one point, when the Soviets advanced a time-filling reversal of a previous position, a U.S. negotiator recalled former senator Stephen Young's (D-OH) classic response to crank letters: "Dear Sir, You should be aware that some madman is signing your name to letters."

Clearly, the U.S. delegation benefited from internal cohesion with clear lines of communications and authority. Information was widely shared throughout the delegation, with judgments and decision making collegial rather than hierarchical. No one will ever pretend that powerful personalities representing agencies with diverging views will always agree, but momentary heat frequently forges solid conclusions. In contrast, Soviet working group members often seemed to lack information being communicated at other levels; more than once a senior Soviet negotiator was openly reversed by his ostensible subordinate.

For the last three months of the INF "end game," the United States was able to reinforce its negotiating team with key technical experts and others with years of INF experience. The Soviets either could not or would not reinforce their delegation to match the U.S. negotiating team and suffered because of it. Consequently, Soviet delegation members were even more pressed by overwork than were their U.S. counterparts. Full Soviet teams were not available for expert working sessions, and the United States largely took control of the drafting process.

U.S. technical experts, for example, conclusively proved that missiles could be safely and quickly destroyed on the ground by a variety of methods, rather than eliminated only by launching as the Soviets originally argued. (In the end, however, a limited number of launches during the first six months of the Treaty were permitted). Likewise, faced with the requirement to devise parameters for a permanent facility to monitor Soviet missile production at Votkinsk, the United States could draw on past studies and career verification experts to quickly devise a system the Soviets accepted virtually *en toto*.

The Soviets were also remarkably deficient in the technology that supports modern diplomacy: word processors, high-speed photo-copying equipment, and dedicated transportation. Sufficient copies of Soviet proposals were rarely available; reproduction equipment belonging to the Soviet team appeared to be limited to making three poor-quality copies. U.S. word-processing equipment at the Geneva negotiating-team level was hardly state-of-the-art, but the Soviets had nothing to match the secure word processors and high-speed printers standard for the U.S. negotiating team. This capability permitted the United States greater flexibility in drafting, proposing, and integrating elements of the Treaty into final text.

Virtually instantaneous communication with Washington enabled the United States to draw quickly on the skills of a range of technical experts to supplement the expertise of the negotiating team. The U.S. delegation also gained major advantages by repeatedly being the first to introduce Treaty language, beginning with the 4 March 1987, U.S. draft INF Treaty, to which the Soviets were able to respond with a text of their own only six weeks later. While no one could force the Soviets to accept even the most logical argumentation, the Soviets were decidedly weaker in developing strong arguments and adducing facts to support their positions.

When returning to the United States for the Treaty-signing ceremony, the U.S. negotiating team brought a few magnetic disks containing the entire Treaty text. The Soviets, who returned on the same plane with the U.S. delegation, brought their text in an Italian-made word processor the size of a small refrigerator. Indeed, had the United States not offered to transport the Soviets, it is unclear how they would have gotten to Washington, for reproducing the Treaty on official treaty paper in both languages was completed too late for scheduled commercial airlines to carry the Soviet delegation. Further covering every possible, even catastrophic contingency, the U.S. delegation sent additional copies of the Treaty to Washington via Federal Express.

Being technically more advanced gave the U.S. government a decided edge in information and argumentation against its counterparts. These American advantages need to be developed further in future negotiations. Negotiators should have access to extensive, detailed databases and electronic-mail word-processing systems with easy retrieval capability for key documents and telegrams.

Expected Negotiating Delays

The U.S. government gave the Soviets considerable credit for being tough, clever, astute negotiators. The final days of the INF talks, however, provided Americans with a different picture. In retrospect, Soviet negotiating toughness owed more to inflexibility, either personal or Moscow-driven, than to diplomatic skills. Soviet negotiators needed constant guidance from Moscow, even for minor word changes, yet often did not use this guidance (or withheld it for extended periods), anticipating that the U.S. negotiators would unilaterally resolve issues for them.

Our understanding of Soviet motivation for specific moves remained murky. *Glasnost* had yet to produce any day-to-day media insight into Soviet bureaucratic infighting equivalent to *The Washington Post* and *The New York Times* columns, let alone the books published by investigative journalists. Lacking such insights, we had to assume that Soviet positions were shaped both by personality and by institutional interests.

Personality is important in any negotiating situation, at least on the tactical level. Negotiators frequently do not wish to change positions. They believe in them. Changing a position in which one has a vested interest can be viewed as a personal defeat rather than a tactical adjustment. The Soviets were certainly not immune to this problem. Another problem at the human level concerns uncertainty about intentions; for example, when an argument becomes technical, as many inspection-related issues are, one side often grows suspicious about the degree of intrusion necessary for monitoring Treaty compliance. At what point does the desire for verification turn into lust for intelligence collection? Thus, any new idea will most likely be reflexively rejected. Any hope of agreement depends on patient repetition of technical explanation, in order to convince those on the other side of the table that there are no hidden traps, and that the proposal will indeed prove mutually beneficial.

On the strategic level, neither side will knowingly accept an agreement that does not meet its interests. Although many arguments may have led Moscow to accept a zero agreement, the road to the zero option was opened by the Reykjavik agreement that would have eliminated INF in Europe and limited INF warheads worldwide to one hundred for each side. Retaining such a militarily trivial force was ultimately seen as illogical and inefficient. Not only would a residual force have been expensive to maintain and modernize, it also would have aggravated relations with Asian states, while requiring a more stringent inspection regime.

While the U.S. delegation was willing to accept a Reykjavik-style residual force agreement, American negotiators continued to point out the advantages of a global zero agreement, including the ease of monitoring. For their part, the Soviets attempted to trade their remaining one hundred warheads for U.S. nuclear forces in the Far East (land- and carrier-based aircraft and submarines). But when the U.S. team spurned such an offer in Geneva, they dropped positions requiring destruction of U.S. INF systems and shelters, saving the United States hundreds of millions of dollars, and adopted verification proposals that an ideologue would have judged impossible.

Conclusion

Rhetoric surrounding the INF Treaty tended to make the usual mistake of seeing each bend in the road as a major turning point. Valuable as it is, the INF agreement is more important as a precedent than for what it accomplishes in itself. It does, after all, address only three to four percent of the global nuclear arsenal: systems that one U.S. military officer characterized as "rubble bouncers." The INF Treaty is more a cornerstone of a structure yet to be built (the blueprints of which are now being vigorously debated) than it is a prototype for future agreements. It suggests a potential direction for U.S.-Soviet relations rather than firmly establishing such a direction itself.

Nevertheless, from the INF negotiations, we learned that:

- Agreement can be reached to eliminate a weapon system totally, even a newly modernized one;
- The Soviets were willing to accept asymmetrical weapons reductions to equal levels. Knowing this reality will serve U.S. negotiators in good stead in other arms control negotiations (START, chemical weapons, and conventional arms) where Moscow's weapons and stockpiles significantly outnumber those of the West. (Asymmetrical reductions may some day prove a two-edged sword, however, should naval forces ever become a subject of negotiation);
- The Soviets were willing to be more flexible than outsiders previously imagined. The issue no longer is whether there will be inspection, but how to design effective inspection programs;
- The Soviets announced adherence to global zero, while presenting their agreement as something they did out of concern for Asians; and
- An agreement takes time to negotiate. Dealing with the Soviets is only one facet of the process, as negotiators must be simultaneously aware of congressional, media, domestic, and Allied views. INF took a decade to complete and other agreements will not be much faster.

The tendency for Soviet negotiators to be slowed by constantly looking over their shoulders was also exhibited in their intense concern that the agreement gave an appearance of perfect equity. Aware that they were to destroy many more systems than the United States, they sought an ostensible balance in every possible area, apparently anticipating that they would have to defend the agreement against internal critics. Thus the eighty-four Soviet GLCMs (a "system tested but not deployed") had to be balanced against the largely hypothetical U.S. Pershing Ib, for which there was little more than a photograph.

A similar problem of appearances concerned elimination of SS-20 launchers. The Soviet launcher for the SS-20 is an inseparable combination of the prime mover and the mechanism to erect the missile: essentially a launcher on wheels. The U.S. Pershing II launcher, by contrast, is essentially a flatbed trailer, the prime mover is a separable truck employed to pull it. One way to eliminate the launchers would be to cut them in pieces. But this approach would also destroy the Soviet prime mover while leaving the U.S. prime mover (the truck) intact. The Soviets said frankly, "If you drive something away, we want to drive something away." The result was a careful negotiation to modify the SS-20 launcher irreversibly so it could never serve that purpose again. The erector mechanism was removed and cut up, and the rear end of the Soviet prime mover cut off so it could not support an SS-20 erector mechanism (although it could still be used for hauling ordinary loads). So, in the end, both sides drove something away.

Despite its preoccupation with clearing what was said and done with Moscow, the Soviet delegation did, toward the end of the negotiations, display a willingness to sacrifice ideology for solution. Even arch-rhetorician Ambassador Aleksei Obukhov turned pragmatic. Presumably, the reward must be exceedingly attractive in order to justify the forfeit of ideology, but once that decision was made, the Soviets moved quickly.

INF was a test agreement. The manner of its implementation and the scrupulousness of Soviet compliance would suggest whether we could go on to more ambitious agreements with Gorbachev's government. No doubt, a desire to see how INF was working out was one element in the George H.W. Bush administration's review prior to resumption of the START negotiations. Moscow's response to the delay in Washington's review was uncharacteristically reserved. Where Brezhnev could not have passed up the chance to rail against a U.S. "delay," Gorbachev demonstrated a patient willingness to resume negotiations when U.S. decision making was finished. This restraint suggested a useful maturity that could be reflected in future negotiations.

Asian Arms Control Attitudes Post-INF

DAVID T. JONES

The article was originally published in Asian Survey *in May 1990 and slightly revised.*

Background

The Asian and European INF experiences were never alike. Their perceptions of threat were entirely different. Europeans had been corporately looking east toward the Soviet and Warsaw Pact threat since the end of WWII. The NATO Alliance epitomized Europe's concern over the Soviet threat and the SS-20 was just the latest illustration of this concern.

Asia, however, had viewed the Soviet threat differently. With the prominent exceptions of mainland China and Afghanistan, Asian states did not share a land border with the Soviets. Their concept of the Soviet threat was thus more abstract. Protected by water or intervening territory, Japan, Korea, and other Asian states did not suffer from Europe's migraine vision of Soviet armor rolling across open countryside. Yes, the Soviet military forces in the Far East were a potential threat to Asians. And Asian military establishments kept track of the order of battle numbers of Soviet naval vessels and aircraft and their regional military capabilities. But viscerally they were less concerned over the Soviets, who for the past 30 years they had considered Europe-centered in their politics and China-centered in their animosity.

Consequently, the Asian friends and Allies of the United States almost had to be taught the practical effects of the SS-20 and the nature of its unique threat for those within its targeting arc. One (perhaps apocryphal) story suggested that upon a visit by FRG

Chancellor Schmidt, Japanese Prime Minister Ohira did not know what the SS-20 was. Even if overstated, such an attitude marked much of Asian attitudes during the INF decade. As such, INF became and remained primarily an intellectual problem, and was reserved for the domain of arms control specialists in ministries of foreign affairs, defense officials, and think tank denizens. During their deployment, Soviet INF missiles were not and never became a matter of significant public concern. Certainly there was never any suggestion that the U.S. should deploy countervailing systems from Japan or even Korea.

This detached view of the INF threat and negotiations permitted Asian governments to operate independently of public opinion. Thus, such governments were more concerned that the process and outcome of the INF negotiations clearly take their interests into account than that a specific, consciously perceived threat be removed. It was important, for example, that an agreement not result in a transfer of Soviet systems from Europe to the Far East. Likewise, it was important that U.S./NATO proposals could be judged as handling European and Asian interests equally. Consequently, the proposal for an INF agreement stemming from the November 1986 Reykjavik summit that would have left one hundred Soviet INF warheads in Asia as their "global" limit was unsettling, even if explained as an interim measure, as it could be criticized by domestic opponents as discriminating against Asians.

U.S. Diplomatic Efforts

Although initially viewing INF as a NATO/Europe problem, the United States quickly realized its global nature. While the Alliance counter to Soviet INF deployments was limited to Europe (the United States never considered basing outside Europe), the global requirements for agreement were written into the basic Alliance position. Although consultations with Asian friends and allies were not as intense as with the NATO Alliance, following every significant U.S.-Soviet or Alliance meeting, a U.S. briefing team (most frequently headed by Ambassador Edward Rowny) would travel to the Far East to explain the details of the most recent developments. Likewise, U.S. officials in Washington and Geneva frequently briefed Asian colleagues on the status of INF negotiations, putting details of recent developments into context.

Indeed, the United States played the INF issue very carefully and ultimately with considerable success in Asia. We were successful in this regard because we gave Asian concerns real consideration. In particular, the United States was able effectively to stimulate Asian reaction to the concept of a 100 warhead "residual force." This concern was particularly expressed in Japan. Immediately following the Reykjavik Summit, Ambassador Rowny flew to Tokyo and other points in the Far East to outline the proposal. Japanese government officials were unconvinced by the rationales for a residual force, pointing out verification problems as well as their domestic concerns that the agreement would be perceived as discriminatory. Rowny relayed these concerns to Washington, and reportedly President Reagan eventually sent a message to Japanese Prime Minister Nakasonne, assuring him that the United States would continue to press for global zero.

By pointing out that the United States had always preferred global zero for INF systems, we were able to direct Asian critics at Moscow. This effort was ultimately successful, as the Japanese made a variety of demarches in Moscow critical of the residual force. Also of special note was an intervention by the PRC UN ambassador during a UN Conference at the Black Sea resort of Dagomys, between 6-13 June 1987. In the presence of ranking Soviet arms control officials, the Chinese urged global elimination of INF missiles: a point subsequently followed up by the U.S. delegation leader. It is perhaps coincidental, but still telling, that on 23 July Gorbachev announced through an interview published in an Indonesian newspaper that the Soviets were willing to accept global zero.

During the announcement and signature of the INF Treaty, Asian media and "man in the street" interviews aped leadership comment to the effect that the Treaty was a "good thing." Its importance for them personally, however, was regarded as trivial (if it were considered at all) in comparison to the persistent reaction by European publics.

With this background, the following is a review of selected current Asian attitudes toward the INF Treaty and what it may mean for Asia and arms control. Japanese officials were fully aware of the details of the INF Treaty. They were thoroughly informed during the course of the negotiations and vigorously propounded their views. Indeed, Japanese interest in U.S. INF decision-making was so extensive that one U.S. official suggested that a drawback of the INF negotiations was that it had "taught the Japanese to speak German."

Still, some Japanese remained puzzled over the extent of Soviet SS-20 deployments in the Far East. In retrospect, they viewed these missiles as militarily redundant, and presumably designed to send a political signal to U.S. regional allies. But this was not a judgment immediately perceived or acted upon, and it was not until the Williamsburg economic summit that Japanese PM Nakasone openly addressed the issue, and then only indirectly by noting that security was "indivisible." Nevertheless, the INF issue remained an official, rather than a public problem as the Japanese public was and is indifferent to INF.

Nevertheless, managing the Japanese role in the INF negotiations was very difficult for Tokyo. Throughout the negotiations, the essential Japanese requirement remained that any INF agreement not be perceived by the public as disadvantageous to Japan. Asian requirements needed to be given the same consideration as European concerns. This objective potentially put Japan at loggerheads with Europeans, interested in securing an INF agreement which would eliminate the Soviet threat (and coincidentally U.S. INF systems) from Europe. If Tokyo were to be too strident in protesting a potentially unequal agreement, it risked generating European animosity and charges of obstructionism. Japanese diplomats in Bonn in the early 1980's attempted to convince FRG officials that any INF agreement should be global zero (it was after all the official Alliance position) and garnered some intellectual sympathy but no real agreement. Japan, after all, was not hosting U.S. nuclear systems, and was getting a free ride from U.S. nuclear deterrence while paying none of the political costs of accepting U.S. nuclear deployments. Consequently, to make its points, Japan concentrated on consultations with the United States, while rarely discussing the issue in depth with NATO members. The "nightmare" scenario that the Soviets would succeed in playing European and Japanese interests against each other did not come to pass, but dwelt heavily in Japanese calculations throughout the negotiations.

Japanese an INF Winner

With the conclusion of the INF Treaty negotiations, and observing its ongoing implementation, clearly the Japanese believed that they came out of the INF negotiations a winner. They engaged for the first time in detailed consultations with the United States on arms control issues and won their points in Washington. The agreement was of "great historical significance," global in nature, and provided the effective verification vital for any agreement with Moscow. (One Japanese official commented that the Soviets have two means of verification: The *Washington Post* and Congress.) U.S. diplomacy is also credited in Japanese official circles with both having negotiated well and maintaining solidarity with allies: a considerable feat.

Military Judgments

Some military specialists note that as well as the overall SS-20 nuclear threat against Japanese cities, eliminating Soviet SS-20s/12s and SS-23s reduced the Soviet hard target kill capability, and consequently enhanced somewhat the survivability of many military bases. Other Japanese officials were less sanguine, commenting that the Soviets retained enough *theater* military capability to strike all Japanese military targets. Nonetheless, the INF Treaty leaves U.S. nuclear systems in the region unscathed, as they are sea-based. At the same time, Japanese strategic thinkers suggested that the INF outcome also enhanced stability by eliminating "fast flying" Soviet ballistic missiles that compacted the decision-making time for nuclear use.

Political Conclusions

Japanese officials have given considerable thought to the geostrategic circumstances of Northeast Asia and their political relationship with the Soviets. They were able to afford a degree of detachment as militarily they did not face a direct Soviet land threat, and politically they concluded that Japan remained a secondary theater for Soviet foreign policy attention with START and Sino-Soviet relations receiving primary effort. Japanese planners also benefited from public indifference/antipathy to the Soviet Union. An unofficial October 1988 poll suggested that those who felt hostile to the

Soviets outnumbered those who felt friendly by thirty-six percent to sixteen percent, despite some increase in friendly feeling to the Soviets in the previous year. Clearly there is no "Gorbomania" in Tokyo and no other "Western" public has such a negative opinion of Moscow.

Tokyo considers that the primary military balance in the region is naval and air rather than land and missile forces. In this regard, the U.S. naval presence is vital and provides a key element of linkage with the United States. Japanese officials stressed this linkage strongly; they reportedly stated during the INF negotiations that a trade of U.S. Japanese based F-16s and/or aircraft carriers in the region for Asian-based SS-20s would adversely affect U.S. regional strategy. In contrast, Tokyo believed Moscow was over-armed in the size of its Far East fleet, for which they had no strategic need equivalent to the Japanese requirement to protect sea lanes, trade, and maintaining linkage with the United States.

Likewise, Japanese views on nuclear deterrence differ from the European. NATO's doctrine of "flexible response" views Alliance response to Warsaw Pact aggression as potentially nuclear, indeed strategic, from the first moment of aggression. Conventional forces are linked to both tactical and strategic nuclear systems in a seamless web. To make a nuclear response more credible, U.S. nuclear weapons must be based in Europe. The greatest European politico-military concern was that the Soviets could perceive European-based forces as "decoupled" from the U.S. strategic deterrent, leaving Moscow free to fight a war, even at nuclear level, without risking attack from U.S. strategic forces. The Japanese, however, viewed such a philosophy as peculiar to Europe, where the conventional force balance fell against NATO and the potential for Soviet *blitzkrieg* had dominated Alliance military concern for 40 years.

In contrast, U.S./Japanese-Soviet conventional forces in northeast Asia were regarded as in much closer balance, with some quietly suggesting that the United States held an advantage. Under such circumstances, nuclear weapons were closer to being a last military resort (retaliation for a Soviet nuclear attack) than the principal deterrent of Soviet aggression.

Realistically, the Japanese noted a "geographic asymmetry" in Asia in that Japan and the Soviet Far East were not comparable strategic assets. Nuclear threats against targets in the Soviet Maritime Provinces would make little sense when more valuable Japanese targets would suffer from a Soviet response. In contrast, Western Europe and the European portion of the Soviet Union were closer strategic equivalents.

Next Steps

General public indifference to INF, and the current distractions of the "Recruit" scandal combined to continue to give Japanese officials a virtual free hand in determining policy for post INF arms control. Although the Soviets gained some credit for the INF Treaty and there were occasional challenges in the Diet, the Japanese government resisted quick response to assorted Soviet regional arms control proposals. During parliamentary discussion of the INF Treaty, for example, the GOJ responded to a Socialist question on elimination of nuclear systems by emphasizing that the Treaty eliminated a category of forces with deterrence maintained by U.S. and NATO forces. Thus, basic Japanese attitudes tended to emphasize that the Treaty addressed only a small percentage of total nuclear stockpiles and that the basic structure of the international situation, i.e., the Soviet threat, remained unaltered.

Against this backdrop, the Japanese saw no requirement for rapid regional arms control movement. They preferred global solutions, citing Chemical Weapons as the next case, and rejecting regional approaches "except for narrowly defined ground forces," i.e., the recently launched Conventional Armed Forces in Europe (CFE) negotiations (which should not, however, permit force transfers to the Far East). The Japanese saw Gorbachev as maneuvering to stimulate regional conventional force negotiations (which almost by definition would have to include naval forces) through his proposals at Vladivostok and Krasnoyarsk. While the Soviets wanted to switch military spending to civilian concerns, they still sought to remove U.S. military forces from both sides of the Eurasian continent: if not by force, then by arms control. Japanese officials recognized the potential public appeal of an Asian counterpoint to the CFE negotiations, but given the foregoing, saw no advantage to Tokyo. They also noted that Soviet short-range nuclear missiles (SNF) with ranges under 500 kilometers such as the SS-21 or FROG threatened selected Japanese targets, and that consequently Japan could benefit from regional elimination of these systems.

Instead, the Japanese argued, all such negotiations should be delayed until regional political issues had been resolved. They cited the example that in Europe, the Berlin problem and CSCE were agreed before NATO opened conventional forces discussions. In this regard, some officials cited three problems: Kampuchea, the divided Korean peninsula, and the "Northern Territories" (the four Kuril Islands taken by the Soviets at the end of World War II).

Such preconditions, in Japanese view, would defer regional arms control negotiations indefinitely. Vigorously as they sought return of the Northern Territories, Tokyo did not believe the Soviets could release them, fearing both political and military repercussions. For example, heavy Soviet SSBN deployments in the Sea of Okhotsk were protected by the Kuril chain, including the four Northern Territories islands, from U.S. naval penetration.

Still, if any regional CFE were to develop, either through Soviets meeting some or all of the implicit Japanese preconditions or through public pressure to match European arms control action, the Japanese would seek tough conditions including Soviet land and air reductions, not simply naval forces. Indeed, some argued that the United States and Japan as naval powers would suffer substantial disadvantages from any agreement to regional "equality," especially if we accepted a Soviet claim that we should take asymmetrical reductions in, for example, aircraft carriers (as they had accepted conceptually in negotiations such as INF, START, CW, and CFE).

In short, the Japanese government was groping for a post-INF arms control policy for the 1990s. Longstanding public hostility to the Soviets provided time for detailed consideration, and Tokyo was watching Washington closely for signals on how the Soviets were being treated.

A Korea-centric Seoul

Although U.S. diplomats regularly briefed Seoul on INF developments, Korean officials were careful to point out that these exchanges were on the level of information provided rather than "consultations." The U.S. assured Seoul that Asian interests would not be neglected or sacrificed, but it did not seek or suggest Korean diplomatic demarches on the topic. Nor did Seoul seek greater involvement. Such a "listening mode" on INF reflected both the status of the longstanding U.S.-ROK security relationship, in which the United States took care of cosmic issues such as nuclear deterrence, and Seoul focused on persuading Moscow to restrain any North Korean effort to disrupt the Olympic Games.

Consequently Korean officials emphasized the "symbolic" rather than the military effect of the INF Treaty. As Koreans did not view themselves as prospective targets for Soviet SS-20s, they did not view the Treaty as having affected the military balance on the Korean Peninsula. Strategically, they considered that the Treaty is Eurocentric, primarily designed to counter a European concern. The consequent Korean conclusion was psycho-political. They judged the Treaty as a prospective turning point in U.S.-Soviet relations designed to reduce military confrontation and perhaps start a new detente.

What such a relationship would mean for Northeast Asia and what Koreans should do about it was a subject for considerable debate. Would a more amicable U.S.-Soviet relationship be reflected on the Korean peninsula? Cautious ROK officials declared that Pyongyang had not changed its military or political outlook. It had not abandoned its official commitment to reunite Korea by force if necessary. There remained no substantial reduction in North-South military tension.

Pyongyang, in Seoul's view, had happily fished in the troubled waters of the ROK's domestic turmoil and refused the step-by-step process of moving from easier to harder issues in North-South discussions. Moreover, the Soviets had not been particularly helpful in reducing tensions with ROK officials, citing extensive Soviet military assistance and politico-military cooperation since 1985. It was a matter of indifference whether Soviet involvement with Pyongyang was to "control" the North or not. Instead they suggested that the North had succeeded in drawing Moscow deeper into its military affairs.

In prospective discussions with the ROK, Pyongyang maintained its focus on military issues: removal of U.S. nuclear weapons; removal of U.S. troops; end to U.S.-ROK military exercises. The

North's primary argument, i.e., that Soviet and Chinese forces were not stationed in the North and, therefore, U.S. military should leave the South frustrated the ROK, as it both played to growing national-ist sentiment in the South and left conservative officials concerned that any alteration in the formula that had maintained peace for the past 35 years could be profoundly destabilizing.

Official ROK skepticism, however, had not dampened popular Korean anticipation of changes. An inchoate public view suggest-ed that if there can be U.S.-Soviet detente, why not detente on the Korean peninsula? To a degree this attitude reflected an axiomatic challenge to official positions by an emerging domestic opposi-tion that had no policy other than the reverse of the government's. But, additionally, it was a response to the "peace is breaking out all over" international attitude that had characterized much of the analysis of foreign affairs.

Consequently, although bleakly predicting a dark future for substantive arms control in Northeast Asia, some suggested that the 1990s would be a period for arms control both between the United States and ROK as well as North-South. Others suggested a wider process, involving a variety of Northeast Asian states including the Soviets, Japan, and China. Any process, however, would be slow, as Asian experience in arms control negotiations was extremely lim-ited, in contrast to the generation-long series of substantive discus-sions on both nuclear and conventional forces in Europe.

With the United States

The extended U.S. military presence on the Korean peninsula has regularly come under review. At points, e.g., the opening of the Carter administration, this review was traumatic. Then, the im-petus was more likely to come from Seoul than from Washington. Seoul was slowly coming to the opinion that a studied, systemat-ic review of U.S. military presence could be to the advantage of both the United States and Korea. If it was accepted that U.S. forces should not remain "indefinitely," then when and how should they be drawn down? Obviously there were no answers; indeed, the question was barely ready to be posed. An ancillary issue is that of U.S. nuclear weapons in Korea. Despite U.S. official policy of nei-ther confirming nor denying the presence of nuclear weapons at any specific location, "99 percent" of the Korean population" believed nuclear weapons were deployed in Korea. The perception thus became the reality. And, concurrently, popular concern against such deployments was rising with momentum likely to increase.

With the North

The extremely cautious attitude toward Pyongyang appeared to be groping toward proposals for confidence building measures (CBMs). These are the "test drive" mechanisms of arms control, which by creating greater "transparency" between parties to an agreement can open the way for serious reductions proposals.

An Analytical Beijing

Beijing continued to view the INF Treaty positively, even warmly. Particularly appreciated was the global elimination of INF as "world peace is inseparable." But behind the opening statements endorsing the Treaty "wholeheartedly" and praising it as the first agreement to eliminate a class of nuclear weapons, Chinese officials hastened to add that it is only a "first step" dealing with no more than three to five percent of U.S. and Soviet nuclear arsenals, and that nothing had yet limited the qualitative aspects of the arms race.

Indeed, Chinese officials suggested that they had not paid a great deal of attention to SS-20 missiles prior to the Reykjavik Summit. Surprisingly, they viewed the missiles as a U.S.-Soviet issue and noted that they were not widely accepted as a threat to China. They held this view although recognizing that the SS-20 was designed to intimidate and hypothesizing that the Soviets sought both to damage U.S.-PRC-Japan relations and perhaps "detach China from the United States." PRC officials consequently concluded that the Treaty was more important politically than militarily. Its successful negotiation was viewed as an exercise in political will by the United States, but particularly attributed to Moscow. PRC officials concluded that a Soviet policy change toward INF was the basic reason for agreement as the Soviets made "far more concessions" than the United States. This change was attributed to Gorbachev, who was labeled "sincere" in his desire for arms control but, prior to the latter half of 1987, unable to fully control the process.

Chinese officials were reticent about their role in INF. Although some admitted bilateral pressures on Moscow for global elimination, others, perhaps from ignorance, denied it. One suggested that Chinese officials had convinced Ambassador Rowny that it was important to regional security interests to eliminate all SS-20s.

Next Steps

In PRC eyes, Gorbachev was impelled toward further arms control negotiations as serving Soviet national interests, by both assisting in support for national reform and alleviating domestic economic pressures. Conventional force reductions would help create better balance between civil and military budgets, as well as improving the Soviet international image. Nevertheless, the Soviets were most interested in strategic force reductions, as only such forces threatened their national survival (clearly Moscow did not fear a conventional force invasion by NATO).

Consequently, Beijing judged that the West was in a strong position to extract concessions. Although the Soviets would not accept obviously disadvantageous outcomes, e.g., conventional force reductions to NATO levels without NATO reductions, they would take disproportionate reductions. The Chinese believed that an agreement should disband such forces rather than permit their transfer (thus preventing a possible increase in Soviet Asian-based forces). The INF Treaty provided precedents for additional arms control agreements, particularly START, whose proposed reductions Beijing (unsurprisingly) supported. These precedents were partly technical, particularly in verification, where on-site inspection supplemented National Technical Means. Beyond the technical precedents, however, INF demonstrated the precedent of political will necessary for making tough agreements.

Chinese officials had quiet reservations about the depth of U.S. commitment to arms control. They noted the long delay in resuming nuclear arms negotiations consequent to the U.S. domestic review and hypothesized that the United States may have changed negotiating priorities with greater concern for a conventional force agreement in Europe rather than a strategic nuclear accord. They were skeptical that there would be any near term START progress. In reaching this interim conclusion, they observed President

George H.W. Bush's verbal restraint in characterizing Gorbachev and U.S. reluctance to endorse the judgment that "the cold war is over." They were closely watching the evolution of U.S. policy.

A Skeptical Taiwan

During the INF negotiations, U.S. officials did not visit or consult with Taiwan on this issue. Consequently, Taiwanese attitudes toward INF developed largely in isolation. Nevertheless, they essentially reflected the positions taken elsewhere, with distinctive twists reflecting Taiwan's anomalous international position. Thus, officials in the Republic of China (ROC) were blunt about INF. They had had no special concern over Soviet INF systems. Very little was written about INF ("papers don't get 1/20th the stories printed in the United States. People don't read 1/20 of what is printed"). This indifference was not because defense and foreign affairs experts were unaware of SS-20 range and capability, but more due to the ROC's total helplessness with respect to a potential threat. Their judgment was (a) the Soviets were not concerned with Taiwan; (b) if the Soviets ever decided to destroy Taiwan, they could do so virtually with a single SS-20 (or with a single MIRV'd strategic missile; (c) the United States must deal with whatever threat the Soviets posed.

Taiwan could not affect Soviet positions.

Thus in its overall effects, the ROC saw little military result from the INF Treaty. There was clear recognition that the INF Treaty affected only three to four percent of global nuclear forces, and that strategic systems could cover targets previously captured by INF. In their briefings, ROC military apparently used the anecdote of a soldier armed with artillery, machine guns, and pistols. Discarding a pistol, he asked if others felt less threatened. The judgment was that at least it was better than adding more pistols.

In assessing the consequences of the INF Treaty, ROC officials suggested that there were little direct effects on Taiwan, but any effects would be contingent upon PRC perceptions. For Taipei, the question was how Beijing would perceive U.S.-Soviet relations following the INF Treaty and consequently how Beijing would view its relations with Moscow. There are no conclusions yet to these questions.

Thus for the present, Taiwan remained focused on its "main enemy," the PRC, and what needed to be done to maintain independence. Here, they believed they had the ability to affect the outcome, particularly as over the years, the native Taiwanese have grown willing to resist any invasion attempt. At the same time, ROC officials judged that the likelihood of PRC invasion had diminished, and they felt "less threatened" than in the past. They concluded that the costs for Beijing would not be worth the prize, even if an invasion proved successful. Cynically, they suggested that Beijing was already well positioned to pick up the pieces and that Taiwanese (500,000 of whom visited the mainland the previous year) would provide more assistance through economic incentive than through coercion.

Dispute Resolution in Bilateral Arms Control
The INF Experience

JOHN A. WOODWORTH

The following text is a chapter titled "Dispute Resolution in Bilateral Arms Control: The INF Experience" in Peaceful Resolution of Major International Disputes, *edited by Julie Dahlitz and published by the United Nations in 1999.*

Introduction

INF, like any negotiation, had unique circumstances that governed its development. It was also a negotiation of a particular kind, with the purpose being arms control, with the subject being nuclear weapons, and with the participants being the two major powers of the second half of the Twentieth Century. This realm of negotiations was in many respects a world unto itself. Characteristically, the atmosphere was marked less by a sense of urgent crisis than by caution, calculation, and deliberateness. After all, the theoretical workings of nuclear deterrence that both sides had compelling reasons to try to understand have an apocalyptic character. Little wonder that the great debates of the nuclear era have often seemed akin to theology. Moreover, the coins of nuclear arms control negotiations are indeed rather different from the traditional coins of international disputes like land, resources, access, and control.

Within the world of nuclear arms control, INF itself was in many respects *sui generis.* Its political dimension was vast and complex. Its military dimension, although not of the scope and size of the strategic armaments at the heart of the Cold War superpower nuclear rivalry, had a dynamic quality stimulated by new systems and growing deployments. The United States and the Soviet Union as well as other countries with vital interests at stake were wrestling with problems for which there was little precedent.

Although one can readily see the distinctive features of INF, a close examination of the negotiation can also reveal some broad features that are potentially of universal relevance for dispute resolution. It would be a mistake to think that such features could serve as hard and fast rules for other cases. Nevertheless, profit can be gained from insights into how to think about, plan for, and conduct negotiations to resolve a wide range of bilateral as well as other disputes. This paper outlines some lessons that the INF experience may afford for dispute resolution more generally.

INF Overview

To set the stage for this examination, it is useful to highlight in a few words the key events and characteristics of the INF negotiations. The INF story was an intrinsically interesting one, full of international drama. It extended well beyond just the negotiations in Geneva. This short paper cannot begin to do justice to what was one of the defining episodes of the Cold War.

The negotiations themselves stretched over a period of more than seven years. In a little known opening chapter, four weeks of so-called preliminary talks were held in Geneva during October and November 1980. Formal negotiations were finally initiated in November 1981 following a period of extensive policy review at the beginning of the Reagan administration. This stage of talks lasted for two years, until the Soviet team suspended the negotiations in November 1983 when NATO deployed the first Pershing II and ground-launched cruise missiles in the United Kingdom and the Federal Republic of Germany. The INF talks, and the parallel negotiations on strategic arms, remained in suspension for more than a year. After prolonged and difficult diplomatic exchanges, they were resumed in March 1985 in a broadened three-part format that included INF, strategic, and defense and space arms—the so-called NST, or Nuclear and Space Talks.

The newly charged and ultimately successful INF negotiations took place over the next two and one-half years, culminating in the signing of the INF Treaty by President Reagan and General Secretary Gorbachev at their Washington summit on 8 December

1987. The passage of INF through this period was marked by significant ebbs and flows. The prospects for a successful outcome were not firmly in view until late in the talks. The final weeks were especially intense and arduous. The outcome re-wrote much of the book on superpower nuclear arms control, eliminating whole classes of weapons for the first time, breaking new ground in verification, setting new standards for subsequent bilateral as well as multilateral agreements, and marking a significant new phase in the waning of the Cold War era. As a notable event historically, INF offers interesting insights into various dimensions of dispute resolution.

Understanding the Broad Context

Practical results in dispute resolution depend on a correct understanding of the circumstances governing a specific negotiation. In its essence, INF unfolded in the context of competition between Cold War rivals locked in an adversary relationship. The negotiations were directed toward the specific arms control task of lessening the risks and dangers of nuclear competition. But this effort was shaped by much wider political imperatives. Underlying distrust, which could be lessened but not dispelled, dictated much of the pace of the negotiations and many of the issues that had to be solved. INF could affect to only a limited degree the more fundamental differences in U.S.-Soviet relations. Ultimate resolution of these would depend on broader political developments.

One way to understand the achievement of INF, then, was the success the agreement represented in accomplishing bold steps but without engaging still larger stakes. The implication for dispute resolution more generally is the task—indeed art—of securing as much as can be achieved without foundering on goals that reach too far. The broad context of a dispute will determine the limits of what can be accomplished. Step-by-step progress, grounded in existing realities, can pave the way to subsequent and more ambitious endeavors.

Getting to the Negotiating Table

In any dispute situation, the first and often high hurdle is securing agreement to sit down at the negotiating table. INF was no exception.

Exchanges about INF systems between the United States and Soviet Union stretched back to SALT I and SALT II. The Soviet Union sought on various occasions to bring so-called "forward based systems" into these talks. The United States would not consider doing this unless comparable Soviet systems were also considered, e.g., MRBMs and IRBMs. These issues were dropped in both negotiations in the interest of moving forward with agreements on strategic arms.

It was clear from these discussions, though, that both sides were edging toward the likelihood of talks on INF. The precipitating developments were the Soviet deployment of SS-20 missiles beginning in 1977, and the NATO "double track decision" of December 1979 to deploy new missiles in Europe and to call for negotiations on INF between the United States and Soviet Union. These developments changed the political-strategic landscape and led to an eventual convergence of interests to join in talks.

To reach this point, which was far from a linear progression, specific steps were necessary that in their nature could have general relevance for starting negotiations in other cases of dispute.

First, it was necessary for preparations to mature. On the U.S. side, INF was intrinsically linked to NATO security. An extended consultation process was launched to develop a common view of the desirability of INF negotiations and of principles that should govern its conduct. Preparations such as these, although time-consuming in the case of INF, can be important for subsequent effectiveness in negotiations.

Second, preconditions had to be dropped. Typically, preconditions seek to freeze a result on one or more issues in dispute, or to leverage outcomes on unrelated issues. Such moves will generally prove to be barriers to the initiation of negotiations. In INF, the Soviet Union dropped its early insistence that NATO reverse its deployment decision as a condition for talks to begin.

Third, it was necessary to avoid over-definition of subject matter. It was clear from discussions in SALT, public pronouncements, and diplomatic exchanges that there were distinctly differing views about what an INF agreement might cover. However, both countries set these differences aside in deciding to enter into talks, recognizing that such issues would constitute the substantive heart of subsequent negotiations. These moves proved essential to allow talks to get underway.

Fourth, it was necessary to separate one subject from others. In the case of INF, this meant forging agreement to address this category of systems separately from strategic arms. This required changes on both sides. The United States, in consultation with its Allies, initially saw INF as proceeding in the framework of SALT, with the exact meaning of this formulation undefined. With SALT II ratification stalled in the U.S. Congress, however, it was agreed to let INF proceed separately. The Soviet Union, for its part, had to overcome its longstanding preference to lump U.S. "forward based systems" together with U.S. strategic arms. The combination allowed INF talks to begin.

While these steps allowed INF negotiations to get underway, the sides entered the preliminary talks in 1980 and the formal INF negotiations in 1981 with fundamentally contradictory objectives— for the United States, to support INF deployments with a negotiating track and to bolster NATO, and for the Soviet Union, to block INF deployments and to divide NATO. These contradictory objectives notwithstanding, getting a negotiating process in motion set the stage for subsequent progress and ultimate agreement.

Phases of Negotiations

INF progressed through several phases that were distinct in their nature but frequently overlapping in their development. These phases can be seen as characteristic of negotiations in general, with each offering insights into how different levels of issues can be solved. Each phase in INF confronted the task of resolving differences by sorting essential interests from lesser ones, and broadening convergence through persuasion or compromise. Core issues were settled largely as a result of shifting incentives rather than through concessions. Other differences yielded to logic and facts, or were settled through trade-offs. Typically, the resolution of larger issues moved lesser issues forward in significance and frequently in difficulty. Real bottom-lines were opaque, but in retrospect proved malleable over time.

The first phase in INF involved the presentation and exploration of basic positions. This was accomplished during the opening stages, through formal statements and then intensive questioning and discussion of rationale, facts, and priorities. These explorations were essential in clarifying positions, identifying differences, and testing the seriousness of interests. At different points in the negotiation, when basic positions underwent change, as they did for both sides, this process was replayed. There were no fixed timelines. Indeed, during the first two years of INF, the negotiations never got substantially beyond this first phase. The differences were marked and, during this period, irreconcilable.

The second and most critical phase of INF involved resolution of core issues about what the agreement would cover. This was the substantive heart of the negotiation. Settlement of these issues was necessary before other phases could progress, although the sequence overlapped as new core issues emerged during the course of the talks. Perhaps the most interesting question—and perhaps the most difficult to answer—is what caused the eventual convergence on core issues that permitted an agreement to emerge.

The key core issues in INF involved (1) the systems to be included; (2) the principle of equal outcomes; (3) the level of limitations, that is, a finite number or zero; (4) the geographic coverage of an agreement; and (5) verification. The first three of these issues could not be finally settled until agreement was reached to exclude accounting for third-country systems, i.e., French and British nuclear forces. The overall process was long and arduous, with core issues passing through various bargaining stages. Most were not settled in their final form until the last months of a seven-year negotiation.

How, then, were core issues resolved, and what implications are there for dispute resolution more generally? The resolution of these issues in INF rested fundamentally on shifting incentives. One of the critical variables here were changing facts on the ground reflected in the deployment of Pershing II and ground-launched cruise missiles. For NATO this represented the demonstration of political will and the commitment of resources and endeavor. The Soviet position remained consistent throughout the negotiations in ultimately refusing to condone these deployments in Europe. This led inexorably to final agreement on zero.

Factors other than shifting incentives also played a part in the settlement of core issues. One was use of facts and logic. This was necessary in setting the foundation for and sustaining the defense of basic positions; it was also essential in convincing publics of the merits of negotiating proposals. For example, arguments over the bedeviling question of third-country systems were largely carried out in terms of logic. In another example, the Soviet effort to include aircraft in an agreement ultimately yielded to explanations of the complexities and difficulties in finding equitable and practicable solutions. Both sides ultimately agreed to put the aircraft issue aside.

Compromises and trade-offs also had a part in helping to solve some core issues. Soviet demands for a solution to the deployment and modernization of Federal Republic of Germany Pershing I missiles was settled through a tacit compromise outside the negotiation, wherein the Federal Republic announced a decision to eliminate its Pershing I missiles in parallel with implementation of a zero INF agreement. The final push to the so-called double global zero outcome was aided at least in part by a trade-off in which the Soviet Union agreed to go to zero and the United States dropped the most intrusive measures from its verification position. Other complex factors also contributed to this outcome.

The third phase of negotiations dealt with settlement of issues of substantive content and technical detail derived from the solutions to core issues. It is here that one meets the challenges reflected in the old saying that "the devil is in the details." There were innumerable issues in this phase, ranging from agreeing on criteria for establishing the range boundaries for the missiles covered by the agreement, to defining the specific elements for an ambitious Memorandum of Understanding on Data. Of interest to discussion are the methods that were used to resolve these kinds of issues.

This phase depended more than any other on argumentation of fact. Distrust and security considerations impeded gaining full value from use of facts by both sides. But on many of these issues, there were relatively objective answers to solutions for particular problems. Thus, trade-offs and compromises were often not a useful or effective way to resolve them. In other cases, where the changes would not put important interests at risk, these negotiating methods could be used to varying degrees.

A large proportion of issues in this phase, especially in the last stages of negotiations, centered on verification. The United States was demandeur on most of these issues, but the Soviet Union insisted on equal application of measures. A critical example where this came into play concerned permanent monitoring. The United States demanded a permanent monitoring arrangement at Votkinsk in the Urals to ensure that SS-20 missiles were not produced under cover of production of the outwardly similar SS-25 ICBM. The U.S. agreed to establish a comparable monitoring arrangement at Magna, Utah, where Pershing rocket motors were previously produced, not because the Soviet Union had serious concerns about Pershing production in violation of the agreement, but rather in order to meet Soviet demands for equal treatment.

An important process of this phase of the negotiations was breaking down issues into manageable parts so that more important ones could be solved to open the way to the next level of issues. As lesser issues surfaced, their significance took on magnified importance. Issues had to be sorted for those that could prove to be "treaty breakers" and others that did not have this character. The distinction between tactical bargaining and substantive importance was not always clear. Pressure was also augmented by a deadline (the December 1987 summit) under which INF operated in its final stage. Deadlines can have value for forcing closure but can also be susceptible to brinkmanship. The price can be imprecision and later controversy.

The final phase of negotiations was translating the substance of agreement into Treaty legal text. Indeed, this all-important phase is ultimately where all issues come home to roost. In practice, treaty drafting and the prior phase of resolving substantive and technical details often blended together. That is, issues were resolved, and in some cases even identified, in the process of developing agreed formulations for Treaty text. The drafting process, in addition to accomplishing the obvious purpose of producing a formal agreement, has the ancillary benefit of maintaining a rolling record of where a negotiation stands.

An issue in this last phase is when it should or can begin. There is advantage in starting early to codify congruence in small steps. Such work can proceed while core issues still remain outstanding. Typically though (and INF was no exception) the phase of drafting an agreement cannot realistically get underway until the parties have tabled draft treaties reflecting their respective positions. Apart from setting the stage for joint preparation of an agreement, this step serves the valuable purposes of signaling seriousness, clarifying positions, and helping in the identification of differences that must be solved.

Processes for Issue Resolution

A combination of negotiating activities both inside and outside the Geneva talks provided the synergy necessary to reach agreement in INF. The negotiating work in Geneva constituted only a part of the picture. Core issues were largely settled through heads-of-state public statements or summit meetings. Many other substantive issues were resolved through Ministerial or high-level expert meetings. For example, the basic U.S. proposal for the elimination of INF missiles was set out in President Reagan's speech of 18 November 1981. Comparable statements of the Soviet position were enunciated initially by General Secretary Brezhnev.

During the second period of INF negotiations, meetings between President Reagan and General Secretary Gorbachev, in particular at Reykjavik in October 1986, and subsequent public pronouncements by both leaders, marked key milestones in the talks. In the final run-up to the December 1987 U.S.-Soviet summit, Secretary of State Schultz and Foreign Minister Shevardnadze met four times to resolve outstanding issues, most of which concerned verification.

The Geneva delegations were agents of authorities in capitals and conducted negotiations under close instructions. Their role was essential for elaborating positions, clarifying concerns and interests, setting the stage for resolution of core issues, resolving most remaining issues, and preparing the Treaty. The delegations used a full range of procedural tools for carrying out these activities—the stuff of a negotiation. These included formal plenary meetings for presentation and elaboration of positions, meetings of delegation heads and deputies, informal sessions, working groups, and treaty drafting committees.

Using this complex of activities proved essential in forging progress, especially in the critical closing months. Comparable approaches could have value for other dispute resolution cases. It is also critical to have the right quality and scope of expertise that is needed to negotiate effectively and authoritatively. Quite obviously, INF could not have progressed successfully without the combination of political, strategic, military, and technical experts who were available on both delegations.

It is necessary to add a word about *ad referendum* explorations. At critical junctures, a negotiation can profit from the skillful exploration of solutions to issues that differ from formal positions. This can help uncover a deeper understanding of concerns, interests, and even bottom lines, and ultimately can serve to open new avenues to progress. But there can be delicate questions surrounding such efforts. Preserving credibility, avoiding dangers of unwanted or unintended signals, and misreading backing in capitals can prove to be pitfalls with potential dysfunctional effects. In INF lore, the "walk-in-the-woods" was the best known episode of this kind. Without commenting on the merits of the endeavor, which was bold and imaginative, the outcome did not alter the fundamental differences that prevailed in INF at that time.

The Necessity of Innovation

Within the realm of arms control negotiations, INF was notable for the innovations it produced. The elimination of a whole class of weapons systems was unprecedented, requiring agreement on a host of new measures to perform and account for the destruction of missiles, equipment, and facilities. The verification regime was the most stringent ever negotiated, marking a new phase in the capacity of the United States and Soviet Union to deal with increasingly ambitious arms control goals. In another innovation, INF, even though bilateral, had to be accompanied by agreements with third-countries to allow for U.S. and Soviet inspections on their territories. These agreements posed interesting diplomatic challenges that had to be carefully surmounted.

Creativity, willingness to experiment, and extensive technical input were essential to resolution of these and other tasks. Such features have relevance for other negotiations. They point toward the value of embracing innovation for solving specific problems. Success in doing so requires mutual will, of course, but also underscores the importance of openness to new ideas.

The Political Dimension Surrounding Negotiations

INF had a uniquely high political profile as a focal point of Cold War confrontation in Europe. The negotiation of core issues in particular was conducted heavily through high-level public diplomacy. Positions on both sides were developed and argued with an eye to their public impact. The competition for public support had to be played out before negotiations could get down to the serious business of hammering out the terms of an agreement. In short, what was happening outside the negotiations was at least as important as what was happening inside the talks.

In this light, any negotiation must take due account of the surrounding political circumstances. If the governing problem lies outside the talks, then this will dictate a particular strategy. It will also affect the viability of the practice of confidentiality, which otherwise is a desirable ingredient for successful dispute resolution. In INF, the rule was established but in practice was confined to details and to day-to-day negotiations.

With respect to the political dimension, it is also important to note the role of legislative connections. In democratic parliaments where ratification of agreements might be controversial, there are ample grounds for bending efforts to promote contact between legislators, government decision-makers, and negotiators. These efforts can involve delicate questions of the balance between executive and legislative branches, which indeed vary under different democratic systems. But since both branches must play a part in the ultimate success of a negotiation, i.e., consent to ratification, careful attention must be paid to promoting support in the legislature, especially where negotiations are controversial. This was certainly true in the U.S. Congress.

Conclusions

The INF experience points toward a number of lessons that could be useful for future international dispute resolution. The following summary conclusions represent some principal examples:

- Practical results in dispute resolution depend on accurately understanding and taking due account of the limits and possibilities imposed by the prevailing context. This point generally dictates the need for step-by-step agreements;
- Launching negotiations despite fundamentally contradictory objectives can achieve the desirable goal of setting a dispute resolution process in motion. Getting to this point can be facilitated by propelling necessary unilateral preparations, dropping preconditions, avoiding over-definition of subject matter, and separating out one potentially self-standing area of dispute from others;
- Clarity of principles and core positions with defendable *mutual* advantages provide good foundation for a sustained negotiating effort. The contrary point is that positions aimed toward unilateral advantage will stall progress;
- The bottom lines in negotiations are generally opaque, often unformed, and can be susceptible to being shaped and changed. New circumstances can also breed new possibilities;
- *Ad referendum* explorations can be helpful for uncovering positions, interests, and solutions, but also can carry risks if not well grounded and executed;
- Synergy between negotiating activities inside and outside of talks is critical. Also, making full use of a full range of delegation activities—plenaries, informal discussions, working groups, etc.—promotes progress and optimizes use of expertise;
- Linkage of a negotiation to external requirements should be compelling substantively since doing so tactically frequently only impedes progress; and
- Finally, political will is essential to reach any agreement, and ultimately for major issues this must come from top leadership.

Vignette: A Moment at Midnight

It was midnight in the U.S. Mission on 6 December, and time to initial the completed INF Treaty and its Elimination Protocol. The first two of the four Treaty documents had completed the rigorous process of preparation on official treaty paper in both English and Russian and were ready for "initialing" by the U.S. and Soviet ambassadors. By placing their initials on each page of the text, the ambassadors indicated that the text was agreed. Ahead lay the ceremony of Presidential signature; of White House pomp and circumstance; and the sonorous tones of history marching to its documented drumbeat. This moment at midnight, however, was the delegation's time.

There was a mixture of magic and mundane. The room was ablaze with light. The U.S. team, many hearing at the last minute that there would be an initialing ceremony, had gathered. The team that had "done the Treaty," all who were awake and available: officers, secretaries, support technicians, interpreters were there for the highlight of their Geneva experience.

The American negotiator, informal as benefited a midnight mission in flannel shirt and sports jacket, initialed each page with a separate pen. The delegation's Executive Secretary, quietly preparing for the moment for weeks, had purchased scores of pens each appropriately inscribed "INF Treaty 1987."

The Soviet ambassador initialed steadily in quiet formality. He appeared satisfied rather than exhilarated.

There was no official photographer. A few Instamatics flashed. But by and large, it was a moment frozen in the mind's eye rather than trapped on celluloid. And it was a time for tears. Tears of joy; tears of exhaustion; tears that marked the end of tension.

Still later there was champagne—with a taste of salt.

Appendix: INF Treaty Text

What follows is the full English text of the Treaty, including the Memoranda of Understanding on Elimination and Inspection, as well as the Corrigenda and diplomatic exchanges of notes associated with the treaty. The only material not included here is the MOU on Data Exchange, which is too long and complex to include in a memoir of this nature. For those interested, it can be found in the State Department's online archives at <http://www.state.gov/t/avc/trty/102360.htm>.

TREATY BETWEEN THE UNITED STATES OF AMERICA AND THE UNION OF SOVIET SOCIALIST REPUBLICS ON THE ELIMINATION OF THEIR INTERMEDIATE-RANGE AND SHORTER-RANGE MISSILES

Signed at Washington December 8, 1987
Ratification advised by U.S. Senate May 27, 1988
Instruments of ratification exchanged June 1, 1988
Entered into force June 1, 1988
Proclaimed by U.S. President December 27, 1988

The United States of America and the **Union of Soviet Socialist Republics**, hereinafter referred to as the Parties,

Conscious that nuclear war would have devastating consequences for all mankind,

Guided by the objective of strengthening strategic stability,

Convinced that the measures set forth in this Treaty will help to reduce the risk of outbreak of war and strengthen international peace and security, and

Mindful of their obligations under Article VI of the Treaty on the Non-Proliferation of Nuclear Weapons,

Have agreed as follows:

Article I

In accordance with the provisions of this Treaty which includes the Memorandum of Understanding and Protocols which form an integral part thereof, each Party shall eliminate its intermediate-range and shorter-range missiles, not have such systems thereafter, and carry out the other obligations set forth in this Treaty.

Article II

For the purposes of this Treaty:

1. The term "ballistic missile" means a missile that has a ballistic trajectory over most of its flight path. The term "ground-launched ballistic missile (GLBM)" means a ground-launched ballistic missile that is a weapon-delivery vehicle.

2. The term "cruise missile" means an unmanned, self-propelled vehicle that sustains flight through the use of aerodynamic lift over most of its flight path. The term "ground-launched cruise missile (GLCM)" means a ground-launched cruise missile that is a weapon-delivery vehicle.

3. The term "GLBM launcher" means a fixed launcher or a mobile land-based transporter-erector-launcher mechanism for launching a GLBM.

4. The term "GLCM launcher" means a fixed launcher or a mobile land-based transporter-erector-launcher mechanism for launching a GLCM.

5. The term "intermediate-range missile" means a GLBM or a GLCM having a range capability in excess of 1000 kilometers but not in excess of 5500 kilometers.

6. The term "shorter-range missile" means a GLBM or a GLCM having a range capability equal to or in excess of 500 kilometers but not in excess of 1000 kilometers.

7. The term "deployment area" means a designated area within which intermediate-range missiles and launchers of such missiles may operate and within which one or more missile operating bases are located.

8. The term "missile operating base" means:

   (a) in the case of intermediate-range missiles, a complex of facilities, located within a deployment area, at which intermediate-range missiles and launchers of such missiles normally operate, in which support structures associated with such missiles and launchers are also located and in which support equipment associated with such missiles and launchers is normally located; and

   (b) in the case of shorter-range missiles, a complex of facilities, located any place, at which shorter-range missiles and launchers of such missiles normally operate and in which support equipment associated with such missiles and launchers is normally located.

9. The term "missile support facility," as regards intermediate-range or shorter-range missiles and launchers of such missiles, means a missile production facility or a launcher production facility, a missile repair facility or a launcher repair facility, a training facility, a missile storage facility or a launcher storage facility, a test range, or an elimination facility as those terms are defined in the Memorandum of Understanding.

10. The term "transit" means movement, notified in accordance with paragraph 5(f) of Article IX of this Treaty, of an intermediate-range missile or a launcher of such a missile between missile support facilities, between such a facility and a deployment area or between deployment areas, or of a shorter-range missile or a launcher of such a missile from a missile support facility or a missile operating base to an elimination facility.

11. The term "deployed missile" means an intermediate-range missile located within a deployment area or a shorter-range missile located at a missile operating base.

12. The term "non-deployed missile" means an intermediate-range missile located outside a deployment area or a shorter-range missile located outside a missile operating base.

13. The term "deployed launcher" means a launcher of an intermediate-range missile located within a deployment area or a launcher of a shorter-range missile located at a missile operating base.

14. The term "non-deployed launcher" means a launcher of an intermediate-range missile located outside a deployment area or a launcher of a shorter-range missile located outside a missile operating base.

15. The term "basing country" means a country other than the United States of America or the Union of Soviet Socialist Republics on whose territory intermediate-range or shorter-range missiles of the Parties, launchers of such missiles or support structures associated with such missiles and launchers

were located at any time after November 1, 1987. Missiles or launchers in transit are not considered to be "located."

Article III

1. For the purposes of this Treaty, existing types of intermediate-range missiles are:

   (a) for the United States of America, missiles of the types designated by the United States of America as the Pershing II and the BGM-109G, which are known to the Union of Soviet Socialist Republics by the same designations; and

   (b) for the Union of Soviet Socialist Republics, missiles of the types designated by the Union of Soviet Socialist Republics as the RSD-10, the R-12 and the R-14, which are known to the United States of America as the SS-20, the SS-4 and the SS-5, respectively.

2. For the purposes of this Treaty, existing types of shorter-range missiles are:

   (a) for the United States of America, missiles of the type designated by the United States of America as the Pershing IA, which is known to the Union of Soviet Socialist Republics by the same designation; and

   (b) for the Union of Soviet Socialist Republics, missiles of the types designated by the Union of Soviet Socialist Republics as the OTR-22 and the OTR-23, which are known to the United States of America as the SS-12 and the SS-23, respectively.

Article IV

1. Each Party shall eliminate all its intermediate-range missiles and launchers of such missiles, and all support structures and support equipment of the categories listed in the Memorandum of Understanding associated with such missiles and launchers, so that no later than three years after entry into force of this Treaty and thereafter no such missiles, launchers, support structures or support equipment shall be possessed by either Party.

2. To implement paragraph 1 of this Article, upon entry into force of this Treaty, both Parties shall begin and continue throughout the duration of each phase, the reduction of all types of their deployed and non-deployed intermediate-range missiles and deployed and non-deployed launchers of such missiles and support structures and support equipment associated with such missiles and launchers in accordance with the provisions of this Treaty. These reductions shall be implemented in two phases so that:

(a) by the end of the first phase, that is, no later than 29 months after entry into force of this Treaty:

    (i) the number of deployed launchers of intermediate-range missiles for each Party shall not exceed the number of launchers that are capable of carrying or containing at one time missiles considered by the Parties to carry 171 warheads;

    (ii) the number of deployed intermediate-range missiles for each Party shall not exceed the number of such missiles considered by the Parties to carry 180 warheads;

    (iii) the aggregate number of deployed and non-deployed launchers of intermediate-range missiles for each Party shall not exceed the number of launchers that are capable of carrying or containing at one time missiles considered by the Parties to carry 200 warheads;

    (iv) the aggregate number of deployed and non-deployed intermediate-range missiles for each Party shall not exceed the number of such missiles considered by the Parties to carry 200 warheads; and

    (v) the ratio of the aggregate number of deployed and non-deployed intermediate-range GLBMs of existing types for each Party to the aggregate number of deployed and non-deployed intermediate-range missiles of existing types possessed by that Party shall not exceed the ratio of such intermediate-range GLBMs to such intermediate-range missiles for that Party as of November 1, 1987, as set forth in the Memorandum of Understanding; and

(b) by the end of the second phase, that is, no later than three years after entry into force of this Treaty, all intermediate-range missiles of each Party, launchers of such missiles and all support structures and support equipment of the categories listed in the Memorandum of Understanding associated with such missiles and launchers, shall be eliminated.

Article V

1. Each Party shall eliminate all its shorter-range missiles and launchers of such missiles, and all support equipment of the categories listed in the Memorandum of Understanding associated with such missiles and launchers, so that no later than 18 months after entry into force of this Treaty and thereafter no such missiles, launchers or support equipment shall be possessed by either Party.

2. No later than 90 days after entry into force of this Treaty, each Party shall complete the removal of all its deployed shorter-range missiles and deployed and non-deployed launchers of such missiles to elimination facilities and shall retain them at those locations until they are eliminated in accordance with the procedures set forth in the Protocol on Elimination. No later than 12 months after entry into force of this Treaty, each Party shall complete the removal of all its non-deployed shorter-range missiles to elimination facilities and shall retain them at those locations until they are eliminated in accordance with the procedures set forth in the Protocol on Elimination.

3. Shorter-range missiles and launchers of such missiles shall not be located at the same elimination facility. Such facilities shall be separated by no less than 1000 kilometers.

Article VI

1. Upon entry into force of this Treaty and thereafter, neither Party shall:

   (a) produce or flight-test any intermediate-range missiles or produce any stages of such missiles or any launchers of such missiles; or

(b) produce, flight-test or launch any shorter-range missiles or produce any stages of such missiles or any launchers of such missiles.

2. Notwithstanding paragraph 1 of this Article, each Party shall have the right to produce a type of GLBM not limited by this Treaty which uses a stage which is outwardly similar to, but not interchangeable with, a stage of an existing type of intermediate-range GLBM having more than one stage, providing that that Party does not produce any other stage which is outwardly similar to, but not interchangeable with, any other stage of an existing type of intermediate-range GLBM.

Article VII

For the purposes of this Treaty:

1. If a ballistic missile or a cruise missile has been flight-tested or deployed for weapon delivery, all missiles of that type shall be considered to be weapon-delivery vehicles.

2. If a GLBM or GLCM is an intermediate-range missile, all GLBMs or GLCMs of that type shall be considered to be intermediate-range missiles. If a GLBM or GLCM is a shorter-range missile, all GLBMs or GLCMs of that type shall be considered to be shorter-range missiles.

3. If a GLBM is of a type developed and tested solely to intercept and counter objects not located on the surface of the earth, it shall not be considered to be a missile to which the limitations of this Treaty apply.

4. The range capability of a GLBM not listed in Article III of this Treaty shall be considered to be the maximum range to which it has been tested. The range capability of a GLCM not listed in Article III of this Treaty shall be considered to be the maximum distance which can be covered by the missile in its standard design mode flying until fuel exhaustion, determined by projecting its flight path onto the earth's sphere from the point of launch to the point of impact. GLBMs or GLCMs that have a range capability equal to or in excess of 500 kilometers but not

in excess of 1000 kilometers shall be considered to be shorter-range missiles. GLBMs or GLCMs that have a range capability in excess of 1000 kilometers but not in excess of 5500 kilometers shall be considered to be intermediate-range missiles.

5. The maximum number of warheads an existing type of inter-mediate-range missile or shorter-range missile carries shall be considered to be the number listed for missiles of that type in the Memorandum of Understanding.

6. Each GLBM or GLCM shall be considered to carry the maximum number of warheads listed for a GLBM or GLCM of the type in the Memorandum of Understanding.

7. If a launcher has been tested for launching a GLBM or a GLCM, all launchers of that type shall be considered to have been tested for launching GLBMs or GLCMs.

8. If a launcher has contained or launched a particular type of GLBM or GLCM, all launchers of that type shall be considered to be launchers of that type of GLBM or GLCM.

9. The number of missiles each launcher of an existing type of inter-mediate-range missile or shorter-range missile shall be considered to be capable of carrying or containing at one time is the number listed for launchers of missiles of that type in the Memorandum of Understanding.

10. Except in the case of elimination in accordance with the procedures set forth in the Protocol on Elimination, the following shall apply:

    (a) for GLBMs which are stored or moved in separate stages, the longest stage of an intermediate-range or shorter-range GLBM shall be counted as a complete missile;

    (b) for GLBMs which are not stored or moved in separate stages, a canister of the type used in the launch of an intermediate-range GLBM, unless a Party proves to the satisfaction of the other Party that it does not contain such a missile, or an assembled intermediate-range or shorter-range GLBM, shall be counted as a complete missile; and

    (c) for GLCMs, the airframe of an intermediate-range or shorter-range GLCM shall be counted as a complete missile.

11. A ballistic missile which is not a missile to be used in a ground-based mode shall not be considered to be a GLBM if it is test-launched at a test site from a fixed land-based launcher which is used solely for test purposes and which is distinguishable from GLBM launchers. A cruise missile which is not a missile to be used in a ground-based mode shall not be considered to be a GLCM if it is test-launched at a test site from a fixed land-based launcher which is used solely for test purposes and which is distinguishable from GLCM launchers.

12. Each Party shall have the right to produce and use for booster systems, which might otherwise be considered to be intermediate-range or shorter-range missiles, only existing types of booster stages for such booster systems. Launches of such booster systems shall not be considered to be flight-testing of intermediate-range or shorter-range missiles provided that:

    (a) stages used in such booster systems are different from stages used in those missiles listed as existing types of intermediate-range or shorter-range missiles in Article III of this Treaty;

    (b) such booster systems are used only for research and development purposes to test objects other than the booster systems themselves;

    (c) the aggregate number of launchers for such booster systems shall not exceed 35 for each Party at any one time; and

    (d) the launchers for such booster systems are fixed, emplaced above ground and located only at research and development launch sites which are specified in the Memorandum of Understanding.

Research and development launch sites shall not be subject to inspection pursuant to Article XI of this Treaty.

Article VIII

1. All intermediate-range missiles and launchers of such missiles shall be located in deployment areas, at missile support facilities or shall be in transit. Intermediate-range missiles or launchers of such missiles shall not be located elsewhere.

2. Stages of intermediate-range missiles shall be located in deployment areas, at missile support facilities or moving between deployment areas, between missile support facilities or between missile support facilities and deployment areas.

3. Until their removal to elimination facilities as required by paragraph 2 of Article V of this Treaty, all shorter-range missiles and launchers of such missiles shall be located at missile operating bases, at missile support facilities or shall be in transit. Shorter-range missiles or launchers of such missiles shall not be located elsewhere.

4. Transit of a missile or launcher subject to the provisions of this Treaty shall be completed within 25 days.

5. All deployment areas, missile operating bases and missile support facilities are specified in the Memorandum of Understanding or in subsequent updates of data pursuant to paragraphs 3, 5(a) or 5(b) of Article IX of this Treaty. Neither Party shall increase the number of, or change the location or boundaries of, deployment areas, missile operating bases or missile support facilities, except for elimination facilities, from those set forth in the Memorandum of Understanding. A missile support facility shall not be considered to be part of a deployment area even though it may be located within the geographic boundaries of a deployment area.

6. Beginning 30 days after entry into force of this Treaty, neither Party shall locate intermediate-range or shorter-range missiles, including stages of such missiles, or launchers of such missiles at missile production facilities, launcher production facilities or test ranges listed in the Memorandum of Understanding.

7. Neither Party shall locate any intermediate-range or shorter-range missiles at training facilities.

8. A non-deployed intermediate-range or shorter-range missile shall not be carried on or contained within a launcher of such a type of missile, except as required for maintenance conducted at repair facilities or for elimination by means of launching conducted at elimination facilities.

9. Training missiles and training launchers for intermediate-range or shorter-range missiles shall be subject to the same locational

restrictions as are set forth for intermediate-range and shorter-range missiles and launchers of such missiles in paragraphs 1 and 3 of this Article.

Article IX

1. The Memorandum of Understanding contains categories of data relevant to obligations undertaken with regard to this Treaty and lists all intermediate-range and shorter-range missiles, launchers of such missiles, and support structures and support equipment associated with such missiles and launchers, possessed by the Parties as of November 1, 1987. Updates of that data and notifications required by this Article shall be provided according to the categories of data contained in the Memorandum of Understanding.

2. The Parties shall update that data and provide the notifications required by this Treaty through the Nuclear Risk Reduction Centers, established pursuant to the Agreement Between the United States of America and the Union of Soviet Socialist Republics on the Establishment of Nuclear Risk Reduction Centers of September 15, 1987.

3. No later than 30 days after entry into force of this Treaty, each Party shall provide the other Party with updated data, as of the date of entry into force of this Treaty, for all categories of data contained in the Memorandum of Understanding.

4. No later than 30 days after the end of each six-month interval following the entry into force of this Treaty, each Party shall provide updated data for all categories of data contained in the Memorandum of Understanding by informing the other Party of all changes, completed and in process, in that data, which have occurred during the six-month interval since the preceding data exchange, and the net effect of those changes.

5. Upon entry into force of this Treaty and thereafter, each Party shall provide the following notifications to the other Party:

   (a) notification, no less than 30 days in advance, of the scheduled date of the elimination of a specific deployment area, missile operating base or missile support facility;

(b) notification, no less than 30 days in advance, of changes in the number or location of elimination facilities, including the location and scheduled date of each change;

(c) notification, except with respect to launches of intermediate-range missiles for the purpose of their elimination, no less than 30 days in advance, of the scheduled date of the initiation of the elimination of intermediate-range and shorter-range missiles, and stages of such missiles, and launchers of such missiles and support structures and support equipment associated with such missiles and launchers, including:

  (i) the number and type of items of missile systems to be eliminated;

  (ii) the elimination site;

  (iii) for intermediate-range missiles, the location from which such missiles, launchers of such missiles and support equipment associated with such missiles and launchers are moved to the elimination facility; and

  (iv) except in the case of support structures, the point of entry to be used by an inspection team conducting an inspection pursuant to paragraph 7 of Article XI of this Treaty and the estimated time of departure of an inspection team from the point of entry to the elimination facility;

(d) notification, no less than ten days in advance, of the scheduled date of the launch, or the scheduled date of the initiation of a series of launches, of intermediate-range missiles for the purpose of their elimination, including:

  (i) the type of missiles to be eliminated;

  (ii) the location of the launch, or, if elimination is by a series of launches, the location of such launches and the number of launches in the series;

  (iii) the point of entry to be used by an inspection team conducting an inspection pursuant to paragraph 7 of Article XI of this Treaty; and

(iv) the estimated time of departure of an inspection team from the point of entry to the elimination facility;

(e) notification, no later than 48 hours after they occur, of changes in the number of intermediate-range and shorter-range missiles, launchers of such missiles and support structures and support equipment associated with such missiles and launchers resulting from elimination as described in the Protocol on Elimination, including:

(i) the number and type of items of a missile system which were eliminated; and

(ii) the date and location of such elimination; and

(f) notification of transit of intermediate-range or shorter-range missiles or launchers of such missiles, or the movement of training missiles or training launchers for such intermediate-range and shorter-range missiles, no later than 48 hours after it has been completed, including:

(i) the number of missiles or launchers;

(ii) the points, dates, and times of departure and arrival;

(iii) the mode of transport; and

(iv) the location and time at that location at least once every four days during the period of transit.

6. Upon entry into force of this Treaty and thereafter, each Party shall notify the other Party, no less than ten days in advance, of the scheduled date and location of the launch of a research and development booster system as described in paragraph 12 of Article VII of this Treaty.

Article X

1. Each Party shall eliminate its intermediate-range and shorter-range missiles and launchers of such missiles and support structures and support equipment associated with such missiles and launchers in accordance with the procedures set forth in the Protocol on Elimination.

2. Verification by on-site inspection of the elimination of items of

missile systems specified in the Protocol on Elimination shall be carried out in accordance with Article XI of this Treaty, the Protocol on Elimination and the Protocol on Inspection.

3. When a Party removes its intermediate-range missiles, launchers of such missiles and support equipment associated with such missiles and launchers from deployment areas to elimination facilities for the purpose of their elimination, it shall do so in complete deployed organizational units. For the United States of America, these units shall be Pershing II batteries and BGM-109G flights. For the Union of Soviet Socialist Republics, these units shall be SS-20 regiments composed of two or three battalions.

4. Elimination of intermediate-range and shorter-range missiles and launchers of such missiles and support equipment associated with such missiles and launchers shall be carried out at the facilities that are specified in the Memorandum of Understanding or notified in accordance with paragraph 5(b) of Article IX of this Treaty, unless eliminated in accordance with Sections IV or V of the Protocol on Elimination. Support structures, associated with the missiles and launchers subject to this Treaty, that are subject to elimination shall be eliminated *in situ*.

5. Each Party shall have the right, during the first six months after entry into force of this Treaty, to eliminate by means of launching no more than 100 of its intermediate-range missiles.

6. Intermediate-range and shorter-range missiles which have been tested prior to entry into force of this Treaty, but never deployed, and which are not existing types of intermediate-range or shorter-range missiles listed in Article III of this Treaty, and launchers of such missiles, shall be eliminated within six months after entry into force of this Treaty in accordance with the procedures set forth in the Protocol on Elimination. Such missiles are:

    (a) for the United States of America, missiles of the type designated by the United States of America as the Pershing IB, which is known to the Union of Soviet Socialist Republics by the same designation; and

(b) for the Union of Soviet Socialist Republics, missiles of the type designated by the Union of Soviet Socialist Republics as the RK-55, which is known to the United States of America as the SSC-X-4.

7. Intermediate-range and shorter-range missiles and launchers of such missiles and support structures and support equipment associated with such missiles and launchers shall be considered to be eliminated after completion of the procedures set forth in the Protocol on Elimination and upon the notification provided for in paragraph 5(e) of Article IX of this Treaty.

8. Each Party shall eliminate its deployment areas, missile operating bases and missile support facilities. A Party shall notify the other Party pursuant to paragraph 5(a) of Article IX of this Treaty once the conditions set forth below are fulfilled:

    (a) all intermediate-range and shorter-range missiles, launchers of such missiles and support equipment associated with such missiles and launchers located there have been removed;

    (b) all support structures associated with such missiles and launchers located there have been eliminated; and

    (c) all activity related to production, flight-testing, training, repair, storage or deployment of such missiles and launchers has ceased there.

    Such deployment areas, missile operating bases and missile support facilities shall be considered to be eliminated either when they have been inspected pursuant to paragraph 4 of Article XI of this Treaty or when 60 days have elapsed since the date of the scheduled elimination which was notified pursuant to paragraph 5(a) of Article IX of this Treaty. A deployment area, missile operating base or missile support facility listed in the Memorandum of Understanding that met the above conditions prior to entry into force of this Treaty, and is not included in the initial data exchange pursuant to paragraph 3 of Article IX of this Treaty, shall be considered to be eliminated.

9. If a Party intends to convert a missile operating base listed in the Memorandum of Understanding for use as a base associated

with GLBM or GLCM systems not subject to this Treaty, then that Party shall notify the other Party, no less than 30 days in advance of the scheduled date of the initiation of the conversion, of the scheduled date and the purpose for which the base will be converted.

Article XI

1. For the purpose of ensuring verification of compliance with the provisions of this Treaty, each Party shall have the right to conduct on-site inspections. The Parties shall implement on-site inspections in accordance with this Article, the Protocol on Inspection and the Protocol on Elimination.

2. Each Party shall have the right to conduct inspections provided for by this Article both within the territory of the other Party and within the territories of basing countries.

3. Beginning 30 days after entry into force of this Treaty, each Party shall have the right to conduct inspections at all missile operating bases and missile support facilities specified in the Memorandum of Understanding other than missile production facilities, and at all elimination facilities included in the initial data update required by paragraph 3 of Article IX of this Treaty. These inspections shall be completed no later than 90 days after entry into force of this Treaty. The purpose of these inspections shall be to verify the number of missiles, launchers, support structures and support equipment and other data, as of the date of entry into force of this Treaty, provided pursuant to paragraph 3 of Article IX of this Treaty.

4. Each Party shall have the right to conduct inspections to verify the elimination, notified pursuant to paragraph 5(a) of Article IX of this Treaty, of missile operating bases and missile support facilities other than missile production facilities, which are thus no longer subject to inspections pursuant to paragraph 5(a) of this Article. Such an inspection shall be carried out within 60 days after the scheduled date of the elimination of that facility. If a Party conducts an inspection at a particular facility pursuant to paragraph 3 of this Article after the scheduled date of the

elimination of that facility, then no additional inspection of that facility pursuant to this paragraph shall be permitted.

5. Each Party shall have the right to conduct inspections pursuant to this paragraph for 13 years after entry into force of this Treaty. Each Party shall have the right to conduct 20 such inspections per calendar year during the first three years after entry into force of this Treaty, 15 such inspections per calendar year during the subsequent five years, and ten such inspections per calendar year during the last five years. Neither Party shall use more than half of its total number of these inspections per calendar year within the territory of any one basing country. Each Party shall have the right to conduct:

   (a) inspections, beginning 90 days after entry into force of this Treaty, of missile operating bases and missile support facilities other than elimination facilities and missile production facilities, to ascertain, according to the categories of data specified in the Memorandum of Understanding, the numbers of missiles, launchers, support structures and support equipment located at each missile operating base or missile support facility at the time of the inspection; and

   (b) inspections of former missile operating bases and former missile support facilities eliminated pursuant to paragraph 8 of Article X of this Treaty other than former missile production facilities.

6. Beginning 30 days after entry into force of this Treaty, each Party shall have the right, for 13 years after entry into force of this Treaty, to inspect by means of continuous monitoring:

   (a) the portals of any facility of the other Party at which the final assembly of a GLBM using stages, any of which is outwardly similar to a stage of a solid-propellant GLBM listed in Article III of this Treaty, is accomplished; or

   (b) if a Party has no such facility, the portals of an agreed former missile production facility at which existing types of intermediate-range or shorter-range GLBMs were produced.

The Party whose facility is to be inspected pursuant to this paragraph shall ensure that the other Party is able to establish a permanent continuous monitoring system at that facility within six months after entry into force of this Treaty or within six months of initiation of the process of final assembly described in subparagraph (a). If, after the end of the second year after entry into force of this Treaty, neither Party conducts the process of final assembly described in subparagraph (a) for a period of 12 consecutive months, then neither Party shall have the right to inspect by means of continuous monitoring any missile production facility of the other Party unless the process of final assembly as described in subparagraph (a) is initiated again. Upon entry into force of this Treaty, the facilities to be inspected by continuous monitoring shall be: in accordance with subparagraph (b), for the United States of America, Hercules Plant Number 1, at Magna, Utah; in accordance with subparagraph (a), for the Union of Soviet Socialist Republics, the Votkinsk Machine Building Plant, Udmurt Autonomous Soviet Socialist Republic, Russian Soviet Federative Socialist Republic.

7. Each Party shall conduct inspections of the process of elimination, including elimination of intermediate-range missiles by means of launching, of intermediate-range and shorter-range missiles and launchers of such missiles and support equipment associated with such missiles and launchers carried out at elimination facilities in accordance with Article X of this Treaty and the Protocol on Elimination. Inspectors conducting inspections provided for in this paragraph shall determine that the processes specified for the elimination of the missiles, launchers and support equipment have been completed.

8. Each Party shall have the right to conduct inspections to confirm the completion of the process of elimination of intermediate-range and shorter-range missiles and launchers of such missiles and support equipment associated with such missiles and launchers eliminated pursuant to Section V of the Protocol on Elimination, and of training missiles, training missile stages, training launch canisters and training launchers eliminated pursuant to Sections II, IV and V of the Protocol on Elimination.

Article XII

1. For the purpose of ensuring verification of compliance with the provisions of this Treaty, each Party shall use national technical means of verification at its disposal in a manner consistent with generally recognized principles of international law.

2. Neither Party shall:

   (a) interfere with national technical means of verification of the other Party operating in accordance with paragraph 1 of this Article; or

   (b) use concealment measures which impede verification of compliance with the provisions of this Treaty by national technical means of verification carried out in accordance with paragraph 1 of this Article. This obligation does not apply to cover or concealment practices, within a deployment area, associated with normal training, maintenance and operations, including the use of environmental shelters to protect missiles and launchers.

3. To enhance observation by national technical means of verification, each Party shall have the right until a Treaty between the Parties reducing and limiting strategic offensive arms enters into force, but in any event for no more than three years after entry into force of this Treaty, to request the implementation of cooperative measures at deployment bases for road-mobile GLBMs with a range capability in excess of 5500 kilometers, which are not former missile operating bases eliminated pursuant to paragraph 8 of Article X of this Treaty. The Party making such a request shall inform the other Party of the deployment base at which cooperative measures shall be implemented. The Party whose base is to be observed shall carry out the following cooperative measures:

   (a) no later than six hours after such a request, the Party shall have opened the roofs of all fixed structures for launchers located at the base, removed completely all missiles on launchers from such fixed structures for launchers and displayed such missiles on launchers in the open without using concealment measures; and

(b) the Party shall leave the roofs open and the missiles on launchers in place until twelve hours have elapsed from the time of the receipt of a request for such an observation.

Each Party shall have the right to make six such requests per calendar year. Only one deployment base shall be subject to these cooperative measures at any one time.

Article XIII

1. To promote the objectives and implementation of the provisions of this Treaty, the Parties hereby establish the Special Verification Commission. The Parties agree that, if either Party so requests, they shall meet within the framework of the Special Verification Commission to:

   (a) resolve questions relating to compliance with the obligations assumed; and

   (b) agree upon such measures as may be necessary to improve the viability and effectiveness of this Treaty.

2. The Parties shall use the Nuclear Risk Reduction Centers, which provide for continuous communication between the Parties, to:

   (a) exchange data and provide notifications as required by paragraphs 3, 4, 5 and 6 of Article IX of this Treaty and the Protocol on Elimination;

   (b) provide and receive the information required by paragraph 9 of Article X of this Treaty;

   (c) provide and receive notifications of inspections as required by Article XI of this Treaty and the Protocol on Inspection; and

   (d) provide and receive requests for cooperative measures as provided for in paragraph 3 of Article XII of this Treaty.

Article XIV

The Parties shall comply with this Treaty and shall not assume any international obligations or undertakings which would conflict with its provisions.

Article XV

1. This Treaty shall be of unlimited duration.

2. Each Party shall, in exercising its national sovereignty, have the right to withdraw from this Treaty if it decides that extraordinary events related to the subject matter of this Treaty have jeopardized its supreme interests. It shall give notice of its decision to withdraw to the other Party six months prior to withdrawal from this Treaty. Such notice shall include a statement of the extraordinary events the notifying Party regards as having jeopardized its supreme interests.

Article XVI

Each Party may propose amendments to this Treaty. Agreed amendments shall enter into force in accordance with the procedures set forth in Article XVII governing the entry into force of this Treaty.

Article XVII

1. This Treaty, including the Memorandum of Understanding and Protocols, which form an integral part thereof, shall be subject to ratification in accordance with the constitutional procedures of each Party. This Treaty shall enter into force on the date of the exchange of instruments of ratification.

2. This Treaty shall be registered pursuant to Article 102 of the Charter of the United Nations.

DONE at Washington on December 8, 1987, in two copies, each in the English and Russian languages, both texts being equally authentic.

FOR THE UNITED STATES OF AMERICA:
Ronald Reagan
President of the United States of America

FOR THE UNION OF SOVIET SOCIALIST REPUBLICS:
Mikhail Gorbachev
General Secretary of the Central Committee of the CPSU

PROTOCOL ON PROCEDURES GOVERNING THE
ELIMINATION OF THE MISSILE SYSTEMS SUBJECT TO THE
TREATY BETWEEN THE UNITED STATES OF AMERICA AND
THE UNION OF SOVIET SOCIALIST REPUBLICS ON THE
ELIMINATION OF THEIR INTERMEDIATE-RANGE AND
SHORTER-RANGE MISSILES

*Pursuant to and in implementation of the Treaty Between the United
States of America and the Union of Soviet Socialist Republics on the
Elimination of Their Intermediate-Range and Shorter-Range Missiles of
December 8, 1987, hereinafter referred to as the Treaty, the Parties hereby
agree upon procedures governing the elimination of the missile systems
subject to the Treaty.*

I. Items of Missile Systems Subject to Elimination

The specific items for each type of missile system to be eliminated
are:

1. For the United States of America:

Pershing II:	missile, launcher and launch pad shelter
BGM-109G:	missile, launch canister and launcher,
Pershing IA:	missile and launcher, and
Pershing IB:	missile

2. For the Union of Soviet Socialist Republics

SS-20:	missile, launch canister, launcher, missile transporter vehicle and fixed structure for a launcher,
SS-4:	missile, missile transporter vehicle, missile erector, launch stand and propellant tanks;
SS-5:	missile;

SSC-X-4:	missile, launch canister and launcher,
SS-12:	missile, launcher and missile transporter vehicle, and
SS-23:	missile, launcher and missile transporter vehicle

3. For both Parties, all training missiles, training missile stages, training launch canisters and training launchers shall be subject to elimination.

4. For both Parties, all stages of intermediate-range and shorter-range GLBMs shall be subject to elimination.

5. For both Parties, all front sections of deployed intermediate-range and shorter-range missiles shall be subject to elimination.

II. Procedures for Elimination at Elimination Facilities

1. In order to ensure the reliable determination of the type and number of missiles, missile stages, front sections, launch canisters, launchers, missile transporter vehicles, missile erectors and launch stands, as well as training missiles, training missile stages, training launch canisters and training launchers, indicated in Section I of this Protocol, being eliminated at elimination facilities, and to preclude the possibility of restoration of such items for purposes inconsistent with the provisions of the Treaty, the Parties shall fulfill the requirements below.

2. The conduct of the elimination procedures for the items of missile systems listed in paragraph 1 of this Section, except for training missiles, training missile stages, training launch canisters and training launchers, shall be subject to on-site inspection in accordance with Article XI of the Treaty and the Protocol on Inspection. The Parties shall have the right to conduct on-site inspections to confirm the completion of the elimination procedures set forth in paragraph 11 of this Section for training missiles, training missile stages, training launch canisters and training launchers. The Party possessing such a

training missile, training missile stage, training launch canister or training launcher shall inform the other Party of the name and coordinates of the elimination facility at which the on-site inspection may be conducted as well as the date on which it may be conducted. Such information shall be provided no less than 30 days in advance of that date.

3. Prior to a missiles arrival at the elimination facility, its nuclear warhead device and guidance elements may be removed.

4. Each Party shall select the particular technological means necessary to implement the procedures required in paragraphs 10 and 11 of this Section and to allow for on-site inspection of the conduct of the elimination procedures required in paragraph 10 of this Section in accordance with Article XI of the Treaty, this Protocol and the Protocol on Inspection.

5. The initiation of the elimination of the items of missile systems subject to this Section shall be considered to be the commencement of the procedures set forth in paragraph 10 or 11 of this Section.

6. Immediately prior to the initiation of the elimination procedures set forth in paragraph 10 of this Section, an inspector from the Party receiving the pertinent notification required by paragraph 5(c) of Article IX of the Treaty shall confirm and record the type and number of items of missile systems, listed in paragraph 1 of this Section, which are to be eliminated. If the inspecting Party deems it necessary, this shall include a visual inspection of the contents of launch canisters.

7. A missile stage being eliminated by burning in accordance with the procedures set forth in paragraph 10 of this Section shall not be instrumented for data collection. Prior to the initiation of the elimination procedures set forth in paragraph 10 of this Section, an inspector from the inspecting Party shall confirm that such missile stages are not instrumented for data collection. Those missile stages shall be subject to continuous observation by such an inspector from the time of that inspection until the burning is completed.

8. The completion of the elimination procedures set forth in this

Section, except those for training missiles, training missile stages, training launch canisters and training launchers, along with the type and number of items of missile systems for which those procedures have been completed, shall be confirmed in writing by the representative of the Party carrying out the elimination and by the inspection team leader of the other Party. The elimination of a training missile, training missile stage, training launch canister or training launcher shall be considered to have been completed upon completion of the procedures set forth in paragraph 11 of this Section and notification as required by paragraph 5(e) of Article IX of the Treaty following the date specified pursuant to paragraph 2 of this Section.

9. The Parties agree that all United States and Soviet intermediate-range and shorter-range missiles and their associated reentry vehicles shall be eliminated within an agreed overall period of elimination. It is further agreed that all such missiles shall, in fact, be eliminated fifteen days prior to the end of the overall period of elimination. During the last fifteen days, a Party shall withdraw to its national territory reentry vehicles which, by unilateral decision, have been released from existing programs of cooperation and eliminate them during the same timeframe in accordance with the procedures set forth in this Section.

10. The specific procedures for the elimination of the items of missile systems listed in paragraph 1 of this Section shall be as follows, unless the Parties agree upon different procedures to achieve the same result as the procedures identified in this paragraph:

For the Pershing II:

Missile:

(a) missile stages shall be eliminated by explosive demolition or burning;

(b) solid fuel, rocket nozzles and motor cases not destroyed in this process shall be burned, crushed, flattened or destroyed by explosion; and

(c) front section, minus nuclear warhead device and guidance elements, shall be crushed or flattened.

Launcher:

(a) erector-launcher mechanism shall be removed from launcher chassis;

(b) all components of erector-launcher mechanism shall be cut at locations that are not assembly joints into two pieces of approximately equal size;

(c) missile launch support equipment, including external instrumentation compartments, shall be removed from launcher chassis; and

(d) launcher chassis shall be cut at a location that is not an assembly joint into two pieces of approximately equal size.

For the BGM-109G:

Missile:

(a) missile airframe shall be cut longitudinally into two pieces;

(b) wings and tail section shall be severed from missile airframe at locations that are not assembly joints; and

(c) front section, minus nuclear warhead device and guidance elements, shall be crushed or flattened.

Launch Canister:

(a) launch canister shall be crushed, flattened, cut into two pieces of approximately equal size or destroyed by explosion.

Launcher:

(a) erector-launcher mechanism shall be removed from launcher chassis;

(b) all components of erector-launcher mechanism shall be cut at locations that are not assembly joints into two pieces of approximately equal size;

(c) missile launch support equipment, including external instrumentation compartments, shall be removed from launcher chassis; and

(d) launcher chassis shall be cut at a location that is not an assembly joint into two pieces of approximately equal size.

For the Pershing IA:

Missile:

(a) missile stages shall be eliminated by explosive demolition or burning;

(b) solid fuel, rocket nozzles and motor cases not destroyed in this process shall be burned, crushed, flattened or destroyed by explosion; and

(c) front section, minus nuclear warhead device and guidance elements, shall be crushed or flattened.

Launcher:

(a) erector-launcher mechanism shall be removed from launcher chassis;

(b) all components of erector-launcher mechanism shall be cut at locations that are not assembly joints into two pieces of approximately equal size;

(c) missile launch support equipment, including external instrumentation compartments, shall be removed from launcher chassis; and

(d) launcher chassis shall be cut at a location that is not an assembly joint into two pieces of approximately equal size.

For the Pershing IB:

Missile:

(a) missile stage shall be eliminated by explosive demolition or burning;

(b) solid fuel, rocket nozzle and motor case not destroyed in this process shall be burned, crushed, flattened or destroyed by explosion; and

(c) front section, minus nuclear warhead device and guidance elements, shall be crushed or flattened.

For the SS-20:

Missile:

(a) missile shall be eliminated by explosive demolition of the missile in its launch canister or by burning missile stages;

(b) solid fuel, rocket nozzles and motor cases not destroyed in this process shall be burned, crushed, flattened or destroyed by explosion; and

(c) front section, including reentry vehicles, minus nuclear warhead devices, and instrumentation compartment, minus guidance elements, shall be crushed or flattened.

Launch Canister:

(a) launch canister shall be destroyed by explosive demolition together with a missile, or shall be destroyed separately by explosion, cut into two pieces of approximately equal size, crushed or flattened.

Launcher:

(a) erector-launcher mechanism shall be removed from launcher chassis;

(b) all components of erector-launcher mechanism shall be cut at locations that are not assembly joints into two pieces of approximately equal size;

(c) missile launch support equipment, including external instrumentation compartments, shall be removed from launcher chassis;

(d) mountings of erector-launcher mechanism and launcher leveling supports shall be cut off launcher chassis;

(e) launcher leveling supports shall be cut at locations that are not assembly joints into two pieces of approximately equal size; and

(f) a portion of the launcher chassis, at least 0.78 meters in length, shall be cut off aft of the rear axle.

Missile Transporter Vehicle:

(a) all mechanisms associated with missile loading and mounting shall be removed from transporter vehicle chassis;

(b) all mountings of such mechanisms shall be cut off transporter vehicle chassis;

(c) all components of the mechanisms associated with missile loading and mounting shall be cut at locations that are not assembly joints into two pieces of approximately equal size;

(d) external instrumentation compartments shall be removed from transporter vehicle chassis;

(e) transporter vehicle leveling supports shall be cut off transporter vehicle chassis and cut at locations that are not assembly joints into two pieces of approximately equal size; and

(f) a portion of the transporter vehicle chassis, at least 0.78 meters in length, shall be cut off aft of the rear axle.

For the SS-4:

Missile:

(a) nozzles of propulsion system shall be cut off at locations that are not assembly joints;

(b) all propellant tanks shall be cut into two pieces of approximately equal size;

(c) instrumentation compartment, minus guidance elements, shall be cut into two pieces of approximately equal size; and

(d) front section, minus nuclear warhead device, shall be crushed or flattened.

Launch Stand:

(a) launch stand components shall be cut at locations that are not assembly joints into two pieces of approximately equal size.

Missile Erector:

(a) jib, missile erector leveling supports and missile erector mechanism shall be cut off missile erector at locations that are not assembly joints; and

(b) jib and missile erector leveling supports shall be cut into two pieces of approximately equal size.

Missile Transporter Vehicle:

(a) mounting components for a missile and for a missile erector mechanism as well as supports for erecting a missile onto a launcher shall be cut off transporter vehicle at locations that are not assembly joints.

For the SS-5:

Missile:

(a) nozzles of propulsion system shall be cut off at locations that are not assembly joints;

(b) all propellant tanks shall be cut into two pieces of approximately equal size; and

(c) instrumentation compartment, minus guidance elements, shall be cut into two pieces of approximately equal size.

For the SSC-X-4:

Missile:

(a) missile airframe shall be cut longitudinally into two pieces;

(b) wings and tail section shall be severed from missile airframe at locations that are not assembly joints; and

(c) front section, minus nuclear warhead device and guidance elements, shall be crushed or flattened.

Launch Canister:

(a) launch canister shall be crushed, flattened, cut into two pieces of approximately equal size or destroyed by explosion.

Launcher:

(a) erector-launcher mechanism shall be removed from launcher chassis;

(b) all components of erector-launcher mechanism shall be cut at locations that are not assembly joints into two pieces of approximately equal size;

(c) missile launch support equipment, including external instrumentation compartments, shall be removed from launcher chassis;

(d) mountings of erector-launcher mechanism and launcher leveling supports shall be cut off launcher chassis;

(e) launcher leveling supports shall be cut at locations that are not assembly joints into two pieces of approximately equal size; and

(f) the launcher chassis shall be severed at a location determined by measuring no more than 0.70 meters rearward from the rear axle.

For the SS-12:

Missile:

(a) missile shall be eliminated by explosive demolition or by burning missile stages;

(b) solid fuel, rocket nozzles and motor cases not destroyed in this process shall be burned, crushed, flattened or destroyed by explosion; and

(c) front section, minus nuclear warhead device, and instrumentation compartment, minus guidance elements, shall be crushed, flattened or destroyed by explosive demolition together with a missile.

Launcher:

(a) erector-launcher mechanism shall be removed from launcher chassis;

(b) all components of erector-launcher mechanism shall be cut at locations that are not assembly joints into two pieces of approximately equal size;

(c) missile launch support equipment, including external instrumentation compartments, shall be removed from launcher chassis;

(d) mountings of erector-launcher mechanism and launcher leveling supports shall be cut off launcher chassis;

(e) launcher leveling supports shall be cut at locations that are not assembly joints into two pieces of approximately equal size; and

(f) a portion of the launcher chassis, at least 1.10 meters in length, shall be cut off aft of the rear axle.

Missile Transporter Vehicle:

(a) all mechanisms associated with missile loading and mounting shall be removed from transporter vehicle chassis;

(b) all mountings of such mechanisms shall be cut off transporter vehicle chassis;

(c) all components of the mechanisms associated with missile loading and mounting shall be cut at locations that are not assembly joints into two pieces of approximately equal size;

(d) external instrumentation compartments shall be removed from transporter vehicle chassis;

(e) transporter vehicle leveling supports shall be cut off transporter vehicle chassis and cut at locations that are not assembly joints into two pieces of approximately equal size; and

(f) a portion of the transporter vehicle chassis, at least 1.10 meters in length, shall be cut off aft of the rear axle.

For the SS-23:

Missile:

(a) missile shall be eliminated by explosive demolition or by burning the missile stage;

(b) solid fuel, rocket nozzle and motor case not destroyed in this process shall be burned, crushed, flattened or destroyed by explosion; and

(c) front section, minus nuclear warhead device, and instrumentation compartment, minus guidance elements, shall be crushed, flattened, or destroyed by explosive demolition together with a missile.

Launcher:

(a) erector-launcher mechanism shall be removed from launcher body;

(b) all components of erector-launcher mechanism shall be cut at locations that are not assembly joints into two pieces of approximately equal size;

(c) missile launch support equipment shall be removed from launcher body;

(d) mountings of erector-launcher mechanism and launcher leveling supports shall be cut off launcher body;

(e) launcher leveling supports shall be cut at locations that are not assembly joints into two pieces of approximately equal size;

(f) each environmental cover of the launcher body shall be removed and cut into two pieces of approximately equal size; and

(g) a portion of the launcher body, at least 0.85 meters in length, shall be cut off aft of the rear axle.

Missile Transporter Vehicle:

(a) all mechanisms associated with missile loading and mounting shall be removed from transporter vehicle body;

(b) all mountings of such mechanisms shall be cut off transporter vehicle body;

(c) all components of mechanisms associated with missile loading and mounting shall be cut at locations that are not assembly joints into two pieces of approximately equal size;

(d) control equipment of the mechanism associated with missile loading shall be removed from transporter vehicle body;

(e) transporter vehicle leveling supports shall be cut off transporter vehicle body and cut at locations that are not assembly joints into two pieces of approximately equal size; and

(f) a portion of the transporter vehicle body, at least 0.85 meters in length, shall be cut off aft of the rear axle.

11. The specific procedures for the elimination of the training missiles, training missile stages, training launch canisters and training launchers indicated in paragraph 1 of this Section shall be as follows:

Training Missile and Training Missile Stage:

(a) training missile and training missile stage shall be crushed, flattened, cut into two pieces of approximately equal size or destroyed by explosion.

Training Launch Canister:

(a) training launch canister shall be crushed, flattened, cut into two pieces of approximately equal size or destroyed by explosion.

Training Launcher:

(a) training launcher chassis shall be cut at the same location designated in paragraph 10 of this Section for launcher of the same type of missile.

III. Elimination of Missiles by Means of Launching

1. Elimination of missiles by means of launching pursuant to paragraph 5 of Article X of the Treaty shall be subject to on-site inspection in accordance with paragraph 7 of Article XI of the Treaty and the Protocol on Inspection. Immediately prior to each launch conducted for the purpose of elimination, an inspector from the inspecting Party shall confirm by visual observation the type of missile to be launched.

2. All missiles being eliminated by means of launching shall be launched from designated elimination facilities to existing impact areas for such missiles. No such missile shall be used as a target vehicle for a ballistic missile interceptor.

3. Missiles being eliminated by means of launching shall be launched one at a time, and no less than six hours shall elapse between such launches.

4. Such launches shall involve ignition of all missile stages. Neither Party shall transmit or recover data from missiles being eliminated by means of launching except for unencrypted data used for range safety purposes.

5. The completion of the elimination procedures set forth in this Section, and the type and number of missiles for which those procedures have been completed, shall be confirmed in writing by the representative of the Party carrying out the elimination and by the inspection team leader of the other Party.

6. A missile shall be considered to be eliminated by means of launching after completion of the procedures set forth in this Section and upon notification required by paragraph 5(e) of Article IX of the Treaty.

IV. Procedures for Elimination *In Situ*

1. Support Structures

   (a) Support structures listed in Section I of this Protocol shall be eliminated *in situ*.

   (b) The initiation of the elimination of support structures shall be considered to be the commencement of the elimination procedures required in paragraph 1(d) of this Section.

   (c) The elimination of support structures shall be subject to verification by on-site inspection in accordance with paragraph 4 of Article XI of the Treaty.

   (d) The specific elimination procedures for support structures shall be as follows:

      (i) the superstructure of the fixed structure or shelter shall be dismantled or demolished, and removed from its base or foundation;

      (ii) the base or foundation of the fixed structure or shelter shall be destroyed by excavation or explosion;

      (iii) the destroyed base or foundation of a fixed structure or shelter shall remain visible to national technical means of verification for six months or until completion of an on-site inspection conducted in accordance with Article XI of the Treaty; and

      (iv) upon completion of the above requirements, the elimination procedures shall be considered to have been completed.

2. Propellant Tanks for SS-4 Missiles: Fixed and transportable propellant tanks for SS-4 missiles shall be removed from launch sites.

3. Training Missiles, Training Missile Stages, Training Launch

Canisters and Training Launchers

(a) Training missiles, training missile stages, training launch canisters and training launchers not eliminated at elimination facilities shall be eliminated *in situ.*

(b) Training missiles, training missile stages, training launch canisters and training launchers being eliminated *in situ* shall be eliminated in accordance with the specific procedures set forth in paragraph 11 of Section II of this Protocol.

(c) Each Party shall have the right to conduct on-site inspection to confirm the completion of the elimination procedures for training missiles, training missile stages, training launch canisters and training launchers.

(d) The Party possessing such a training missile, training missile stage, training launch canister or training launcher shall inform the other Party of the place-name and coordinates of the location at which the on-site inspection provided for in paragraph 3(c) of this Section may be conducted as well as the date on which it may be conducted. Such information shall be provided no less than 30 days in advance of that date.

(e) Elimination of a training missile, training missile stage, training launch canister or training launcher shall be considered to have been completed upon the completion of the procedures required by this paragraph and upon notification as required by paragraph 5(e) of Article IX of the Treaty following the date specified pursuant to paragraph 3(d) of this Section.

V. Other Types of Elimination

1. Loss or Accidental Destruction

(a) If an item listed in Section I of this Protocol is lost or destroyed as a result of an accident, the possessing Party shall notify the other Party within 48 hours, as required in paragraph 5(e) of Article IX of the Treaty, that the item has been eliminated.

(b) Such notification shall include the type of the eliminated item, its approximate or assumed location and the circumstances related to the loss or accidental destruction.

(c) In such case, the other Party shall have the right to conduct an inspection of the specific point at which the accident occurred to provide confidence that the item has been eliminated.

2. Static Display

(a) The Parties shall have the right to eliminate missiles, launch canisters and launchers, as well as training missiles, training launch canisters and training launchers, listed in Section I of this Protocol by placing them on static display. Each Party shall be limited to a total of 15 missiles, 15 launch canisters and 15 launchers on such static display.

(b) Prior to being placed on static display, a missile, launch canister or launcher shall be rendered unusable for purposes inconsistent with the Treaty. Missile propellant shall be removed and erector-launcher mechanisms shall be rendered inoperative.

(c) The Party possessing a missile, launch canister or launcher, as well as a training missile, training launch canister or training launcher that is to be eliminated by placing it on static display shall provide the other Party with the place-name and coordinates of the location at which such a missile, launch canister or launcher is to be on static display, as well as the location at which the on-site inspection provided for in paragraph 2(d) of this Section, may take place.

(d) Each Party shall have the right to conduct an on-site inspection of such a missile, launch canister or launcher within 60 days of receipt of the notification required in paragraph 2(c) of this Section.

(e) Elimination of a missile, launch canister or launcher, as well as a training missile, training launch canister or training launcher, by placing it on static display shall be considered to have been completed upon completion of the procedures required by this paragraph and notification as required by paragraph 5(e) of Article IX of the Treaty.

This Protocol is an integral part of the Treaty. It shall enter into force on the date of the entry into force of the Treaty and shall remain in force so long as the Treaty remains in force. As provided for in paragraph 1(b) of Article XIII of the Treaty, the Parties may agree upon such measures as may be necessary to improve the viability and effectiveness of this Protocol. Such measures shall not be deemed amendments to the Treaty.

DONE at Washington on December 8, 1987, in two copies, each in the English and Russian languages, both texts being equally authentic.

FOR THE UNITED STATES OF AMERICA:
RONALD REAGAN
President of the United States of America

FOR THE UNION OF SOVIET SOCIALIST REPUBLICS:
M.S. GORBACHEV
General Secretary of the Central
Committee of the CPSU

PROTOCOL REGARDING INSPECTIONS RELATING TO THE TREATY BETWEEN THE UNITED STATES OF AMERICA AND THE UNION OF SOVIET SOCIALIST REPUBLICS ON THE ELIMINATION OF THEIR INTERMEDIATE-RANGE AND SHORTER-RANGE MISSILES

Pursuant to and in implementation of the Treaty Between the United States of America and the Union of Soviet Socialist Republics on the Elimination of Their Intermediate-Range and Shorter-Range Missiles of December 8, 1987, hereinafter referred to as the Treaty, the Parties hereby agree upon procedures governing the conduct of inspections provided for in Article XI of the Treaty.

I. Definitions

For the purposes of this Protocol, the Treaty, the Memorandum of Understanding and the Protocol on Elimination:

1. The term "inspected Party" means the Party to the Treaty whose sites are subject to inspection as provided for by Article XI of the Treaty.

2. The term "inspecting Party" means the Party to the Treaty carrying out an inspection.

3. The term "inspector" means an individual designated by one of the Parties to carry out inspections and included on that Party's list of inspectors in accordance with the provisions of Section III of this Protocol.

4. The term "inspection team" means the group of inspectors assigned by the inspecting Party to conduct a particular inspection.

5. The term "inspection site" means an area, location or facility at which an inspection is carried out.

6. The term "period of inspection" means the period of time from arrival of the inspection team at the inspection site until its departure from the inspection site, exclusive of time spent on any pre-and post-inspection procedures.

7. The term "point of entry" means: Washington, D.C., or San Francisco, California, the United States of America; Brussels (National Airport), The Kingdom of Belgium; Frankfurt (Rhein Main Airbase), The Federal Republic of Germany; Rome (Ciampino), The Republic of Italy; Schiphol, The Kingdom of the Netherlands; RAF Greenham Common, The United Kingdom of Great Britain and Northern Ireland; Moscow, or Irkutsk, the Union of Soviet Socialist Republics; Schkeuditz Airport, the German Democratic Republic; and International Airport Ruzyne, the Czechoslovak Socialist Republic.

8. The term "in-country period" means the period from the arrival of the inspection team at the point of entry until its departure from the country through the point of entry.

9. The term "in-country escort" means individuals specified by the inspected Party to accompany and assist inspectors and aircrew members as necessary throughout the in-country period.

10. The term "aircrew member" means an individual who performs duties related to the operation of an airplane and who is included on a Party's list of aircrew members in accordance with the provisions of Section III of this Protocol.

II. General Obligations

1. For the purpose of ensuring verification of compliance with the provisions of the Treaty, each Party shall facilitate inspection by the other Party pursuant to this Protocol.

2. Each Party takes note of the assurances received from the other Party regarding understandings reached between the other Party and the basing countries to the effect that the basing countries have agreed to the conduct of inspections, in accordance with the provisions of this Protocol, on their territories.

III. Pre-Inspection Requirements

1. Inspections to ensure verification of compliance by the Parties with the obligations assumed under the Treaty shall be carried out by inspectors designated in accordance with paragraphs 3 and 4 of this Section.

2. No later than one day after entry into force of the Treaty, each Party shall provide to the other Party: a list of its proposed aircrew members; a list of its proposed inspectors who will carry out inspections pursuant to paragraphs 3, 4, 5, 7 and 8 of Article XI of the Treaty; and a list of its proposed inspectors who will carry out inspection activities pursuant to paragraph 6 of Article XI of the Treaty. None of these lists shall contain at any time more than 200 individuals.

3. Each Party shall review the lists of inspectors and aircrew members proposed by the other Party. With respect to an individual included on the list of proposed inspectors who will carry out inspection activities pursuant to paragraph 6 of Article XI of the Treaty, if such an individual is unacceptable to the Party reviewing the list, that Party shall, within 20 days, so inform the Party providing the list, and the individual shall be deemed not accepted and shall be deleted from the list. With respect to an individual on the list of proposed aircrew members or the list of proposed inspectors who will carry out inspections pursuant to paragraphs 3, 4, 5, 7 and 8 of Article XI of the Treaty, each Party, within 20 days after the receipt of such lists, shall inform the other Party of its agreement to the designation of each inspector and aircrew member proposed. Inspectors shall be citizens of the inspecting Party.

4. Each Party shall have the right to amend its lists of inspectors and aircrew members. New inspectors and aircrew members shall be designated in the same manner as set forth in paragraph 3 of this Section with respect to the initial lists.

5. Within 30 days of receipt of the initial lists of inspectors and aircrew members, or of subsequent changes thereto, the Party receiving such information shall provide, or shall ensure the provision of, such visas and other documents to each individual to whom it has agreed as may be required to ensure that each inspector or aircrew member may enter and remain in the territory of the Party or basing country in which an inspection site is located throughout the in-country period for the purpose of carrying out inspection activities in accordance with the provisions of this Protocol. Such visas and documents shall be valid for a period of at least 24 months.

6. To exercise their functions effectively, inspectors and aircrew members shall be accorded, throughout the in-country period, privileges and immunities in the country of the inspection site as set forth in the Annex to this Protocol.

7. Without prejudice to their privileges and immunities, inspectors and aircrew members shall be obliged to respect the laws and regulations of the State on whose territory an inspection is carried out and shall be obliged not to interfere in the internal affairs of that State. In the event the inspected Party determines that an inspector or aircrew member of the other Party has violated the conditions governing inspection activities set forth in this Protocol, or has ever committed a criminal offense on the territory of the inspected Party or a basing country, or has ever been sentenced for committing a criminal offense or expelled by the inspected Party or a basing country, the inspected Party making such a determination shall so notify the inspecting Party, which shall immediately strike the individual from the lists of inspectors or the list of aircrew members. If, at that time, the individual is on the territory of the inspected Party or a basing country, the inspecting Party shall immediately remove that individual from the country.

8. Within 30 days after entry into force of the Treaty, each Party shall inform the other Party of the standing diplomatic clearance number for airplanes of the Party transporting inspectors and equipment necessary for inspection into and out of the territory of the Party or basing country in which an inspection site is located. Aircraft routings to and from the designated point of entry shall be along established international airways that are agreed upon by the Parties as the basis for such diplomatic clearance.

IV. Notifications

1. Notification of an intention to conduct an inspection shall be made through the Nuclear Risk Reduction Centers. The receipt of this notification shall be acknowledged through the Nuclear Risk Reduction Centers by the inspected Party within one hour of its receipt.

(a) For inspections conducted pursuant to paragraphs 3, 4 or 5 of Article XI of the Treaty, such notifications shall be made no less than 16 hours in advance of the estimated time of arrival of the inspection team at the point of entry and shall include:

(i) the point of entry;

(ii) the date and estimated time of arrival at the point of entry;

(iii) the date and time when the specification of the inspection site will be provided; and

(iv) the names of inspectors and aircrew members.

(b) For inspections conducted pursuant to paragraphs 7 or 8 of Article XI of the Treaty, such notifications shall be made no less than 72 hours in advance of the estimated time of arrival of the inspection team at the point of entry and shall include:

(i) the point of entry;

(ii) the date and estimated time of arrival at the point of entry;

(iii) the site to be inspected and the type of inspection; and

(iv) the names of inspectors and aircrew members.

2. The date and time of the specification of the inspection site as notified pursuant to paragraph 1(a) of this Section shall fall within the following time intervals:

(a) for inspections conducted pursuant to paragraphs 4 or 5 of Article XI of the Treaty, neither less than four hours nor more than 24 hours after the estimated date and time of arrival at the point of entry; and

(b) for inspections conducted pursuant to paragraph 3 of Article XI of the Treaty, neither less than four hours nor more than 48 hours after the estimated date and time of arrival at the point of entry.

3. The inspecting Party shall provide the inspected Party with a flight plan, through the Nuclear Risk Reduction Centers, for its

flight from the last airfield prior to entering the airspace of the country in which the inspection site is located to the point of entry, no less than six hours before the scheduled departure time from that airfield. Such a plan shall be filed in accordance with the procedures of the International Civil Aviation Organization applicable to civil aircraft. The inspecting Party shall include in the remarks section of each flight plan the standing diplomatic clearance number and the notation: "Inspection aircraft. Priority clearance processing required."

4. No less than three hours prior to the scheduled departure of the inspection team from the last airfield prior to entering the airspace of the country in which the inspection is to take place, the inspected Party shall ensure that the flight plan filed in accordance with paragraph 3 of this Section is approved so that the inspection team may arrive at the point of entry by the estimated arrival time.

5. Either Party may change the point or points of entry to the territories of the countries within which its deployment areas, missile operating bases or missile support facilities are located, by giving notice of such change to the other Party. A change in a point of entry shall become effective five months after receipt of such notification by the other Party.

V. Activities Beginning Upon Arrival at the Point of Entry

1. The in-country escort and a diplomatic aircrew escort accredited to the Government of either the inspected Party or the basing country in which the inspection site is located shall meet the inspection team and aircrew members at the point of entry as soon as the airplane of the inspecting Party lands. The number of aircrew members for each airplane shall not exceed ten. The in-country escort shall expedite the entry of the inspection team and aircrew, their baggage, and equipment and supplies necessary for inspection, into the country in which the inspection site is located. A diplomatic aircrew escort shall have the right to accompany and assist aircrew members throughout the in-country period. In the case of an inspection taking place on the territory of a basing country, the in-country escort may include representatives of that basing country.

2. An inspector shall be considered to have assumed his duties upon arrival at the point of entry on the territory of the inspected Party or a basing country, and shall be considered to have ceased performing those duties when he has left the territory of the inspected Party or basing country.

3. Each Party shall ensure that equipment and supplies are exempt from all customs duties.

4. Equipment and supplies which the inspecting Party brings into the country in which an inspection site is located shall be subject to examination at the point of entry each time they are brought into that country. This examination shall be completed prior to the departure of the inspection team from the point of entry to conduct an inspection. Such equipment and supplies shall be examined by the in-country escort in the presence of the inspection team members to ascertain to the satisfaction of each Party that the equipment and supplies cannot perform functions unconnected with the inspection requirements of the Treaty. If it is established upon examination that the equipment or supplies are unconnected with these inspection requirements, then they shall not be cleared for use and shall be impounded at the point of entry until the departure of the inspection team from the country where the inspection is conducted. Storage of the inspecting Party's equipment and supplies at each point of entry shall be within tamper-proof containers within a secure facility. Access to each secure facility shall be controlled by a "dual key" system requiring the presence of both Parties to gain access to the equipment and supplies.

5. Throughout the in-country period, the inspected Party shall provide, or arrange for the provision of, meals, lodging, work space, transportation and, as necessary, medical care for the inspection team and aircrew of the inspecting Party. All the costs in connection with the stay of inspectors carrying out inspection activities pursuant to paragraph 6 of Article XI of the Treaty, on the territory of the inspected Party, including meals, services, lodging, work space, transportation and medical care shall be borne by the inspecting Party.

6. The inspected Party shall provide parking, security protection, servicing and fuel for the airplane of the inspecting Party at the point of entry. The inspecting Party shall bear the cost of such fuel and servicing.

7. For inspections conducted on the territory of the Parties, the inspection team shall enter at the point of entry on the territory of the inspected Party that is closest to the inspection site. In the case of inspections carried out in accordance with paragraphs 3, 4 or 5 of Article XI of the Treaty, the inspection team leader shall, at or before the time notified, pursuant to paragraph 1(a)(iii) of Section IV of this Protocol, inform the inspected Party at the point of entry through the in-country escort of the type of inspection and the inspection site, by place-name and geographic coordinates.

VI. General Rules for Conducting Inspections

1. Inspectors shall discharge their functions in accordance with this Protocol.

2. Inspectors shall not disclose information received during inspections except with the express permission of the inspecting Party. They shall remain bound by this obligation after their assignment as inspectors has ended.

3. In discharging their functions, inspectors shall not interfere directly with on-going activities at the inspection site and shall avoid unnecessarily hampering or delaying the operation of a facility or taking actions affecting its safe operation.

4. Inspections shall be conducted in accordance with the objectives set forth in Article XI of the Treaty as applicable for the type of inspection specified by the inspecting Party under paragraph 1(b) of Section IV or paragraph 7 of Section V of this Protocol.

5. The in-country escort shall have the right to accompany and assist inspectors and aircrew members as considered necessary by the inspected Party throughout the in-country period. Except as otherwise provided in this Protocol, the movement and travel of inspectors and aircrew members shall be at the discretion of the in-country escort.

6. Inspectors carrying out inspection activities pursuant to paragraph 6 of Article XI of the Treaty shall be allowed to travel within 50 kilometers from the inspection site with the permission of the in-country escort, and as considered necessary by the inspected Party, shall be accompanied by the in-country escort. Such travel shall be taken solely as a leisure activity.

7. Inspectors shall have the right throughout the period of inspection to be in communication with the embassy of the inspecting Party located within the territory of the country where the inspection is taking place using the telephone communications provided by the inspected Party.

8. At the inspection site, representatives of the inspected facility shall be included among the in-country escort.

9. The inspection team may bring onto the inspection site such documents as needed to conduct the inspection, as well as linear measurement devices; cameras; portable weighing devices; radiation detection devices; and other equipment, as agreed by the Parties. The characteristics and method of use of the equipment listed above, shall also be agreed upon within 30 days after entry into force of the Treaty. During inspections conducted pursuant to paragraphs 3, 4, 5(a), 7 or 8 of Article XI of the Treaty, the inspection team may use any of the equipment listed above, except for cameras, which shall be for use only by the inspected Party at the request of the inspecting Party. During inspections conducted pursuant to paragraph 5(b) of Article XI of the Treaty, all measurements shall be made by the inspected Party at the request of the inspecting Party. At the request of inspectors, the in-country escort shall take photographs of the inspected facilities using the inspecting Party's camera systems which are capable of producing duplicate, instant development photographic prints. Each Party shall receive one copy of every photograph.

10. For inspections conducted pursuant to paragraphs 3, 4, 5, 7 or 8 of Article XI of the Treaty, inspectors shall permit the in-country escort to observe the equipment used during the inspection by the inspection team.

11. Measurements recorded during inspections shall be certified by the signature of a member of the inspection team and a member of the in-country escort when they are taken. Such certified data shall be included in the inspection report.

12. Inspectors shall have the right to request clarifications in connection with ambiguities that arise during an inspection. Such requests shall be made promptly through the in-country escort. The in-country escort shall provide the inspection team, during the inspection, with such clarifications as may be necessary to remove the ambiguity. In the event questions relating to an object or building located within the inspection site are not resolved, the inspected Party shall photograph the object or building as requested by the inspecting Party for the purpose of clarifying its nature and function. If the ambiguity cannot be removed during the inspection, then the question, relevant clarifications and a copy of any photographs taken shall be included in the inspection report.

13. In carrying out their activities, inspectors shall observe safety regulations established at the inspection site, including those for the protection of controlled environments within a facility and for personal safety. Individual protective clothing and equipment shall be provided by the inspected Party, as necessary.

14. For inspections pursuant to paragraphs 3, 4, 5, 7 or 8 of Article XI of the Treaty, pre-inspection procedures, including briefings and safety-related activities, shall begin upon arrival of the inspection team at the inspection site and shall be completed within one hour. The inspection team shall begin the inspection immediately upon completion of the pre-inspection procedures. The period of inspection shall not exceed 24 hours, except for inspections pursuant to paragraphs 6, 7 or 8 of Article XI of the Treaty. The period of inspection may be extended, by agreement with the in-country escort, by no more than eight hours. Post-inspection procedures, which include completing the inspection report in accordance with the provisions of Section XI of this Protocol, shall begin immediately upon completion of the inspection and shall be completed at the inspection site within four hours.

15. An inspection team conducting an inspection pursuant to Article XI of the Treaty shall include no more than ten inspectors, except for an inspection team conducting an inspection pursuant to paragraphs 7 or 8 of that Article, which shall include no more than 20 inspectors and an inspection team conducting inspection activities pursuant to paragraph 6 of that Article, which shall include no more than 30 inspectors. At least two inspectors on each team must speak the language of the inspected Party. An inspection team shall operate under the direction of the team leader and deputy team leader. Upon arrival at the inspection site, the inspection team may divide itself into subgroups consisting of no fewer than two inspectors each. There shall be no more than one inspection team at an inspection site at any one time.

16. Except in the case of inspections conducted pursuant to paragraphs 3, 4, 7 or 8 of Article XI of the Treaty, upon completion of the post-inspection procedures, the inspection team shall return promptly to the point of entry from which it commenced inspection activities and shall then leave, within 24 hours, the territory of the country in which the inspection site is located, using its own airplane. In the case of inspections conducted pursuant to paragraphs 3, 4, 7 or 8 of Article XI of the Treaty, if the inspection team intends to conduct another inspection it shall either:

   (a) notify the inspected Party of its intent upon return to the point of entry; or

   (b) notify the inspected Party of the type of inspection and the inspection site upon completion of the post-inspection procedures. In this case it shall be the responsibility of the inspected Party to ensure that the inspection team reaches the next inspection site without unjustified delay. The inspected Party shall determine the means of transportation and route involved in such travel.

   With respect to subparagraph (a), the procedures set forth in paragraph 7 of Section V of this Protocol and paragraphs 1 and 2 of Section VII of this Protocol shall apply.

VII. Inspections Conducted Pursuant to Paragraphs 3, 4 or 5 of Article XI of the Treaty

1.   Within one hour after the time for the specification of the inspection site notified pursuant to paragraph 1(a) of Section IV of this Protocol, the inspected Party shall implement pre-inspection movement restrictions at the inspection site, which shall remain in effect until the inspection team arrives at the inspection site. During the period that pre-inspection movement restrictions are in effect, missiles, stages of such missiles, launchers or support equipment subject to the Treaty shall not be removed from the inspection site.

2.   The inspected Party shall transport the inspection team from the point of entry to the inspection site so that the inspection team arrives at the inspection site no later than nine hours after the time for the specification of the inspection site notified pursuant to paragraph 1(a) of Section IV of this Protocol.

3.   In the event that an inspection is conducted in a basing country, the aircrew of the inspected Party may include representatives of the basing country.

4.   Neither Party shall conduct more than one inspection pursuant to paragraph 5(a) of Article XI of the Treaty at any one time, more than one inspection pursuant to paragraph 5(b) of Article XI of the Treaty at any one time, or more than 10 inspections pursuant to paragraph 3 of Article XI of the Treaty at any one time.

5.   The boundaries of the inspection site at the facility to be inspected shall be the boundaries of that facility set forth in the Memorandum of Understanding.

6.   Except in the case of an inspection conducted pursuant to paragraphs 4 or 5(b) of Article XI of the Treaty, upon arrival of the inspection team at the inspection site, the in-country escort shall inform the inspection team leader of the number of missiles, stages of missiles, launchers, support structures and support equipment at the site that are subject to the Treaty and provide the inspection team leader with a diagram of the inspection site indicating the location of these missiles, stages of missiles,

launchers, support structures and support equipment at the inspection site.

7. Subject to the procedures of paragraphs 8 through 14 of this Section, inspectors shall have the right to inspect the entire inspection site, including the interior of structures, containers or vehicles, or including covered objects, whose dimensions are equal to or greater than the dimensions specified in Section VI of the Memorandum of Understanding for the missiles, stages of such missiles, launchers or support equipment of the inspected Party.

8. A missile, a stage of such a missile or a launcher subject to the Treaty shall be subject to inspection only by external visual observation, including measuring, as necessary, the dimensions of such a missile, stage of such a missile or launcher. A container that the inspected Party declares to contain a missile or stage of a missile subject to the Treaty, and which is not sufficiently large to be capable of containing more than one missile or stage of such a missile of the inspected Party subject to the Treaty, shall be subject to inspection only by external visual observation, including measuring, as necessary, the dimensions of such a container to confirm that it cannot contain more than one missile or stage of such a missile of the inspected Party subject to the Treaty. Except as provided for in paragraph 14 of this Section, a container that is sufficiently large to contain a missile or stage of such a missile of the inspected Party subject to the Treaty that the inspected Party declares not to contain a missile or stage of such a missile subject to the Treaty shall be subject to inspection only by means of weighing or visual observation of the interior of the container, as necessary, to confirm that it does not, in fact, contain a missile or stage of such a missile of the inspected Party subject to the Treaty. If such a container is a launch canister associated with a type of missile not subject to the Treaty, and declared by the inspected Party to contain such a missile, it shall be subject to external inspection only, including use of radiation detection devices, visual observation and linear measurement, as necessary, of the dimensions of such a canister.

9. A structure or container that is not sufficiently large to contain a missile, stage of such a missile or launcher of the inspected

Party subject to the Treaty shall be subject to inspection only by external visual observation including measuring, as necessary, the dimensions of such a structure or container to confirm that it is not sufficiently large to be capable of containing a missile, stage of such a missile or launcher of the inspected Party subject to the Treaty.

10. Within a structure, a space which is sufficiently large to contain a missile, stage of such a missile or launcher of the inspected Party subject to the Treaty, but which is demonstrated to the satisfaction of the inspection team not to be accessible by the smallest missile, stage of a missile or launcher of the inspected Party subject to the Treaty shall not be subject to further inspection. If the inspected Party demonstrates to the satisfaction of the inspection team by means of a visual inspection of the interior of an enclosed space from its entrance that the enclosed space does not contain any missile, stage of such a missile or launcher of the inspected Party subject to the Treaty, such an enclosed space shall not be subject to further inspection.

11. The inspection team shall be permitted to patrol the perimeter of the inspection site and station inspectors at the exits of the site for the duration of the inspection.

12. The inspection team shall be permitted to inspect any vehicle capable of carrying missiles, stages of such missiles, launchers or support equipment of the inspected Party subject to the Treaty at any time during the course of an inspection and no such vehicle shall leave the inspection site during the course of the inspection until inspected at site exits by the inspection team.

13. Prior to inspection of a building within the inspection site, the inspection team may station subgroups at the exits of the building that are large enough to permit passage of any missile, stage of such a missile, launcher or support equipment of the inspected Party subject to the Treaty. During the time that the building is being inspected, no vehicle or object capable of containing any missile, stage of such a missile, launcher or support equipment of the inspected Party subject to the Treaty shall be permitted to leave the building until inspected.

14. During an inspection conducted pursuant to paragraph 5(b) of Article XI of the Treaty, it shall be the responsibility of the inspected Party to demonstrate that a shrouded or environmentally protected object which is equal to or larger than the smallest missile, stage of a missile or launcher of the inspected Party subject to the Treaty is not, in fact, a missile, stage of such a missile or launcher of the inspected Party subject to the Treaty. This may be accomplished by partial removal of the shroud or environmental protection cover, measuring, or weighing the covered object or by other methods. If the inspected Party satisfies the inspection team by its demonstration that the object is not a missile, stage of such a missile or launcher of the inspected Party subject to the Treaty, then there shall be no further inspection of that object. If the container is a launch canister associated with a type of missile not subject to the Treaty, and declared by the inspected Party to contain such a missile, then it shall be subject to external inspection only, including use of radiation detection devices, visual observation and linear measurement, as necessary, of the dimensions of such a canister.

VIII. Inspections Conducted Pursuant to Paragraphs 7 or 8 of Article XI of the Treaty

1. Inspections of the process of elimination of items of missile systems specified in the Protocol on Elimination carried out pursuant to paragraph 7 of Article XI of the Treaty shall be conducted in accordance with the procedures set forth in this paragraph and the Protocol on Elimination.

   (a) Upon arrival at the elimination facility, inspectors shall be provided with a schedule of elimination activities.

   (b) Inspectors shall check the data which are specified in the notification provided by the inspected Party regarding the number and type of items of missile systems to be eliminated against the number and type of such items which are at the elimination facility prior to the initiation of the elimination procedures.

   (c) Subject to paragraphs 3 and 11 of Section VI of this Protocol, inspectors shall observe the execution of the specific procedures for the elimination of the items of missile systems as provided for in the Protocol on Elimination. If any deviations from the agreed elimination procedures are found, the inspectors shall have the right to call the attention of the in-country escort to the need for strict compliance with the above-mentioned procedures. The completion of such procedures shall be confirmed in accordance with the procedures specified in the Protocol on Elimination.

(d) During the elimination of missiles by means of launching, the inspectors shall have the right to ascertain by visual observation that a missile prepared for launch is a missile of the type subject to elimination. The inspectors shall also be allowed to observe such a missile from a safe location specified by the inspected Party until the completion of its launch. During the inspection of a series of launches for the elimination of missiles by means of launching, the inspected Party shall determine the means of transport and route for the transportation of inspectors between inspection sites.

2. Inspections of the elimination of items of missile systems specified in the Protocol on Elimination carried out pursuant to paragraph 8 of Article XI of the Treaty shall be conducted in accordance with the procedures set forth in Sections II, IV, and V of the Protocol on Elimination or as otherwise agreed by the Parties.

IX. Inspection Activities Conducted Pursuant to Paragraph 6 of Article XI of the Treaty

1. The inspected Party shall maintain an agreed perimeter around the periphery of the inspection site and shall designate a portal with not more than one rail line and one road which shall be within 50 meters of each other. All vehicles which can contain an intermediate-range GLBM or longest stage of such a GLBM of the inspected Party shall exit only through this portal.

2. For the purposes of this Section, the provisions of paragraph 10 of Article VII of the Treaty shall be applied to intermediate-

range GLBMs of the inspected Party and the longest stage of such GLBMs.

3. There shall not be more than two other exits from the inspection site. Such exits shall be monitored by appropriate sensors. The perimeter of and exits from the inspection site may be monitored as provided for by paragraph 11 of Section VII of this Protocol.

4. The inspecting Party shall have the right to establish continuous monitoring systems at the portal specified in paragraph 1 of this Section and appropriate sensors at the exits specified in paragraph 3 of this Section and carry out necessary engineering surveys, construction, repair and replacement of monitoring systems.

5. The inspected Party shall, at the request of and at the expense of the inspecting Party, provide the following:

   (a) all necessary utilities for the construction and operation of the monitoring systems, including electrical power, water, fuel, heating and sewage;

   (b) basic construction materials including concrete and lumber;

   (c) the site preparation necessary to accommodate the installation of continuously operating systems for monitoring the portal specified in paragraph 1 of this Section, appropriate sensors for other exits specified in paragraph 3 of this Section and the center for collecting data obtained during inspections. Such preparation may include ground excavation, laying of concrete foundations, trenching between equipment locations and utility connections;

   (d) transportation for necessary installation tools, materials and equipment from the point of entry to the inspection site; and

   (e) a minimum of two telephone lines and, as necessary, high frequency radio equipment capable of allowing direct communication with the embassy of the inspecting Party in the country in which the site is located.

6. Outside the perimeter of the inspection site, the inspecting Party shall have the right to:

(a) build no more than three buildings with a total floor space of not more than 150 square meters for a data center and inspection team headquarters, and one additional building with floor space not to exceed 500 square meters for the storage of supplies and equipment;

(b) install systems to monitor the exits to include weight sensors, vehicle sensors, surveillance systems and vehicle dimensional measuring equipment;

(c) install at the portal specified in paragraph 1 of this Section equipment for measuring the length and diameter of missile stages contained inside of launch canisters or shipping containers;

(d) install at the portal specified in paragraph 1 of this Section non-damaging image producing equipment for imaging the contents of launch canisters or shipping containers declared to contain missiles or missile stages as provided for in paragraph 11 of this Section;

(e) install a primary and back-up power source; and

(f) use, as necessary, data authentication devices.

7. During the installation or operation of the monitoring systems, the inspecting Party shall not deny the inspected Party access to any existing structures or security systems. The inspecting Party shall not take any actions with respect to such structures without consent of the inspected Party. If the Parties agree that such structures are to be rebuilt or demolished, either partially or completely, the inspecting Party shall provide the necessary compensation.

8. The inspected Party shall not interfere with the installed equipment or restrict the access of the inspection team to such equipment.

9. The inspecting Party shall have the right to use its own two-way systems of radio communication between inspectors patrolling the perimeter and the data collection center. Such systems shall conform to power and frequency restrictions established on the territory of the inspected Party.

10. Aircraft shall not be permitted to land within the perimeter of the monitored site except for emergencies at the site and with prior notification to the inspection team.

11. Any shipment exiting through the portal specified in paragraph 1 of this Section which is large enough and heavy enough to contain an intermediate-range GLBM or longest stage of such a GLBM of the inspected Party shall be declared by the inspected Party to the inspection team before the shipment arrives at the portal. The declaration shall state whether such a shipment contains a missile or missile stage as large or larger than and as heavy or heavier than an intermediate-range GLBM or longest stage of such a GLBM of the inspected Party.

12. The inspection team shall have the right to weigh and measure the dimensions of any vehicle, including railcars, exiting the site to ascertain whether it is large enough and heavy enough to contain an intermediate-range GLBM or longest stage of such a GLBM of the inspected Party. These measurements shall be performed so as to minimize the delay of vehicles exiting the site. Vehicles that are either not large enough or not heavy enough to contain an intermediate-range GLBM or longest stage of such a GLBM of the inspected Party shall not be subject to further inspection.

13. Vehicles exiting through the portal specified in paragraph 1 of this Section that are large enough and heavy enough to contain an intermediate-range GLBM or longest stage of such a GLBM of the inspected Party but that are declared not to contain a missile or missile stage as large or larger than and as heavy or heavier than an intermediate-range GLBM or longest stage of such a GLBM of the inspected Party shall be subject to the following procedures.

(a) The inspecting Party shall have the right to inspect the interior of all such vehicles.

(b) If the inspecting Party can determine by visual observation or dimensional measurement that, inside a particular vehicle, there are no containers or shrouded objects large enough to be or to contain an intermediate-range GLBM or longest stage of such a GLBM of the inspected Party, then that vehicle shall not be subject to further inspection.

(c) If inside a vehicle there are one or more containers or shrouded objects large enough to be or to contain an intermediate-range GLBM or longest stage of such a GLBM of the inspected Party, it shall be the responsibility of the inspected Party to demonstrate that such containers or shrouded objects are not and do not contain intermediate-range GLBMs or the longest stages of such GLBMs of the inspected Party.

14. Vehicles exiting through the portal specified in paragraph 1 of this Section that are declared to contain a missile or missile stage as large or larger than and as heavy or heavier than an intermediate-range GLBM or longest stage of such a GLBM of the inspected Party shall be subject to the following procedures.

(a) The inspecting Party shall preserve the integrity of the inspected missile or stage of a missile.

(b) Measuring equipment shall be placed only outside of the launch canister or shipping container; all measurements shall be made by the inspecting Party using the equipment provided for in paragraph 6 of this Section. Such measurements shall be observed and certified by the in-country escort.

(c) The inspecting Party shall have the right to weigh and measure the dimensions of any launch canister or of any shipping container declared to contain such a missile or missile stage and to image the contents of any launch canister or of any shipping container declared to contain such a missile or missile stage; it shall have the right to view such missiles or missile stages contained in launch canisters or shipping containers eight times per calendar year. The in-country escort shall be present during all phases of such viewing. During such interior viewing:

(i) the front end of the launch canister or the cover of the shipping container shall be opened;

(ii) the missile or missile stage shall not be removed from its launch canister or shipping container; and

(iii) the length and diameter of the stages of the missile shall be measured in accordance with the methods agreed by the Parties so as to ascertain that the missile or missile stage is not an intermediate-range GLBM of the inspected Party, or the longest stage of such a GLBM, and that the missile has no more than one stage which is outwardly similar to a stage of an existing type of intermediate-range GLBM.

(d) The inspecting Party shall also have the right to inspect any other containers or shrouded objects inside the vehicle containing such a missile or missile stage in accordance with the procedures in paragraph 13 of this Section.

X. Cancellation of Inspection

An inspection shall be cancelled if, due to circumstances brought about by *force majeure*, it cannot be carried out. In the case of a delay that prevents an inspection team performing an inspection pursuant to paragraphs 3, 4, or 5 of Article XI of the Treaty, from arriving at the inspection site during the time specified in paragraph 2 of Section VII of this Protocol, the inspecting Party may either cancel or carry out the inspection. If an inspection is cancelled due to circumstances brought about by *force majeure* or delay, then the number of inspections to which the inspecting Party is entitled shall not be reduced.

XI. Inspection Report

1. For inspections conducted pursuant to paragraphs 3, 4, 5, 7, or 8 of Article XI of the Treaty, during post-inspection procedures, and no later than two hours after the inspection has been completed, the inspection team leader shall provide the in-country escort with a written inspection report in both the English and Russian languages. The report shall be factual. It shall include the type of inspection carried out, the inspection site, the number of missiles, stages of missiles, launchers and items of support equipment subject to the Treaty observed during the period of inspection and any measurements recorded pursuant to paragraph 11 of Section VI of this Protocol. Photographs taken

during the inspection in accordance with agreed procedures, as well as the inspection site diagram provided for by paragraph 6 of Section VII of this Protocol, shall be attached to this report.

2. For inspection activities conducted pursuant to paragraph 6 of Article XI of the Treaty, within 3 days after the end of each month, the inspection team leader shall provide the in-country escort with a written inspection report both in the English and Russian languages. The report shall be factual. It shall include the number of vehicles declared to contain a missile or stage of a missile as large or larger than and as heavy or heavier than an intermediate-range GLBM or longest stage of such a GLBM of the inspected Party that left the inspection site through the portal specified in paragraph 1 of Section IX of this Protocol during that month. The report shall also include any measurements of launch canisters or shipping containers contained in these vehicles recorded pursuant to paragraph 11 of Section VI of this Protocol. In the event the inspecting Party, under the provisions of paragraph 14(c) of Section IX of this Protocol, has viewed the interior of a launch canister or shipping container declared to contain a missile or stage of a missile as large or larger than and as heavy or heavier than an intermediate-range GLBM or longest stage of such a GLBM of the inspected Party, the report shall also include the measurements of the length and diameter of missile stages obtained during the inspection and recorded pursuant to paragraph 11 of Section VI of this Protocol. Photographs taken during the inspection in accordance with agreed procedures shall be attached to this report.

3. The inspected Party shall have the right to include written comments in the report.

4. The Parties shall, when possible, resolve ambiguities regarding factual information contained in the inspection report. Relevant clarifications shall be recorded in the report. The report shall be signed by the inspection team leader and by one of the members of the in-country escort. Each Party shall retain one copy of the report.

This Protocol is an integral part of the Treaty. It shall enter into force on the date of entry into force of the Treaty and shall remain in force as long as the Treaty remains in force. As provided for in paragraph 1(b) of Article XIII of the Treaty, the Parties may agree upon such measures as may be necessary to improve the viability and effectiveness of this Protocol. Such measures shall not be deemed amendments to the Treaty.

DONE at Washington on December 8, 1987, in two copies, each in the English and Russian languages, both texts being equally authentic.

FOR THE UNITED STATES OF AMERICA:
RONALD REAGAN
President of the United States of America

FOR THE UNION OF SOVIET SOCIALIST REPUBLICS:
M.S. GORBACHEV
General Secretary of the Central
Committee of the CPSU

ANNEX PROVISIONS ON PRIVILEGES AND IMMUNITIES OF INSPECTORS AND AIRCREW MEMBERS

In order to exercise their function effectively, for the purpose of implementing the Treaty and not for their personal benefit, the inspectors and aircrew members referred to in Section III of this Protocol shall be accorded the privileges and immunities contained in this Annex. Privileges and immunities shall be accorded for the entire in-country period in the country in which an inspection site is located, and thereafter with respect to acts previously performed in the exercise of official functions as an inspector or aircrew member.

1. Inspectors and aircrew members shall be accorded the inviolability enjoyed by diplomatic agents pursuant to Article 29 of the Vienna Convention on Diplomatic Relations of April 18, 1961.

2. The living quarters and office premises occupied by an inspector carrying out inspection activities pursuant to paragraph 6 of Article XI of the Treaty shall be accorded the inviolability and protection accorded the premises of diplomatic agents pursuant to Article 30 of the Vienna Convention on Diplomatic Relations.

3. The papers and correspondence of inspectors and aircrew members shall enjoy the inviolability accorded to the papers and correspondence of diplomatic agents pursuant to Article 30 of the Vienna Convention on Diplomatic Relations. In addition, the aircraft of the inspection team shall be inviolable.

4. Inspectors and aircrew members shall be accorded the immunities accorded diplomatic agents pursuant to paragraphs 1, 2 and 3 of Article 31 of the Vienna Convention on Diplomatic Relations. The immunity from jurisdiction of an inspector or an aircrew member may be waived by the inspecting Party in those cases when it is of the opinion that immunity would impede the course of justice and that it can be waived without prejudice to the implementation of the provisions of the Treaty. Waiver must always be express.

5. Inspectors carrying out inspection activities pursuant to paragraph 6 of Article XI of the Treaty shall be accorded the exemption from dues and taxes accorded to diplomatic agents pur-

suant to Article 34 of the Vienna Convention on Diplomatic Relations.

6. Inspectors and aircrew members of a Party shall be permitted to bring into the territory of the other Party or a basing country in which an inspection site is located, without payment of any customs duties or related charges, articles for their personal use, with the exception of articles the import or export of which is prohibited by law or controlled by quarantine regulations.

7. An inspector or aircrew member shall not engage in any professional or commercial activity for personal profit on the territory of the inspected Party or that of the basing countries.

8. If the inspected Party considers that there has been an abuse of privileges and immunities specified in this Annex, consultations shall be held between the Parties to determine whether such an abuse has occurred and, if so determined, to prevent a repetition of such an abuse.

CORRIGENDA

The following are corrections to the text of the Treaty that were agreed between the Parties in an exchange of diplomatic notes on May 21, 1988.

1. In the Memorandum of Understanding (MOU) regarding the establishment of a data base for the Treaty, Section II, paragraph 1, concerning intermediate-range missiles and launchers, for the United States: the number of non-deployed missiles should read "266," the aggregate number of deployed and non-deployed missiles should read "695," and the aggregate number of second stages should read "238."

2. In the MOU, Section III, paragraph 1(A)(II), for missile operating base Wueschheim — the geographic coordinates should read, in the pertinent part, 007 25 40 E., and the number of launchers should read "21."

3. In the MOU, Section III, paragraph 2(A)(I), for launcher production facilities: Martin Marietta — the geographic coordinates should read, in the pertinent part, 39 19 N. For missile storage facilities: Pueblo Depot activity — the number of missiles should read "120"; Redstone Arsenal — the number of training missile stages should read "0"; Weilerbach — the number of missiles should read "9." For launcher storage facilities: Redstone Arsenal — the number of training stages should read "4." For launcher repair facilities: Redstone Arsenal —the number of training missile stages should read "20"; Ft. Sill — the number of launchers should read "1"; Pueblo Depot activity — the geographic coordinates should read, in the pertinent part, 38 17 N. For training facilities: Ft. Sill — the number of training missile stages should read "76."

4. In paragraph 2(b)(i) of Section III and in paragraph 2(b)(i) of Section IV of the Memorandum of Understanding, the geographic coordinates for the Barrikady Plant, Volgograd, should be 48 46' 50" N and 44 35' 44" E.

5. In paragraph 2(b)(i) of Section III of the Memorandum of Understanding, the Elimination Facility at Aralsk with the coordinates 46 50′ N and 61 18′ E should be changed to the Elimination Facility at Kapustin Yar with the coordinates 48 46N and 45 59′ E.

6. In the MOU, Section VI, paragraph 2(A)(I), for missile production facilities: Longhorn Army Ammunition Plant — the number of missiles should read "8" and the number of training missile stages should read "1." For launcher production facilities: Martin Marietta — the geographic coordinates should read, in the pertinent part, 39 19 N. For missile storage facilities: Pueblo Depot activity — the number of missiles should read "162" and the number of training missile stages should read "63." For missiles, launchers, and support equipment in transit the number of missiles should read "0" and the number of training missile stages should read "6."

7. In paragraph 2(b)(ii) of Section IV of the Memorandum of Understanding, the geographic coordinates for the V.I. Lenin Petropavlovsk Heavy Machine Building Plant, Petropavlovsk, should be 54 54′ 20″ N and 69 09′ 58″ E.

8. In the MOU, Section VI, paragraph 1(A)(IV) for the BGM 109G, the maximum diameter of the missile should read "0.52."

9. In the MOU, Section VI, paragraph 1(B)(I), for the BGM 109G launcher the maximum length should read "10.80" and the maximum height should read "3.5."

10. In the MOU, Section VI, paragraph 1(D)(I) for the BGM 109G launch canister the maximum length should read "6.97" and the maximum diameter should read "0.54."

11. In the Protocol Regarding Inspections, paragraph 7 of Section I regarding points of entry for the Union of Soviet Socialist Republics should read "Moscow or Ulan Ude."

12. In the Protocol Regarding Inspections, Section XI, paragraph 1, the reference to "paragraph 10 of Section VI of this protocol" should read "paragraph 11 of Section VI of this protocol."

AGREED MINUTE

Geneva
May 12, 1988

Representatives of the United States of America and the Union of Soviet Socialist Republics discussed the following issues related to the Treaty Between the United States of America and the Union of Soviet Socialist Republics on the Elimination of Their Intermediate-Range and Shorter-Range Missiles, signed in Washington on 8 December, 1987, during the meeting between Secretary Shultz and Foreign Minister Shevardnadze in Geneva on 11-12 May 1988. As a result of these discussions, the Parties agreed on the points that follow.

1. In accordance with paragraph 7 of Section VII of the Inspection Protocol, during baseline, close-out and short-notice inspections, the Parties will be inspecting the entire inspection site, including the interior of structures, containers or vehicles, or including covered objects, capable of containing: for the United States — the second stage of the Pershing II, and the BGM-109G cruise missile; for the USSR — the first stage of the SS-12 missile, the stage of the SS-23 missile, the SSC-X-4 cruise missile and the SS-4 launch stand.

2. Regarding the second stages of United States GLBMs, the aggregate numbers of these stages are listed in the Memorandum of Understanding and will be updated in accordance with Article IX of the Treaty no later than 30 days after entry into force of the Treaty and at six-month intervals thereafter. Except in the case of close-out inspections and inspections of formerly declared facilities, the United States in-country escort is obliged to provide the Soviet inspection team leader with the number of such second stages at the inspection site as well as a diagram of the inspection site indicating the location of those stages. Finally, as set forth in the Elimination Protocol, Soviet inspectors will observe the elimination of all the stages of United States GLBMs.

3. The entire area of an inspection site, including all buildings,

within the outer boundaries depicted on the site diagrams are subject to inspection. In addition, anything depicted outside these outer boundaries on the site diagrams is subject to inspection. Any technical corrections to the site diagrams appended to the Memorandum of Understanding will be made via the corrigendum exchange of notes prior to entry into force of the Treaty. Such corrections will not involve the exclusion of buildings, structures or roads within or depicted outside the outer boundaries depicted on the site diagrams currently appended to the Memorandum of Understanding.

4. The Soviet side assured the United States side that, during the period of continuous monitoring of facilities under the Treaty, no shipment shall exit a continuous monitoring facility on the territory of the USSR whose dimensions are equal to or greater than the dimensions of the SS-20 missile without its front section but less than the dimensions of an SS-20 launch canister, as those dimensions are listed in the Memorandum of Understanding. For the purposes of this assurance, the length of the SS-20 missile without its front section will be considered to be 14.00 meters. In the context of this assurance, the United States side will not be inspecting any shipment whose dimensions are less than those of an SS-20 launch canister, as listed in the Memorandum of Understanding.

5. Inspection teams may bring to the inspection site the equipment provided for in the Inspection Protocol. Use of such equipment will be implemented in accordance with the procedures set forth in that Protocol. For example, if the inspecting Party believes that an ambiguity has not been removed, upon request the inspected Party shall take a photograph of the object or building about which a question remains.

6. During baseline inspections, the Parties will have the opportunity, on a one-time basis, to verify the technical characteristics listed in Section VI of the Memorandum of Understanding, including the weights and dimensions of SS-20 stages, at an elimination facility. Inspectors will select at random one of each type of item to weigh and measure from a sample presented by the inspected Party at a site designated by the inspected Party.

To ensure that the items selected are indeed representative, the sample presented by the inspected Party must contain an adequate number of each item (i.e., at least 8-12, except in the case of the United States Pershing IA launcher, only one of which exists).

7. Immediately prior to the initiation of elimination procedures, an inspector shall confirm and record the type and number of items of missile systems which are to be eliminated. If the inspecting Party deems it necessary, this shall include a visual inspection of the contents of launch canisters. This visual inspection can include looking into the launch canister once it is opened at both ends. It can also include use of the equipment and procedures that will be used eight times per year at Votkinsk and Magna to measure missile stages inside launch canisters (i.e., an optical or mechanical measuring device). If it should turn out, in particular situations, that the inspector is unable to confirm the missile type using the above techniques, the inspected Party is obligated to remove the inspectors doubts so that the inspector is satisfied as to the contents of the launch canister.

8. The length of the SS-23 missile stage will be changed, in a corrigendum to the Memorandum of Understanding, to 4.56 meters. The length of the SS-12 first stage will continue to be listed as 4.38 meters, which includes an interstage structure.

9. The sides will exchange additional photographs no later than May 15, 1988. For the United States side, these photographs will be of the Pershing IA missile and the Pershing II missile with their front sections attached and including a scale. For the Soviet side, these photographs will be of the SS-23, SS-12, and SS-4 with their front sections attached, and of the front section of the SS-20.

10. In providing notifications of transit points in accordance with paragraph 5(f)(iv) of Article IX of the Treaty, the Parties will specify such intermediate locations by providing the place-name and its center coordinates in minutes.

11. The United States side has informed the Soviet side that Davis

Monthan Air Force Base, Arizona will serve as the elimination facility for the United States BGM-109G cruise missile. In order to address Soviet concerns on a related matter, the United States will formally inform the Soviet side before entry into force of the Treaty, of an elimination facility for each of its Treaty-limited items.

These points reflect the understandings of the two Parties regarding their obligations under the Treaty.

Ambassador Maynard W. Glitman
United States Chief Negotiator
on Intermediate-Range Nuclear Forces

Colonel General N. Chervov
Chief of Directorate General Staff
of the Soviet Armed Forces

NOTE OF THE GOVERNMENT OF THE UNITED STATES
OF AMERICA TO THE GOVERNMENT OF THE UNION OF
SOVIET SOCIALIST REPUBLICS

In light of the discussions between the Secretary of State of the
United States of America and the Foreign Minister of the Union of
Soviet Socialist Republics in Geneva and Moscow on April 14 and
April 21-22, 1988, and the Foreign Ministers letter to the Secretary of
State, dated April 15, 1988, the Government of the United States of
America wished to record in an agreement concluded by exchange
of notes the common understanding reached between the two
Governments as to the application of the Treaty Between the United
States of America and the Union of Soviet Socialist Republics on the
Elimination of Their Intermediate-range and Shorter-range Missiles
(hereinafter referred to as "the Treaty"), signed at Washington on
December 8, 1987, to intermediate-range and shorter-range missiles
flight-tested or deployed to carry weapons based on either current
or future technologies and as to the related question of the definition of the term "weapon-delivery vehicle" as used in the Treaty.

It is the position of the Government of the United States of
America that the Parties share a common understanding that all
their intermediate-range and shorter-range missiles as defined by
the Treaty, both at present and in the future, are subject to the provisions of the Treaty.

In this connection, it is also the position of the Government of
the United States of America that the Parties share a common understanding that the term "weapon-delivery vehicle" in the Treaty
means any ground-launched ballistic or cruise missile in the 500
kilometer to 5500 kilometer range that has been flight-tested or deployed to carry or be used as a weapon — that is, any warhead,
mechanism or device, which, when directed against any target, is
designed to damage or destroy it. Therefore, the Treaty requires
elimination and bans production and flight-testing of all such missiles tested or deployed to carry or be used as weapons based on
either current or future technologies, with the exception of missiles
mentioned in paragraph 3 of Article VII of the Treaty. It is also the
position of the Government of the United States of America that

the Parties share a common understanding that the Treaty does not cover non-weapon-delivery vehicles.

It is the understanding of the Government of the United States of America that the above reflects the common view of the two Governments on these matters. If so, the Government of the United States of America proposes that this note and the Soviet reply note confirming that the Government of the Union of Soviet Socialist Republics shares the understanding of the Government of the United States of America, as set forth above, shall constitute an agreement between the Government of the United States of America and the Government of the Union of Soviet Socialist Republics.

Max M. Kampelman
Geneva, May 12, 1988

NOTE OF THE GOVERNMENT OF THE UNION OF SOVIET
SOCIALIST REPUBLICS TO THE GOVERNMENT OF THE
UNITED STATES OF AMERICA

The Government of the Union of Soviet Socialist Republics acknowledges receipt of the note of the Government of the United States of America of May 12, 1988, as follows:

"In light of the discussion between the Secretary of State of the United States of America and the Foreign Minister of the Union of Soviet Socialist Republics in Geneva and Moscow on April 14 and April 21-22, 1988, and the Foreign Ministers letter to the Secretary of State, dated April 15, 1988, the Government of the United States of America wished to record in an agreement concluded by exchange of notes the common understanding reached between the two Governments as to the application of the Treaty Between the United States of America and the Union of Soviet Socialist Republics on the Elimination of Their Intermediate-range and Shorter-range Missiles (hereinafter referred to as "the Treaty"), signed at Washington on December 8, 1987, to intermediate-range and shorter-range missiles flight-tested or deployed to carry weapons based on either current or future technologies and as to the related question of the definition of the term "weapon-delivery vehicle" as used in the Treaty.

It is the position of the Government of the United States of America that the Parties share a common understanding that all their intermediate-range and shorter-range missiles as defined by the Treaty, both at present and in the future, are subject to the provisions of the Treaty.

In this connection, it is also the position of the Government of the United States of America that the Parties share a common understanding that the term "weapon-delivery vehicle" in the Treaty means any ground-launched ballistic or cruise missile in the 500 kilometer to 5500 kilometer range that has been flight-tested or deployed to carry or be used as a weapon—that is, any warhead, mechanism or device, which, when directed against any target, is designed to damage or destroy it. Therefore, the Treaty requires elimination and bans production and flight-testing of all such missiles tested or deployed to carry or be used as weapons based on either current or future technologies, with the exception of missiles mentioned in paragraph 3 of Article VII of the Treaty. It is also the position of the Government of the United States of America that the Parties share a common understanding that the Treaty does not cover non-weapon-delivery vehicles.

It is the understanding of the Government of the United States of America that the above reflects the common view of the two Governments on these matters. If so, the Government of the United States of America proposes that this note and the Soviet reply note confirming that the Government of the Union of Soviet Socialist Republics shares the understanding of the Government of the United States of America, as set forth above, shall constitute an agreement between the Government of the United States of America and the Government of the Union of Soviet Socialist Republics."

The Government of the Union of Soviet Socialist Republics states that it is in full accord with the text and contents of the note of the Government of the United States of America as quoted above and fully shares the understanding of the Government of the United States of America set forth in the above note.

The Government of the Union of Soviet Socialist Republics agrees that the note of the Government of the United States of America of May 12, 1988, and this note in reply thereto, constitute an agreement between the Government of the Union of Soviet Socialist Republics and the Government of the United States of America that the Treaty Between the United States of America and the Union of Soviet Socialist Republics on the Elimination of Their Intermediate-range and Shorter-range Missiles is applicable to intermediate-range and shorter-range missiles flight-tested or deployed to carry weapons based on either current or future technologies, and also regarding the related question of the definition of the term "weapon-delivery vehicle" as used in the Treaty.

Geneva, May 12, 1988

EXCHANGE OF NOTES AT MOSCOW MAY 28, 1988
IDENTIFYING AND CONFIRMING WHICH DOCUMENTS, IN
ADDITION TO THE TREATY, HAVE THE SAME FORCE AND
EFFECT AS THE TREATY

Embassy of the United States of America
Moscow, May 28, 1988

No. MFA/148/88

The Government of the United States of America has the honor to refer:

1. to the notes exchanged in Geneva on May 12, 1988, between the United States and the Union of Soviet Socialist Republics concerning the application of the Treaty Between the United States of America and the Union of Soviet Socialist Republics on the Elimination of Their Intermediate-range and Shorter-range Missiles (the INF Treaty);

2. to the agreed minute concluded in Geneva on May 12, 1988, concerning certain issues related to the Treaty; and

3. to the agreements concluded by exchanges of notes, signed on May 21, 1988, in Vienna and Moscow, respectively, correcting the site diagrams and certain technical errors in the Treaty.

The Government of the United States proposes, in connection with the exchange of the instruments of ratification of the INF Treaty, that the two Governments signify their agreement that these documents are of the same force and effect as the provisions of the Treaty, and that this note together with the reply of the Union of Soviet Socialist Republics, shall constitute an agreement between the two Governments to that effect.

John M. Joyce
Charge d'Affaires a.i.

UNION OF SOVIET SOCIALIST REPUBLICS

May 29, 1988

The Government of the Union of Soviet Socialist Republics confirms receipt of U.S. Government Note no. MFA/148/88, which reads as follows:

[The Russian text of Note no. MFA/148/88 of May 28, 1988, agrees in all substantive respects with the original English text]

The Government of the Union of Soviet Socialist Republics agrees that documents mentioned in U.S. Government Note no. MFA/148/88 of May 28, 1988, are of the same force and effect as the provisions of the Treaty Between the Union of Soviet Republics and the United States of America on the Elimination of Their Intermediate-Range and Shorter-Range Missiles, and that this note and the reply thereto shall constitute an agreement between the Governments of the Union of Soviet Socialist Republics and the United States of America to that effect.

V. Karpov
Moscow
May 29, 1988
/Seal of the Ministry of Foreign Affairs of the USSR/

INF TREATY: BASING COUNTRIES AGREEMENT

Article I: General Obligations
Article II: Definitions
Article III: Notifications
Article IV: Pre-Inspection Arrangements
Article V: Conduct of Inspections
Article VI: Consultations
Article VII: Entry into Force and Duration
Annex

Agreement among the United States of America and The Kingdom of Belgium, the Federal Republic of Germany, the Republic of Italy, the Kingdom of the Netherlands, and the United Kingdom of Great Britain and Northern Ireland
    Regarding Inspections Relating to the Treaty Between the United States of America and The Union of Soviet Socialist Republics on the Elimination of their Intermediate-Range and Shorter-Range Missiles
December 1997

The United States of America and The Kingdom of Belgium, the Federal Republic of Germany, the Republic of Italy, the Kingdom of the Netherlands, and the United Kingdom of Great Britain and Northern Ireland, noting the terms agreed between the United States of America and the Union of Soviet Socialist Republics for the elimination of their intermediate-range and shorter-range missiles,
    Have agreed as follows:

Article I: General Obligations

1. Inspection activities related to Article XI of the Treaty between the United States of America and the Union of Soviet Socialist Republics on the Elimination of Their Intermediate-Range and Shorter-Range Missiles, signed at Washington on December 8, 1987, may take place on the territory of the Kingdom of Belgium, the Federal Republic of Germany, the Republic of Italy, the Kingdom of the Netherlands and the

United Kingdom of Great Britain and Northern Ireland and shall be carried out in accordance with the requirements, procedures and arrangements set forth in the Protocol Regarding Inspections Relating to the Treaty between the United States of America and the Union of Soviet Socialist Republics on the Elimination of Their Intermediate-Range and Shorter-Range Missiles and this Agreement.

2. The Kingdom of Belgium, the Federal Republic of Germany, the Republic of Italy, the Kingdom of the Netherlands and the United Kingdom of Great Britain and Northern Ireland, hereinafter the Basing Countries, hereby agree to facilitate the implementation by the United States of America of its obligations under the Treaty, including the Inspection Protocol thereto, on their territories in accordance with the requirements, procedures and arrangements set forth in this Agreement.

3. Except as herein agreed by the United States of America and the Basing Countries, nothing shall affect the sovereign authority of each state to enforce its laws and regulations with respect to persons entering, and activities taking place within, its jurisdiction.

4. The Basing Countries do not by this Agreement assume any obligations or grant any rights deriving from the Treaty or the Inspection Protocol other than those expressly undertaken or granted in this Agreement or otherwise with their specific consent.

5. The United States of America:

   a) Remains fully responsible towards the Soviet Union for the implementation of its obligations under the Treaty and the Inspection Protocol in respect of United States facilities located on the territories of the Basing Countries;

   b) Undertakes on request at any time to take such action, in exercise of its rights under the Treaty, including the Inspection Protocol, as may be required to protect and preserve the rights of the basing Countries under this agreement.

Article II: Definitions

For purposes of the present Agreement:

1. The term "Treaty" means the Treaty between the United States of America and the Union of Soviet Socialist Republics on the Elimination of Their Intermediate-Range and Shorter-Range Missiles;

2. The term "Inspection Protocol" means the Protocol regarding Inspections Relating to the Treaty between the United States of America and the Union of Soviet Socialist Republics on the Elimination of Their Intermediate-Range and Shorter-Range Missiles;

3. The Term "Inspected Party" means the United States of America;

4. The Term "Inspecting Party" means the Union of Soviet Socialist Republics;

5. The term "inspection team" means those inspectors designated by the Inspecting Party to conduct a particular inspection activity;

6. The term "inspector" means an individual proposed by the Union of Soviet Socialist Republics to carry out inspections pursuant to Article XI of the Treaty, and included on its list of inspectors in accordance with Section III of the Inspection Protocol;

7. The term "diplomatic aircrew escort" means that individual accredited to the government of the Basing Country in which the inspection site is located who is designated by the Inspecting Party to assist the aircrew of the Inspecting Party.

8. The term "inspection site" means the area, facility, or location in a Basing Country at which an inspection provided for in Article XI of the Treaty is carried out;

9. The term "period of inspection" means the period from initiation of the inspection at the inspection site until completion of the inspection at the inspection site, exclusive of time spent on any pre- and post-inspection procedures;

10. The term "point of entry" means: in respect of Belgium, Brussels (National); in respect of the Federal Republic of Germany, Frankfurt (Rhein Main Airbase); in respect of Italy, Rome (Ciampino); in respect of the Kingdom of the Netherlands, Schiphol; and in respect of the United Kingdom of Great Britain and Northern Ireland, RAF Greenham Common;

11. The term "in-country period" means the period from the arrival of the inspection team at the point of entry until departure of the inspection team from the point of entry to depart the country;

12. The term "in-country escort" means the official or officials specified by the Inspected Party, one or more of whom may be nominated by the Basing Country within whose territory the inspection site is located who shall accompany an inspection team throughout the in-country period and provide appropriate assistance to an inspection team, in accordance with the provisions of the Inspection Protocol, throughout the in-country period;

13. The term "aircrew member" means an individual, other than the members of an inspection team, diplomatic aircrew escort and in-country escort, on the aircraft of the Inspecting Party. The number of aircrew members per aircraft shall not exceed ten.

Article III: Notifications

1. Upon entry into force of this Agreement, the Inspected Party and each Basing Country shall establish channels which shall be available to receive and acknowledge receipt of notification on a 24-hour continuous basis.

2. Immediately upon receipt of notice from the Inspecting Party of its intention to conduct an inspection in a Basing Country, the Inspected Party shall notify the Basing Country concerned thereof and of the date and estimated time of arrival of the inspection team at the point of entry, the date and estimated time of departure from the point of entry to the inspection site, the

names of the aircrew and inspection team members, the flight plan (including the type of aircraft as specified therein) filed by the Inspecting Party in accordance with the International Civil Aviation Organization, hereinafter ICAO, procedures applicable to civil aircraft, and any other information relevant to the inspection provided by the Inspecting Party.

3. No less than one hour prior to the estimated time of departure of the inspection team from the point of entry for the inspection site, or in the case of successive inspections conducted pursuant to paragraphs 3, 4, 7 or 8 of Article XI of the Treaty no less than one hour prior to the inspection team's departure from an inspection site for another inspection site, the Inspected Party shall inform the Basing Country of the inspection site, described by place name and geographic coordinates, at which the inspection will be carried out.

Article IV: Pre-Inspection Arrangements

1. The Inspected Party shall provide the Basing Countries with the initial lists of inspectors and aircrew members, or any modification thereto, proposed by the Inspecting Party immediately upon receipt thereof. Within 15 days of receipt of the initial lists or proposed additions thereto, each Basing Country shall notify the Inspected Party if it objects to the inclusion of any inspector or aircrew member on the basis that such individual had ever committed a criminal offense on the territory of the Inspected Party or the Basing Country, or been sentenced for committing a criminal offense or expelled by the Inspected Party or the Basing Country.

2. Within 25 days of receipt of the initial lists of inspectors or aircrew members, or of any subsequent change thereto, each Basing Country shall provide such visas and related documentation as may be necessary to ensure that each inspector or aircrew member may enter its territory for the purpose of carrying out inspection activities in accordance with the provisions of the Treaty and the Inspection Protocol. Such visas and documentation shall be valid for a period of at least 24 months. The Inspected Party shall immediately notify the Basing Countries

of the removal of any individual from the Inspecting Party's lists of inspectors or aircrew members, and the Basing Countries may there upon cancel forthwith any visas and related documentation issued to such persons pursuant to this paragraph.

3. Within 25 days after entry into force of this Agreement, each Basing Country shall inform the Inspected Party of the standing diplomatic clearance number for the aircraft of the Inspecting Party which will transport inspectors and equipment into its territory. At the same time each Basing Country shall inform the Inspected Party of the established international airways along with which aircraft of the Inspecting Party shall enter the airspace of the Basing Country for the purpose of carrying out inspection activities under the Treaty.

4. Each Basing Country shall accord inspectors and aircrew members of the Inspecting Party entering into its territory for the purpose of conducting inspection activities pursuant to the Treaty, including the Inspection Protocol, the privileges and immunities set forth in the Privileges and Immunities Annex to this Agreement. In the event the Inspecting Party refuses or fails to carry out its obligation under Section III, paragraph 7 of the Inspection Protocol to remove an inspector or aircrew member who has violated the conditions governing inspections, the inspector or aircrew member may be refused continued recognition as being entitled to such privileges and immunities.

5. Each Basing Country shall issue, at the point of entry, appropriate authorizations waiving customs duties and expediting customs processing requirements in respect of all equipment relating to inspection activities.

6. Each Basing Country shall provide, if requested, facilities at the point of entry for lodging and the provision of food for inspectors and aircrew members.

7. The Basing Country in which the inspection is to take place shall have the right to examine jointly with the Inspected Party each item of equipment brought in by the Inspecting Party to ascertain that the equipment cannot be used to perform functions unconnected with the inspection requirements of the Treaty. If

it is established upon examination that a piece of equipment is unconnected with these inspection requirements, it shall not be cleaned for use and shall be impounded at the point of entry until the departure of the inspection team from the country.

Article V: Conduct of Inspections

1. Within 90 minutes of receipt from the Inspected Party of notification that a flight plan for an aircraft of the Inspecting Party has been filed in accordance with ICAO procedures applicable to civil aircraft, the Basing Country in whose territory the inspection site is located shall provide the Inspected Party with its approval for the aircraft of the Inspecting Party to proceed to the point of entry via the filed routing, or an amended routing if necessary.

2. The Basing Country in whose territory the inspection site is located shall facilitate the entry of inspectors and aircrew into the country, and shall take the steps necessary to ensure that the baggage and equipment of the inspection team is identified and transported expeditiously through customs.

3. Upon notification by the Inspected Party, in accordance with Article II above, of the inspection site, the Basing Country in whose territory the inspection is to take place shall take the steps necessary to ensure that the inspection team is granted all clearance and assistance necessary to enable it to proceed expeditiously to the inspection site and to arrive at the inspection site within nine hours of the Inspecting Party's notification of the site to be inspected. The Inspected Party and the Basing Country in which the inspection site is located shall consult with respect to the mode of transport to be utilized, and the Basing Country shall have the right to designate the routing between the point of entry and the inspection site.

4. Each Basing Country shall assist the Inspected Party, as necessary in providing two-way voice communication capability for an inspection team between an inspection site within its territory and the embassy of the Inspecting Party.

5. The Inspected Party and the Basing Country within whose ter-

ritory an inspection site is located shall consult with respect to aircraft servicing and the provision of meals, lodging, and services for inspectors and aircrew members at the point of entry and inspection site. The cost of the foregoing requested by the Inspected Party and provided by the Basing Country shall be borne by the Inspected Party.

6. In the event the Inspecting Party requests an extension, which shall not exceed eight hours beyond the original 24-hour period of inspection as provided for in Section VI, paragraph 14 of the Inspection Protocol, the Inspected Party shall immediately notify the Basing Country in whose territory the inspection site is located of the extension.

Article VI: Consultations

1. Within five days after entry into force of this Agreement, the Inspected Party and the Basing Countries shall meet to coordinate implementation of the inspection activities provided for by Article XI of the Treaty, the Inspection Protocol and this Agreement.

2. A meeting between the Inspected Party and any Basing Country to discuss implementation of this Agreement shall be held within five days of a request for such a meeting by the Inspected Party or a Basing Country.

3. Should any question arise which in the opinion of a Basing Country requires immediate attention, the Basing Country may contact the inspection notification authority of the Inspected Party. The Inspected Party will immediately acknowledge receipt of the inquiry or question and give urgent attention to the question or problem.

4. In the event that a Basing Country determines that an inspector or aircrew members has violated the conditions governing inspection within its territory, the Basing Country may notify the Inspected Party which shall inform the Inspecting Party of the disqualification of the inspector or aircraft crew member. The name of the individual will be removed from the list of inspectors or aircrew members.

5.   A Basing Country may change the point of entry for its territory by giving six months' notice of such change to the Inspected Party.

6.   Upon completion of an inspection, the Inspected Party shall advise the Basing Country within whose territory the inspection took place that the inspection has been completed, and upon request of the Basing Country provide a briefing for the Basing Country on the inspection.

7.   The United States of America shall not, without the express agreement of the Basing Countries, propose or accept any amendment to Article XI of the Treaty or to the Inspection Protocol that directly affects the rights, interests or obligations of the Basing Countries.

Article VII: Entry Into Force And Duration

This Agreement shall be subject to approval in accordance with the constitutional procedures of each Party, which approval shall be notified by each Party to each of the other Parties. Following such notification by all Parties, the Agreement shall enter into force simultaneously with the entry into force of the Treaty and shall remain in force for a period of thirteen years.

DONE at Brussels, on the eleventh of December, 1987, in a single original which shall be deposited in the archives of the Government of the United States of America, which shall transmit a duly certified copy thereof to each of the other signatory Governments.

IN WITNESS THEREOF, the undersigned, being duly authorized, have signed the agreement.

FOR THE GOVERNMENT OF THE KINGDOM OF BELGIUM:

FOR THE GOVERNMENT OF THE FEDERAL REPUBLIC OF GERMANY:

FOR THE GOVERNMENT OF THE REPUBLIC OF ITALY:

FOR THE GOVERNMENT OF THE KINGDOM OF THE NETHERLANDS:

FOR THE GOVERNMENT OF THE UNITED KINGDOM OF
GREAT BRITAIN AND NORTHERN IRELAND:

FOR THE GOVERNMENT OF THE UNITED STATES OF
AMERICA:

Annex

PROVISIONS ON PRIVILEGES AND IMMUNITIES OF
INSPECTORS AND AIRCREW MEMBERS

In order to exercise their functions effectively, for the purpose of
implementing the Treaty and not for their personal benefit, inspectors and aircrew members shall be accorded the privileges and immunities contained herein. Privileges and immunities shall be accorded for the entire in-country period in the country in which an
inspection site is located, and thereafter with respect to acts previously performed in the exercise of official functions as an inspector
or aircrew member.

1. Inspectors and aircrew members shall be accorded the inviolability enjoyed by diplomatic agents pursuant to Article 29 of the
   Vienna Convention on Diplomatic Relations on April 18, 1961.

2. The papers and correspondence of inspectors and aircrew
   members shall enjoy the inviolability accorded to the papers
   and correspondence of diplomatic agents pursuant to Article 30
   of the Vienna Convention on Diplomatic Relations. In addition,
   the aircraft of the inspection team shall be inviolable.

3. Inspectors and aircrew members shall be accorded the immunities accorded diplomatic agents pursuant to paragraphs (1), (2),
   and (3) of Article 31 of the Vienna Convention on Diplomatic
   Relations. The immunity from jurisdiction of an inspector or
   an aircrew member may be waived by the Inspecting Party in
   those cases when it is of the opinion that immunity would impede the course of justice and that it can be waived without
   prejudice to the implementation of the provisions of the Treaty.
   Waiver must always be express.

4. Inspectors and aircrew members of the Inspecting Party shall

be permitted to bring into the territory of a Basing Country in which an inspection site is located, without payment of any customs duties or related charges, articles for their personal use, with the exception of articles the import or export of which is prohibited by law or controlled by quarantine regulations.

5. An inspector or aircrew member shall not engage in any professional or commercial activity for personal profit on the territory of the Basing Countries.

OFFICIAL PHOTOS OF INF MISSILES

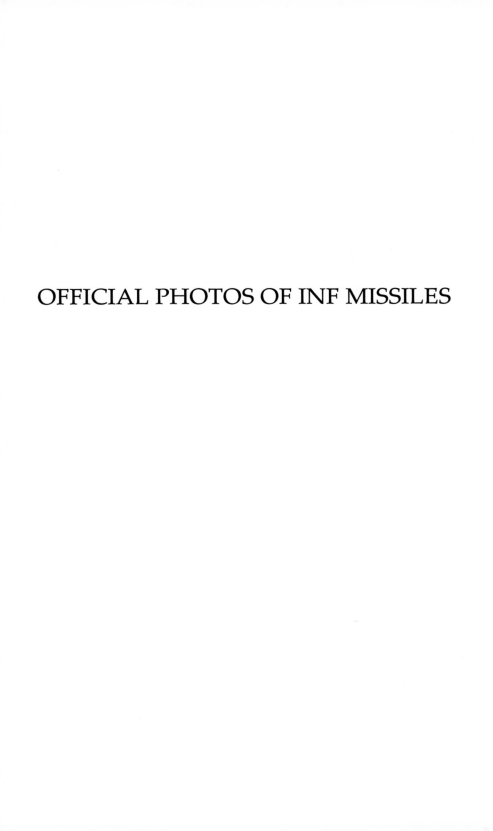

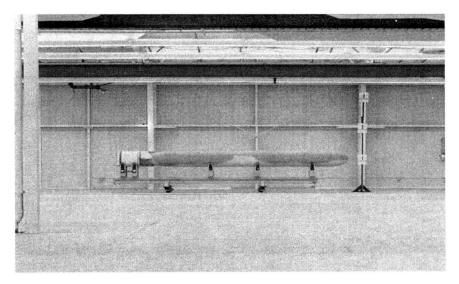

BGM-109G: Fully Assembled Missile (Ground Launcher Cruise Missile)

BGM-109G Launcher

Pershing 1A: Fully Assembled Missile

Pershing 1B: Fully Assembled Missile

Pershing II: Fully Assembled Missile

Pershing II: First Stage

SS-12 Missile Transporter Vehicle

SS-23 Launcher

SS-23 Missile

SSC-X-4 Launcher

SSC-X-4 Missile

SS-4 Missile

SS-4 Missile Transporter

SS-5 Missile

SS-20 Launch Canister

SS-20 Launcher

SS-20: Missile Transporter Vehicle

SS-20 Missile Outside Container

Endnotes

Levitt, Selected Legal Issues in the Negotiation of the Intermediate Range Nuclear Forces Treaty

1 The INF Treaty, Report of the Committee on Foreign Relations, U.S. Senate, Executive Report 100-15, April 14, 1988, at 100, 101.
2 Letter of President Ronald Reagan to the Senate of the United States, June 8, 1988.
3 Resolution of Ratification, May 27, 1988, paragraph (b)(2)(C).

Jones, The INF Treaty, NATO Nuclear Strategy, And Arms Control

4 The third in the NATO Military Committee series, previous editions being MC 14/1 and 14/2, the document is officially entitled "Report by the Military Committee to the Defense Planning Committee on an Overall Strategic Concept for the Defense of the Atlantic Treaty Organization Area."
5 The "Single Integrated Operations Plan," presumably coordinated with U.S. strategic nuclear planning, designed to attack a large array of targets in the Soviet Union.
6 "NATO's Comprehensive Concept of Arms Control & Disarmament," published 30 May 1989.

Jones, How to Negotiate with Gorbachev's Team

7 Jiri Valenta and John Cunningham, "How Moscow Votes in U.S. Presidential Election," *ORBIS,* Winter 1989, p. 14.

Index

CPSIA information can be obtained at www.ICGtesting.com
Printed in the USA
BVOW080645021112

304412BV00001B/6/P